DUCK SOUP IN THE BLACK SEA

Further Collected Travels

DUCK SOUP IN THE BLACK SEA

Further Collected Travels

by

JOSEPH HONE

HAMISH HAMILTON
London

HAMISH HAMILTON LTD

Published by the Penguin Group
27 Wrights Lane, London W8 5TZ, England
Viking Penguin Inc, 40 West 23rd Street, New York, New York 10010, U.S.A.
Penguin Books Australia Ltd, Ringwood, Victoria, Australia
Penguin Books Canada Ltd, 2801 John Street, Markham, Ontario, Canada L3R 1B4
Penguin Books (N.Z.) Ltd, 182–190 Wairau Road, Auckland 10, New Zealand
Penguin Books Ltd, Registered Offices: Harmondsworth, Middlesex, England

First published in Great Britain 1988 by
Hamish Hamilton Ltd

British Library Cataloguing in Publication Data

Hone, Joseph
    Duck soup in the Black Sea.
    1. Voyages and travels — 1951–
    I. Title
    910.4   G465
    ISBN 0–241–12248–1

Typeset in 10/12pt Plantin at The Spartan Press Ltd,
Lymington, Hants
Printed and bound in Great Britain by
Richard Clay Ltd, Bungay, Suffolk

I Went

I was not bound. I let myself go completely, went
To those indulgences, half actual,
And half were turned about in my own brain;
Went into the illuminated night;
And drank strong wines, as when
The champions of pleasure drink strong wine.

C. P. Cavafy – Translated by John Mavrogordato.

For Joy Hatwood

CONTENTS

Contents

FLASHBACK

AUTHOR'S FOREWORD

Since I went to the countries and places described here – two, three, four years ago – things have changed in them all, no doubt, and most obviously so in the Soviet Union under Gorbachev's new regime. Thus some of these essays, from a political standpoint at least, are out of date. Local 'colour' writing, too, can be a most perishable commodity – and there is a deal of that here as well. Tourist and travel advice? – the circumstances on site notoriously change from month to month, and many of my itineraries may no longer be possible. (Or may be much easier to make now. To judge by some recent colour-supplement articles and photographs, for example, I must believe that some people *have* made it up the Congo river to Kisangani, on steamers I signally failed to locate, and lived to tell the tale.)

Perhaps these pieces may have a slightly longer lease as armchair-travel entertainment and comment on the *bizarreries* of national character and event, things which seem to mutate – in Africa, for example – only towards more fantastic and improbable forms.

My own reasons for going to all these places remain as I described them in the introduction to an earlier travel collection, *The Dancing Waiters*, twelve years ago: 'If there was boredom, fatigue, frustration in my travel, there was also, underlying all this like a soft heartbeat, a euphoric sense of privilege that I was going to this strange place at all, that I had got there safely in the first place; that the plane or car or rickshaw hadn't crashed – on my way to Bangkok, to the Taj, to the fiery ghats at Benares; a sense that these exotic sites, which most of us have to imagine, were here in front of me, which might not always be there, which I could see and touch and hear before passing on; a feeling of quiet excitement before sleep – when tomorrow I would be making for another vision, slouched in a train or aircraft seat, waking to look sleepily out on the Nile or snow-topped Kilimanjaro, on my way to Kisumu or Cairo: the exhausted being cradled away to the inexhaustible. The magic of travel, compensation for its sadness, is to feel sometimes, as I did, that one had found the secret at last: an anonymous peace, that one was linked with the world, was part of its wordless sway, was moving unerringly along the right path. In short, that one was at home in the place, a globe without exile.'

All very fine, no doubt. Yet the more I've travelled, the more I realise what a bad traveller I am. I have not, since then, or only with the very fewest exceptions, found myself in 'a globe without exile'. Quite the contrary – I have more and more sensed that this feeling can only be derived, if at all, from my own native roots, that I must finally play at home, not away.

Not a very startling discovery – and hardly worth the struggles, discomfort and expense of such trips to find out. So it would appear that the reasons for my travel, and my writing about it, have become less and less valid. Perhaps, at fifty in my travels, I may be simply becoming an old bore about it all, and should set up shop at once with slippers and pipe, together with a strict regimen of Trollope and the latest cricket scores, by my Cotswold fireside.

And perhaps that will happen, for if one constant theme does emerge here it must be that of the ever-increasing despoliation, of both landscape and people, in even the most remote places, not just in Rome, Nice, Cairo and Alexandria. A truism, a cliché, I suppose by now – that even on the lower slopes of Everest, as a friend has recently told me, one finds old orange peel and beer cans littered about the tracks: Everest, practically Clapham Junction.

And of course, closer to home, before we even get to these other discomforts and despoliations, we know what Gatwick Airport is like. In short, we are all travellers now, and that is far too many, so that, some time ago, at even the most remote destinations, we have exhausted what once seemed to me inexhaustible. The Cotswold slipper-and-pipe syndrome seems more and more inviting . . .

But there are, there must be, some wonderful places left, and the pessimist must not be allowed to have the final say quite yet.

I believed (for I saw) how the West Indian islands had been largely overrun by the rum-sun-surf-and-sex crowd – until I got to the genuine treasure island of Domenica. I thought that the godless Russians from Moscow must have done for all that remained of the Moslem Samarkand – the superb religious artefacts, the incredible architecture, fixtures and fittings of Tamerlane's celestial city. Instead, when I got there, I found that just the opposite had occurred:

the men from Moscow had turned a shambles of old ruined mosques, fountains and forecourts back into their quite dazzling original forms, so that one saw something not seen for 500 years, experiencing this for so long mythical city in something of its initial forms, its splendours available once more, as Tamerlane himself had conceived and built them. I thought, too, that the Kenyan wildlife was finished, until I flew out over the sensational Maasai Mara game reserve in a balloon and found myself playing God over a Noah's Ark game.

So why not let the real theme here be one of hope? – believing that in every initial or continuing depressing circumstance in travel, there *is* something magic over the hill; that beyond the next crummy station or frantic airport lurks the miracle – genuine paradise island, restored celestial city or dawn-of-creation plainsland: a place that will literally take your breath away, as happened with me one evening, entering the empty Gur-Emir mausoleum in Samarkand, when I first saw Tamerlane's tomb, carved from the largest piece of pure jade ever quarried, the walls filled with all the glittering mosaic texts of a Koranic paradise, doves from a lilac evening sky flapping in to roost far above me inside the turquoise dome. A heavenly paradise for the old monster, certainly – but, suddenly, an earthly one for me.

So if parts of this book – confirming the actual existence of these mythical visions – prompt the reader to see these things for himself, or make similarly spellbinding discoveries, then that will be justification enough for it: assuring others that if they can get out of the packages and give themselves the chance to move haphazardly about the world, as I had the luck to do here, then they will more than likely find the magic castle through the briars, beyond all contemporary sloughs of despond.

A romantic notion? – certainly, for that should be the real reason, the supreme justification for any serious travel – the pursuit of just such notions.

The dates given at the head of each piece are transmission dates, succeeding the actual events described by about six months. I must thank BBC Radio 4 for commissioning these pursuits. Things may have changed greatly in the Corporation since I first worked in Broadcasting House as a producer nearly twenty-five years ago. But there is still (as there certainly was then) a brave willingness there to underwrite what must have seemed pretty vague, even whimsical and hardly cost-effective in my initial travel proposals. Great thanks, too, to Helen Burnett who for ten years now has so cleanly, swiftly and with so many much-needed corrections typed my work. Special thanks to Joy Hatwood, my producer in all these pieces, and many before them, who with her tact, precision and ever good-humoured skills has made, for me, such a happy partnership in this work, so that I have not, indeed, been the 'onlie begetter'. Finally, thanks to my wife, Jacky, for so ably continuing with what I thanked her for twelve years ago in a previous collection of wanderings: for holding the castle at home. And now – for those castles in Spain . . .

Joseph Hone
November 1987

RUSSIAN ROUNDABOUT

I

Lenin's Ghost
(May 1982)

There were no red or green customs exits when I got to Moscow Airport. They were *all* appropriately red – and the results of much careful packing were already piling up on the tables ahead of me, as the enthusiastic Soviet officials got their hands well down into the naughty nighties, unsuitable pink pyjamas and old socks.

A long-haired youth with a backpack was approaching the counters, and next to me a well-dressed, North Country businessman, an old Moscow Airport hand apparently, licked his lips in anticipation. 'He'll be for the chop, I tell you,' he said to me with some relish.

But in the event it was exactly the other way round. The smart fellow from Newcastle had his case taken apart, like a long archaeological dig, with all his old socks finally itemised, while the youth passed through practically untouched. Another appropriate reversal of the old order, I thought. And I was rather pleased.

I'd chosen to stay at the famous National Hotel but was dropped instead at the Metropole Hotel next door. I took this little inefficiency as evidence of some humanity, at least, in Russian affairs, and when I finally got to my large room in the National, on the second floor of this splendid old *belle époque* hotel looking straight out over Red Square, I felt a spasm of triumph. I was in Moscow at last. I'd made it – after months of wondering if I ever would.

I cracked my duty-free bottle of Scotch and wandered into the bathroom. Turning the cold tap on to water the drink I was surprised to hear faint voices coming from somewhere in the ancient plumbing.

3

I put my ear down into the basin. Yes, someone was talking, two people indeed, a dialogue in Russian. The moment I turned the tap off the voices stopped – and didn't start again when I tried to repeat the trick. Bizarre, I thought. Was it some kind of bugging device gone wrong – working in reverse?

I went back into the heavily ornate bedroom, with its moulded ceiling, lace curtains and gilded imitation Louis Quinze armchairs. There were two firmly locked interconnecting doors on either side and a large, bad oil painting over the vast gilded bed, of some downtrodden nineteenth-century Russian peasants caught in a snowstorm. I put an ear to all the walls and then looked up for a microphone up behind the appalling picture. But all I found there was a piece of paper with a message in English, written in mock Cyrillic characters, left by some previous joker: 'Listening Service Suspended', it said.

I took a sip of the Scotch and opened one of the tall windows. It was nearly two o'clock in the morning. But the earlier rain had completely cleared and now there was a marvellous velvet-skied, star-filled night outside – and, yes, a crescent moon was actually dangling over Red Square as well: the Kremlin domes and the magic onions of St Basil's Cathedral spread out like an exotic opera set beneath me. One of the greatest views of the world – and here it was at last, waiting for me, a stage I would happily step out onto in the morning.

Happily, I say, because long before, I'd decided that if I ever did get to Russia – and despite the known horrors – I'd try and enjoy myself a bit, try and see the brighter side of things and not be too much of a dog in the manger about the all-too-obvious political and social drawbacks. Yes, I'd thought, while thumbing through the books and guides before I came, I'm going to try and live a bit here: not too many guided tours through museums or old churches pondering the icons – instead a search for the flavour of life itself, and the better parts of life if possible, which I was sure I must find somewhere in this vast nation. I wanted to get behind the chilling surface of constraint and feel the pulse of inner character – that traditionally dramatic, sensitive, emotional and generous nature of the Russian people which I felt must still exist beneath the drab surfaces of their daily lives.

I'd go to the circus for instance; and avoid too much heavy, incomprehensible opera. I might even give the ballet a miss and try a little caviar and Georgian champagne instead – why not? I'd go shopping in GUM for an astrakhan hat, before a lunchtime vodka-tonic in the hotel's dollar bar with some new Russian acquaintance – perhaps with the famous poet Yevtushenko himself, to whom I had an introduction. And for later in my trip I'd arranged a cruise on the Black Sea, before going on to dance with the Georgians in Tbilisi, and a final visit to the restored miracles of Tamerlane's fabulous city of Samarkand. . . . These were my plans. Oh, and I wanted to get to the races too – a great Soviet pastime, I'd heard. I saw myself up in the stands, sporting my astrakhan hat with a Cuban cigar, cheering a few winners home and collecting my roubles before dinner that night amidst the lush Palm Court surroundings of the National Hotel's restaurant – perhaps with my congenial Intourist guide, a bright dark girl from the Caucasus no doubt, with whom there'd be absolutely no political chat, just an evening spent on sweet nothings to the strains of a Lehar waltz or the lightning rhythms of a balalaika band. . . .

I thought, as I stood by the open window, looking out on this dream view of Red Square – I thought that with luck and tact I'd be able to experience the Soviet Union as one did other countries: in a manner which, since I was an individual tourist, not part of any package group, I'd be perfectly free to come and go; free to savour that rich kaleidoscope of new scenes, chance meetings and agreeable appointments that make for the essential adventure of all travel – all those haphazard, vivid colours that form one's vision of a new world.

I'd avoid any mini East–West confrontations, any boring dialogues on Capitalist or Marxist supremacy or indignant comments on the fate of the dissidents. There were Western commentators enough already devoted to all these issues. Music, *tovarisch*! I thought – on with the Moscow Nights.

An hour later I woke in the darkness. There was a row coming from the next room, the same Russian voices probably that I'd heard in the bathroom plumbing. Next morning I mentioned this unsuitable noise to the receptionist. She looked at her booking sheet: 'That room next to you was empty last night.' I left it at that, not wanting an argument on my first morning, and I crossed over the lobby to the Service Bureau to meet my guide.

She was called Tamara, and she wasn't a dark-eyed girl from the Caucasus, but a petite, blonde thirty-five-year-old Muscovite with several children and a husband in documentary films. Tamara was business-like but friendly from the word go.

'Look,' I said, 'I hope you don't mind. But let's not go to too many museums and things.' And since it had started to rain again that Sunday morning I added that perhaps we could give Lenin a miss as well out in his mausoleum, where the queues were already nearly half a mile long. To all this Tamara agreed. 'But I would like to go to the races this afternoon,' I went on. She looked puzzled. 'You know, the Hippodrome. Look, it's in the guide book: every Sunday and Wednesday evening, it says.'

Tamara wasn't certain. 'Perhaps our driver will know,' she said.

'Or the hall porter,' I added. 'Hall porters always know about horses and racing.'

But he didn't. He seemed to think that I wanted to buy a horse or hire a droshky.

'No, no,' I shook my head, asking Tamara to explain. 'Horse *racing.*' And I mimed a jockey, arms pumping on the reins, coming up fast outside on the last furlong. Tamara and the hall porter stared at me in some surprise. I think they thought I wanted to go swimming.

'Never mind,' I said, and a minute later we were out in a smart Volga car, with a chauffeur, speeding round on my obligatory tour of the city. It was a lightning trip. Yet it still lasted all of three hours. What to say, in brief, but that Moscow is a monstrously large place? Everything – streets, pavements, buildings – all at least twice the normal size, so that the people would have to be twelve feet high to fit the scale, which of course they're not and thus spend most of their time trying to escape the architectural threats, looking for somewhere to hide. I was pleased to be hidden in the car myself that morning, wheeling through the torrents of rain.

Tamara pointed out the gloomy virtues as we sped along. 'That's the Gosplan building,' she said. 'Central Planning. And these – that's the old University Library . . . the Rossiya Hotel . . . and that's the Ministry of Foreign Trade. . . .'

'Splendid!' I said. 'Marvellous. . . .'

We went up the Lenin Hills then, to a vantage point by Moscow University where we got out and had a huge, damp view over the city.

'That's the Olympic Stadium. With the Kremlin behind. And there's your hotel – you can just see it.'

'Marvellous,' I said. 'Splendid, excellent. . . .'

It was distinctly chilly and we were getting very wet up on the hills.

'Well now,' I said. 'What about the Novo Devichy Convent? I'd like to see that.'

What I wanted to see, in fact, was the famous cemetery next door where Gogol and Chekhov and Nikita Krushchev are buried. But Tamara had bad news for me in the car. The cemetery was closed.

'Closed for renewal?' I asked brightly, knowing already that this was a favourite Soviet excuse for every refusal. But Tamara was honest enough to admit that, though this *was* the official reason, the real one had to do with a threatened attempt by some pro-Stalin Georgians to dig up and desecrate Krushchev's tomb.

So instead of the cemetery we went to the gloriously gilded Convent Cathedral where several Tsars were enthroned. We arrived just too late for the Sunday morning service, missing all the haunting Orthodox chants and responses. But then from a small ante-chapel by the main entrance behind me, I heard other sounds – of cries and weeping. And on our way out we ran straight into an Orthodox funeral, the elderly mourners crowding round the bearded priest and the open coffin – and suddenly in the small space we were caught amongst them, and I was right next to the long wooden box staring into the bluish, waxen features of an old man. He looked as if he'd died of cold.

It seemed an unhappy omen. But by the time we got back to the car, the weather had begun to clear so I asked again, 'Well, what about the races now?'

Tamara looked puzzled again – and the driver still knew nothing about them. I didn't pursue it. It was after one now in any case – time for lunch and a vodka-tonic – or a hot toddy – in that dollar bar: time for a little cheer at last in that gloomy, drab, depressing Moscow Sunday.

The dollar bar was closed when I got back to the hotel and all five dining rooms completely booked out apparently, though half the tables were empty. I'd have to wait an hour for a seat. I went downstairs to give Yevtushenko a ring but, wisely enough perhaps, in the chilly, gloomy circumstances, he'd left for Italy the previous day and wouldn't be back for a month. I considered my position. There'd been no Cuban cigars or winners at the races; caviar and champagne were out for the moment, and so too was a merry evening with the convivial poet. It hadn't been the best of starts.

But much later that day, in the middle of the night in fact, things got worse. I was woken up once more. The voices were on the go again – the same Russian voices arguing. But this time the dispute came from the *other* room next to mine. My Russian wasn't half good enough to understand anything in the angry babble. I could only identify the word 'iskra' – meaning 'spark' – which cropped up several times. What were they on about – and who the hell were they? I dozed off. Then the voices woke me once more. But now, apart from the annoyance, there was a sudden chill right down the back of my neck and spine – for this time, the voices were actually moving through my own bedroom, somewhere just ahead of me in the darkness, crossing my room from one interconnecting door to the other. I turned the light on. There was no one there and the place was quite silent.

The next morning I complained to the receptionist again. And she assured me that this room, on the *other* side of mine, was also unoccupied.

The dollar bar finally opened later that morning and I had a drink with a Moscow-based, French radio correspondent I met there. I told him about these midnight visitors.

'What room are you in?' he asked.

'231 on the second floor – right above the dining room.'

'Ah,' he said. 'Those were Lenin's rooms. He had a suite of them, just where you are – just above the dining room. He stayed here for several months, immediately after he returned to Russia in 1917. And that word you heard repeated – "Iskra" – "The Spark" – well, that was the name of the paper he edited at the time.'

The Frenchman was quite prosaic about it all.

I laughed. 'You mean, it was Lenin's ghost?'

'His *voice*, apparently,' he corrected me. 'Why not? The body's just out beyond your windows in Red Square after all.'

'But I'm not psychic,' I said. 'Someone must be playing tricks on me.'

'Unless you're playing tricks on *me*?' the Frenchman asked sourly.

'I wish I was,' I answered.

At that moment I knew I'd properly arrived in Moscow, in Russia – and the next three weeks stretched ahead of me, each day an ambush. I foresaw no bright kaleidoscope of events for me here – no music or dancing, no convivial laughter or agreeable appointments. Without realising it, I'd already experienced something of the nightmare side of Russia today: in the face of the old dead man suddenly looming up at me in the convent, in the disembodied voices in my bedroom. And where the signals had been quite clear, I'd been an optimistic fool. I'd been amused for example, at the airport customs when that smart businessman had had his bags pulled about and the long-haired youth had passed through untouched. I'd seen an innocent inefficiency, a sign of feckless humanity in the fact that no one knew where the races were in Moscow, or that there were no tables free in the almost empty restaurant, that the dollar bar was mostly closed. But now in all these events – in the ghostly voices and human muddle – I saw the workings of some grim and capricious hand, a quite arbitrary order, a malign fate. I'd arrived all right, in a world where all logic would have to be suspended, all initial assumptions reversed. In the past thirty-six hours, without knowing it, I'd moved through the looking glass, from light to dark.

2
Moscow Nights
(May 1982)

On my third morning in Moscow I came down the stairs of my hotel feeling reasonably perky. The strange voices in my bedroom had stopped. I'd had a decent night's sleep at last and had managed to organise my breakfast too. The trick here was to grab a table right next to the kitchen entrance where you could make well placed, tactical lunges at the impossibly tardy waiters. But above all that morning I was happy because I was getting out of a city which I hadn't much enjoyed – for a day in the country, into the depths of a Russian autumn, a trip which I'd booked months before in London, a visit to Leo Tolstoy's family house and estate at Yasnaya Polyana 125 miles south of Moscow.

Here, in this traditional Russian nobleman's country retreat, Tolstoy had written most of his books, and had argued with his wife Sonya at even greater length, before finally walking out on her one stormy winter's night and dying in a stationmaster's cabin a few weeks later. Yasnaya Polyana was where this most difficult genius had made an often more difficult home for himself and his huge family – a place where his dreams had at first flourished and then become a nightmare. I had wanted to see this epicentre of his life for many years and now I had the vital Intourist voucher in my hand; an expensive seventy-two pounds worth, which included a car and driver for the day, with my guide Tamara. But Tamara had bad news for me when I met her in the lobby.

'I have just telephoned down to Yasnaya Polyana – to make sure everything was arranged. But they're not expecting us. The house is all closed up in fact. There's no one down there at all – except the fireman. I spoke to him. He said under no circumstances could we bring anyone down.'

I laughed at first and flourished my voucher. 'There must be some mistake. Look – it was all booked for today, *months* ago. Look!'

'I know,' Tamara said sadly. 'But there seems to have been some – misunderstanding.'

'Well, let's fix it,' I urged optimistically. 'Let's go and see the boss at Intourist. The head office is just next door, isn't it?

Tamara nodded, less optimistically, and I strode out of the hotel with her, fire and brimstone rising in my gut.

The Intourist boss wasn't in that morning – or wasn't in to me at least. But the head of the English language section was, in a little wooden cubicle at the front of the building looking over Red Square where the queues of people – as usual already half a mile long – were seeking a more ready entrance to Lenin's eternal home down beneath us. It was to an attractive, big-boned blonde woman that I put my case – and I put it fairly strongly.

'Unfortunately Intourist does not control Yasnaya Polyana,' she said reasonably enough. 'It's part of the National Museums' Board.'

'But you made and confirmed my booking,' I argued, 'and you took my seventy-two pounds for the trip readily enough.'

'And that, of course, will be returned to you.' The blonde woman was now very conscientious.

'But why?' I asked. 'Isn't this an extraordinary piece of in-efficiency? Couldn't you have told me earlier that the trip was cancelled – not minutes before I was due to set off?'

To this question I got no reasonable reply at all, so that I rambled explosively on, like a damp firecracker, getting absolutely nowhere. Apologies were made and that was that. The big-boned woman looked at me calmly, distantly now, like a successful mother confessor who had done her duty – both to me and to the mysterious Soviet power that had arranged things in just such a disadvantageous, but obviously pre-ordained manner.

It had been laid down that I should not visit Yasnaya Polyana. It was a fate that could not now, by any means whatsoever, be reversed. This was my first taste of what I later found to be a common offering in the Soviet Union: the creation and promulgation by officials of every sort and in every circumstance, of immutable laws derived solely from

their own mismanagement and inefficiency. I was fuming dangerously when I left the Intourist building. Apart from the disembodied
voices in my bedroom, I'd missed the races in Moscow that Sunday,
missed the poet Yevtushenko and now I'd missed Tolstoy. It was
pouring with rain again into the bargain. This Russian trip had all the
makings of a full-scale disaster. I adjourned to the dollar bar in my
hotel to consider matters.

Here I was cheered by a meeting with a Dutch engineer. He was
called Peter and he was, as he put it, in 'man-made yarns and
fabrications', setting up a factory for such things in Russia. It
seemed an appropriate industry for the country. Peter knew the
place well – he came to Moscow every few months. He was a tiny,
suave, lively man, dressed incongruously in a very man-made, very
loud, synthetic, tartan-patterned suit, with such wide padded
shoulders and wasp waist that he had the air of a miniscule Super-
man. Certainly he seemed to know all the Soviet ropes and he
commiserated with me heartily over my cancelled trip, while we
downed a few vodka-tonics and then had lunch together – though,
despite the fact that he spoke Russian well and was a regular guest at
this National Hotel, it was still nearly three in the afternoon before
we were served.

I tried the caviar here for the first time – and I must say, even at
five roubles a small throw, it was worth every kopeck: magnificent! –
the little chilled black beads, translucent edges with a dark heart,
tasted like the distilled essence of every other river and sea food in
the world.

'It's Beluga caviar,' Peter told me, 'the National is one of the very
few places left in Moscow where you can get it now. And at five
roubles it's cheap at the price, too.' We split a bottle of Georgian
champagne to accompany it.

'If only things were as tangible as this,' I said, raising the frothy
glass, 'Outside, in the real Russia. This is all something human at last
– something you can actually see and touch and smell. Everything else
I've tried to do here so far has completely eluded me.'

'Yes,' Peter nodded. 'But it eludes everybody, Russians as much as
foreigners. And almost anything done through official channels will
elude you most of all. You have to seek other means – they do exist.
There are other worlds here, many of them. Private worlds.
Everything real is very private here.'

'Yes?' I queried.

'Yes, of course. You see, things can be arranged here, just as in every other country.'

'But don't you get locked up for a long time, if you get caught?'

'Not unless you deal in black market hard currency exchange, and I don't mean that – that's a fool's game. But if you know your people, trust your sources – and if they trust you, that's the most important thing – then almost anything else can be arranged. What was it you wanted to do particularly?'

'Oh, nothing complicated,' I said. 'I just wanted to go to the races – that sort of simple thing. And I thought I might meet a few Russians, ordinary Russians. I'm tired of officials and old icons.'

'That's not difficult. I'm meeting some Russian friends tonight. You can join us. I'll show you round.'

This was the best piece of news I'd had since I'd arrived in Moscow three days before. I went upstairs afterwards and read Chekhov until it was nearly time to meet my new friend. I took a bath and a nip of Scotch and put on my smart suit, the rust cord that went well with my new red tie. It was like getting ready for a command performance: I was going to meet the real people at last.

Peter's Russian friends turned out to be two attractive young women, Polenka and Natasha, in their mid-twenties, a pair of chalk and cheese girls. While Polenka was stringy and flat with fuzzy fair hair, a retroussé nose and lively, dancing blue eyes – Natasha was just the opposite. She was almost a caricature of traditional Slav beauty; very dark and nearly dumpy in a black sheath dress, with eyes that latched onto you like grappling irons. Her body was just about to run away with her. But her face was thin and beautiful and always would be: distinguished, carefully chiselled, with a small, straight nose and those deep pools for eyes, all framed by velvet hair and a classic jawline. Both of them had real style, character, intelligence. Above all they had *feeling*; they were alive. Here were two real Russians at last, with all those innate Russian attributes of passion and generosity that I had hoped, but so far failed, to unearth on my visit here. It looked like being a splendid evening.

We danced with the girls in the Metropole Night Club, drank some more Georgian champagne and chatted as well as we could above the appalling disco music (the days of the little balaika orchestra are long gone in the Soviet Union). Later on, some other Russians joined our table, men with their wives or girl friends – well dressed, amiable people, certainly part of the city's professional élite. But one youngish man on his own puzzled me. More smartly dressed than the others, in a suit that might have come from Saville Row, he had a heavy-lidded, wan, aristocratic face. He sat opposite me, not apparently drunk, but certainly quite speechless as he stared at me with a torpid, glazed, almost reptilian expression.

A while later I reached inside my coat pocket to get a city map out to ask Natasha something. And for an instant, while I searched for the map, I left a walletful of travellers cheques on the table right in front of me. In the same instant the well dressed zombie opposite sprang to life, snatched my wallet and was half way through a hundred-yard sprint down the bar before I was on my feet as well, shouting 'Stop thief!' after him.

The incident caused a small sensation, but they caught the man soon enough, for instead of making for the exit, he'd run in just the opposite direction, cornering himself in the twisting underground passages among the kitchens of the old hotel. Later, with my wallet safely back, I made a statement to one of the hotel managers.

'No,' I said. 'I don't want to bring any charges. The man had simply had too much to drink – just high spirits. I've got the money back. There's no problem.'

But then, as I looked across at the man himself, such a picture of sheer dejection and appalling unhappiness, I saw that there was indeed a problem.

I asked Peter about it, when we'd all left the hotel.

'What on earth was he up to? He was no small-time sneak thief.'

'No,' Peter agreed. 'He's got a good job somewhere, that's for sure, with those clothes. But all the same, with a few drinks, we were just too much of a temptation for him.'

'How do you mean?'

'Well, we all seemed too happy, too carefree. And when he saw what he thought was a lot of real Western cash in your wallet it was the final straw. He wasn't really stealing it, he was just showing how much he resented our freedom. He didn't need the money. But he needed to make the gesture. It's there, that feeling – deep down – with quite a few Russians. And the drink can bring it out: a sense of complete hopelessness. You see, many Russians haven't just lost their freedom here – they've lost the very substance of life itself: the hours and minutes in a day which you and I can take off to enjoy ourselves – to see new things, meet new people, to travel abroad. All that's lost for them here, sacrificed to an ideology. That's why he took your wallet – not for the money, but for his stolen life which that money represented.'

'I see . . .' I wondered about this. 'But is it all like that in Moscow? Is there nowhere where people really let themselves go?'

'I told you – they only really enjoy themselves in private. But there is one place on the outskirts of the city. It's not official. But we can go there.'

We drove there for nearly an hour, fast, along endless, dreary, empty boulevards, until we turned off into the dark, down old rutted lanes, twisting about between shadowy houses and ruined factories, before coming right to the edge of the countryside, where I could see empty fields and the shadow of birch woods beyond. And here, next to a large wooden barn, we stopped. The big main door had been locked a long time ago, but round the back was another small entrance, and inside, pushing through some heavy curtains, we were suddenly in a quite different, brightly lit, sophisticated world – as if we'd just that moment taken a magic journey from Russia back into the West. There was music, dancing, laughter. It was all real for the first time since I'd been in Moscow – genuine, uninhibited enjoyment.

It was a nightclub of sorts, but with nothing plastic about it; done up in pine wood like the inside of a Swiss chalet, with a well stocked bar, long benched tables with bright check cloths where people were eating steaks and great bowls of stroganoff. But the main attraction just then was a big TV screen to one side where half the company were watching *Butch Cassidy and the Sundance Kid*.

I was taken aback. 'That's not Russian TV?' I asked Peter.

'No. That's video. More or less everything in this place is imported. I told you – it's not official.'

'Well who does it belong to then? It's not a private house?'

'It is – practically. It's a little place for the foreign business community in Moscow, shall we say. But you can meet plenty of Russians here, too.'

Peter was right. We could and I did – and I had a tremendous bowl of real stroganoff as well, along with some fine Georgian red wine, quite unobtainable at my grand hotel. We saw the end of the film, danced with the girls again – now more lively and vivacious then ever –

and no one stole my wallet. It turned out to be a merry evening. Yet, I didn't really enjoy it. I felt like a prisoner on parole. And when Natasha started to cry soulfully in the car on the way back to Moscow, I thought of what Peter had said about their stolen lives.

We were all of us going back into the darkness just then, not just Natasha and Polenka. I'd met some real Russians at last, that was true. But I wouldn't meet them tomorrow. No one would steal my wallet or dance with me then. Tomorrow the big-boned woman from Intourist lay in wait for me, with all her grey excuses and prevarications. So that when the passionate, unhappy Natasha kissed me as I left her, I told her not to be so gloomy, that I, too, was a prisoner, returning to my grand hotel.

3
Odessa:
Bread and Circuses
(May 1982)

Going to Odessa – 1000 miles south of Moscow on the Black Sea – I thought I'd be escaping the northern chill and coming into a little warmth. But instead, there was a great wind rushing in from the steppes to the north, with a cold rain to match, and the colonies of rooks on the tall plane trees which I could see from my top-floor hotel bedroom were being slapped downwards in the gale, like tattered old black gloves, unable to rise into the storm above the city.

These birds had woken and surprised me much earlier that first morning, cawing and cackling away like the rooks around some country rectory in the wilds of Ireland. And I was even more surprised when I'd looked out and seen almost nothing but swaying green tree tops all about me. I took my binoculars and searched for the city itself, but all I could see from this height, pushing up through the sodden, windswept greenery, were the broken tiles of old roofs, smashed masonry, classical arches and pediments and heavy eaves all crumbling away. It seemed as if I'd come to a ruined city, decaying beneath a tropical rainforest.

Odessa, with its famous steps and catacombs; its classic Italianate architecture and great port giving out onto the world through the Black Sea, was once, along with St Petersburg, the most sophisticated, cosmopolitan and Western-orientated city in pre-Revolutionary Russia. And since, under the Soviets, the money hasn't been there to pull down the old city or build any horrific new office blocks, a lot of its physical grandeur remains intact: the long, two-storied, red-stuccoed town houses; the museums and Town Hall built as classical temples; the vast art nouveau stock and corn exchanges; and the wedding-cake opera house by the sea front, where Chaliapin and Caruso sang, copied from the one in Vienna.

The old Odessa remains, a stylish and rather grand place, and certainly a highly visible capitalist monument to the nineteenth-century entrepreneurs who built it. For Odessa was essentially a city of merchant adventurers; particularly of corn barons who ran the grain trade here, from their clubs and vast mansions. You can still see the remains of this extinct race and all their fizzy commercial enterprise when you get down to ground level and walk the grid-plan streets: in the faded signs, done in expansive Cyrillic and Roman lettering, above old restaurants, department stores, oyster bars, ships' chandlers and forgotten Grand Hotels.

Today, the shops have no names and are mostly empty. And the people who walk beneath the classical pillars and arcades and along the decaying side streets are like amateur actors appearing at Covent Garden; a troupe of bemused contemporary players walking a stage where some intensely dramatic performance has taken place over many years, but a drama which they have practically no knowledge of now. For if Russians have lost their freedom, a lot of their history has been taken from them as well.

What remains to them, then? Like the plebeian Romans, little more than bread and circuses, I think – along with a stubborn, patriotic courage. And in Odessa particularly you can experience all three of these traditional Russian virtues.

Whenever I travelled in the Soviet Union there was nearly always plenty of bread, at least, in the shops. And some of it, as in Odessa, was very good: fluffy white baguettes or the compressed black variety like a sour malt loaf. Odessa gives back onto the steppes, the great Ukrainian bread basket of the Soviet Union. And the Ukrainians of this city, the 'Little' or 'New' Russians as they're called, are – by comparison with their dour northern neighbours in Russia proper – a lively, open, imaginative, quick-thinking and genuinely hard-working lot. The Ukrainian Republic is vital to Soviet agriculture and industry, so the people here have a lot of political clout in Moscow. Of course there's a long history of violent separatism in the Ukraine as well, and most Ukrainians would prefer to be a genuine Republic, outside Moscow's clutches, but there's absolutely no hope of that. So instead they eat and dress well; they go to the circus and they remember their recent history – their appalling battles with the Nazis during the last war.

Circuses, of course, we know as a Soviet speciality today, just as they were in Victorian and Edwardian Britain at the height of the Empire, and in America in this century, during that country's most expansive phase. Circuses belong to great colonial powers – to countries who, for example, by conquest, have easy access to elephants and tigers. And the last great power of this sort today is the Soviet Union, with its complete domination of a dozen small nations both inside and around its borders. Besides, as the Soviet authorities realised so pertinently long ago, if you ensure that the suppressed masses have bread and circuses, you'll keep their minds off present impoverishment and future insurrection. This is something which Moscow certainly requires, hence the vast State patronage of the Big Top everywhere you go in the Soviet Union.

I first heard about the Odessa Circus in the dollar bar of my hotel from a British package tourist, a middle-aged, rubicund little man who had been in the business himself with Bertram Mills, years before. 'After the Moscow State,' he told me, 'it's the best circus in the country.'

But unfortunately he couldn't join me that evening. His group was taking a late flight to Tashkent or Samarkand or somewhere: that's part of the excitement of travel in the Soviet Union, you can move about by air to exotic places like Alma Ata or Bokhara or Tbilisi just as we might take a day trip to Brighton or Southend. Anyway, I went to the circus on my own – and what a circus it was.

In Russia circuses never tour. They give daily performances and are housed in permanent buildings – and every city of any size has one, most of them recently built, for money is no object in this vital Soviet enterprise. But the Odessa Circus still occupies a beautiful, rather battered, original late nineteenth-century building; a twelve-sided yellow brick big top, with steeply raked wooden benches inside and a pillared promenade for the customers right round underneath, where they congregate before the show starts, over the beer and tea and chocolate stands. And when the doors opened that evening there was a real bums' rush – hundreds of people storming in, as if for a rock concert, anxious to get their hands on a salami roll or a glass of Georgian champagne before the show started.

Here for the first time in my trip I could feel the real surge of corporate Russian gaiety, enthusiasm, life. These were quite different people from the shadows I'd seen walking in the rain down the splintering side streets: here were people out to enjoy themselves, and quite certain they would. I remember the strange, sweet and sour smell everywhere before the show that evening: a mixture of sweat, cheap Russian perfume, a musky attar of roses, mixed with an odour of sawdust and straw. And behind this, the rank air that came in slight whiffs from beyond the curtains, the dung and urine of wild beasts. I hadn't been to a circus for many years, it's almost an extinct entertainment now in Britain, but that evening in the foyer time started to dissolve for me and I felt myself going backwards – thirty, forty years, to that particular adventure in childhood which can surpass all others in heart-stopping excitement. And when we were in our seats and the tinny, old-fashioned little orchestra suddenly blared out with 'Alexander's Ragtime Band', when the house went dark and the drums rolled and the coloured spotlights spun around the Big Top, we were all of us taken out of ourselves completely, embarked on three hours of sheer magic.

Russian circus acts are run, and follow each other, at an incredible pace – all executed with vast skill and discipline, in the most brilliantly colourful and obviously expensive costumes. In some circuses – and I saw nearly half a dozen different ones – they include what amounts to a lavish floor show, with singers, dancers and cabaret artists. Indeed there's an air of the old MGM musical in many of them, you can see that the main intention is to create as extravagant a spectacle as possible, by way of contrast with the people's drab daily lives.

But in Odessa there were no fripperies, no extras. It was the traditional circus of clowns, jugglers, bare-back horse riders and high-wire acts, but with the difference that each act had an additional polish to it, something extra by way of energy, invention, décor or lighting, which took it way out of the commonplace. You were watching a *production* in short, as carefully and elaborately conceived as that of a Grand Opera.

And yet, despite this intense professionalism, there was no false slickness about it all. That essentially innocent mood of the old circuses had been retained. And when the elephants came in and I looked at the audience rising steeply up beyond them on the rough wooden benches, I was suddenly reminded of an almost exactly similar childhood image of mine, in one of Jean de Brunhoff's Babar books of the early 1930s: that double-page colour illustration of Babar and Celeste, trapped by the cruel circus trainer, cavorting unhappily round the ring in some great southern seaport, with its busy harbour, huge ships at berth, and the white limestone hills behind. That fictional port might well have been Odessa, and here were Babar and Celeste themselves, caught in some timelock, still performing, eternally young.

The mood of innocence was thus complete for me that evening; the experience thrilling, enchanting and finally – as all great artistry is – extraordinarily moving. The high spot was the juggler, either foot on two great white horses, careering about the ring while his partner threw him hoops, nine of them – all of which, incredibly, he kept up in the air, circling at great speed in the swinging limelight. This combined skill of man and beasts was breathtaking and when it was done there were tears in my eyes.

We left the building transformed – confident, happy, lightfooted people; infected ourselves with all the daring and magic of the artistes. And though we were back now in the dark, drab streets, the high octane of the circus worked as a drug in us all, a fix that would keep us happy for the next twenty-four hours, making the food queues next day seem shorter, the mental impoverishment of lesser account.

Of course it's fair to add here that the Soviet political system is only part of the current Russian tragedy. The other part lies in the last war, in their suffering at the hands of Nazi Germany; a suffering which, understandably, is still very much emphasised today. They lost twenty million people in that fray, one or more probably from every family in the Union, and no one either wants, or is allowed to forget this. Odessa, now one of the ten Hero Cities in the Soviet Union, was in the forefront of the battle. As a vital port with equally vital access north and east into the interior, the Germans first laid siege to it for weeks on end, before the city finally capitulated. Then, many of the citizens, joined by other Soviet partisans, took to the catacombs beneath Odessa and fought the occupying Germans for nearly a year from these extraordinary underground passageways.

Excavated throughout the last century for building material, the sandstone catacombs run in serpentine passages for over 500 miles beneath the city and its suburbs. And though most of them (as a danger to the buildings above) have either been closed or filled in now, you can still visit long stretches of them, just outside Odessa, where the partisans had their headquarters. I went to see them the next morning with my guide. And just like the circus, they reflected other Russian virtues which we tend to overlook in the West, intent, as we often are now, only on the bad side of the Soviet coin.

The catacombs ran straight down from an almost invisible entrance in a suburban tomato patch to a level thirty or forty feet below ground, before the passageway divided up into a labyrinth of half a dozen different routes, roughly cut in the sandstone. My guide went on ahead, the two of us with just candles. We circled round for nearly two hours that morning in the chilly gloom. Everything had been left as it was in this Brigade HQ: the cave hospital with its huge chunk of sandstone as an operating table; the children's school with its much smaller blocks as chairs and desks; an old, make-do Tzarist map of the world on one wall; the Commissar's office with its field telephone; the forge where they made guns and bombs out of pipes; the endless male and female dormitories and washrooms, where there were Heath-Robinson devices for heating the water and taking a shower, and the machine-gun nests, set up at crucial corners to repel the Germans.

At the height of the resistance here, something over 20,000 people lived in these dark, almost airless and appallingly cramped caverns, many of them for months on end, so that when they rose above into the strong southern sunlight they had to be sure to tan their ghost-white faces with sandstone powder mixed with engine oil. Those who failed or forgot to do this were almost immediately picked up by the Germans, who in any case managed to trap and execute hundreds of partisans in these grimy tunnels, though they never managed to close them down completely.

When we emerged there was a small museum, with photographs and mementoes of the time, as well as the usual contemporary Marxist slogans emblazoned above all the exhibits. But now I didn't mind this propaganda. It was obvious from what I'd seen that morning that this underground battle for Odessa had been an entirely human affair, a classic of wartime resistance. Tenacit patriotism, endurance – these are the great Russian qualities now, just as during the last war. And beyond their bread and circuses they have little else to sustain them today except this same fortitude in adversity.

4
Yalta:
Chekhov's Garden
(June 1982)

Tourist life in Russia, more than any other country I've been in, is a succession of hotels and hotel bedrooms. Outside of these you're in another country, where more or less everything, if not actually forbidden, is somehow barred to you, inaccessible. It's almost impossible to put your hand on the pulse of any ordinary life going on around. It's a curious and unpleasant phenomenon – this absolute mental weightlessness you feel in Russia once you leave the hotel. Your mind is unable to engage with, or interpret, the reality all about you; there seem to be no entrances into understanding. And of course this phenomenon is one entirely encouraged, even intended by the authorities. As a result of this mental and physical segregation, you can pass the visit not in the Soviet Union at all but in an elaborately contrived, pasteboard country called Intourist.

The initial process in this segregation is simple enough. As a Western visitor, wherever you go you'll be housed in a hotel strictly reserved for you and your kind. The locals are not admitted – and nor will you be, if you forget to bring your bedroom reservation card with you. The principle is quite clear-cut: the 'In' in 'Intourist' is short for 'Inostranyets' in Russian, meaning 'foreigner' – the facilities laid on are entirely for you and not for the Russians.

This apartheid reaches its height at the new thousand-bedroom Hotel Yalta where I had to stay during my visit to that famous old

Crimean resort on the Black Sea. The Hotel Yalta is a real monster of a place – the ultimate in rectangular concrete, aluminium, glass and black marble. Twenty storeys high and nearly a quarter of a mile long, built on a steep slope outside the town, it's so formidable and unnatural an edifice that when the sun gets up in the morning behind the hotel it still seems like night as you peer from your bedroom terrace out into a vast gloomy shadow that runs away down the hill – a shade that keeps the flowers in the front gardens asleep until well after midday. At the Hotel Yalta even nature is retarded and made to keep its distance from you; one half expects the sea itself out in the bay to be emptied and filled like a bath, just for the unique convenience of the Western clients.

This Intourist Hotel, like all the others in the Soviet Union, is a world entirely on its own – a comfortable, almost impregnable ghetto set in the middle of an uncomfortable reality. And the trick you have to play, I found, while travelling in Russia is to try and force yourself – at least mentally – on the world outside their doors. I say mentally: I mean that to get in touch with everyday life in Russia now, without much of the language or other pre-arranged access to the people, you have to go out into the streets and *imagine* yourself as a Russian, actually living in the place at that moment. And so it was that during my first two days in Yalta, I spent most of the time out and about in the parks and streets of this ever-popular resort – watching the people, trying to imagine myself into their individual lives, so that the town itself became a backdrop to a variety of fictional creations.

That old lady, for example, whom I follow along the famous seafront promenade in Yalta – where Chekhov's much smarter, younger *Lady with the Little Dog* walked into such emotional distress eighty years ago – that old crone, with a drab head kerchief and a black shawly dress and a heavy collection of empty shopping bags could well be one of the original Tartar settlers in the Crimea; a farmer's wife in from the country for the day – from the great, jagged high tablelands that rise up right behind Yalta. She's sold some grapes, pimentoes, perhaps a few scabby pears in the market that morning and now she's searching for the right buttons, some ribbons to go with that dress for her granddaughter's wedding. . . .

But no – she's suddenly stopped on the seafront, just beyond the dodgem cars and the rifle range in Luna Park, joining a pushing crowd of people surrounding something or someone. When I reach her I find she's having a flutter for ten kopecks on an old Tzarist gambling machine; a variously coloured clock face with a turning arrow and numbers where you can win a rouble if you hang around long enough. Afterwards she moves to an equally ancient arm-balance weighing scales, administered by an even older crone, where for another ten kopecks and an even longer wait, she finds she is still in the land of the living. The pleasures on the Yalta seafront are of the simplest nature.

But wait – who is this much younger woman, tall, slim, stylishly dressed, carrying a big artist's folio case under her arm. I spot her emerging from the palm trees in Lenin Park, crossing over to the promenade. She walks away down the seafront under the great *belle époque* street lanterns – huge white globes still here after a hundred years – a woman, almost severe, with straw-coloured hair done up in a small bun at the back, wearing a neat pleated tartan skirt and a pretty silk patterned blouse. I see her face clearly enough now: gold-rimmed spectacles bridging a delicate nose, pale skin, thinly-cut features, that very fair nordic hair. . . .

She must come from the far north, from beyond Moscow – from Soviet Karelia perhaps, on the Finnish border? She is smart, but not holiday chic; in her late thirties, I'd say. Certainly she knows what she's doing, where she's going. She has, for a Russian woman, an unusually decisive, liberated step. In the West she could well be an advertising executive or a television producer. But here? No, she doesn't look as if she's on holiday. Yet she's too tall and fair skinned to be a local.

I decide she's called Katya. She's staying with her widowed mother, both of them down from Moscow, in one of the many trade union hostels or sanatoria up on the hills. Yes, that's it: her mother is bronchitic, she's taking a cure in these ever mild southern airs – and Katya, an only daughter (her father died in the Battle of Stalingrad), is down here to visit or look after her. But what's she got in that big folio under her arm? X-ray plates? Maybe she's a doctor?

Here my imagination begins to flag. All the same, as the morning passes with other such encounters, gradually these imagined backgrounds, these little bricks of invention mount up, forming the shape of real lives and I begin to feel at home in Yalta at last, practically among friends, so that the awful initial mental weightlessness disappears. Shadow becomes substance and the crowds on the seafront take on an identity and find a home in common existence –

mine and theirs. I'm living in Yalta myself now – not a foreigner incarcerated in an Intourist Hotel.

Yet there remains but one flaw in all this freshly imagined reality. As I look about me, I am quite obviously not living in the contemporary Soviet Union at all. Yalta, physically untouched by the last war or by the earlier revolution, is a last empty husk of Russia's Imperial wealth, folly, grandeur – in which the old palaces and grand hotels and vast summer villas speak much more of ghosts than living people. When you get to Yalta you are forced to think of a quite recent lifestyle which bears no relationship whatsoever to present circumstances in Russia. It's in Yalta, this largely unchanged Tzarist relic, that the full magnitude of Lenin's revolution strikes home. And if there was something eerie in the sense of distance and inaccessibility which I felt in relation to ordinary Russians today, there was a much stranger feeling here. I felt that in Yalta I was peering through to a recent time when an entirely different species inhabited these buildings and walked this seafront promenade with their little dogs: a different species, because it was impossible to relate the habitat of these Imperial Russians – the mechanism of their thoughts, expectations, assumptions, feeding arrangements or entertainments – with those of their communist successors.

It's not a matter of making a value judgement here – no more than you could ever reasonably say that a dodo was a better or worse animal than a rabbit. It's simply that Yalta exposes you, as in a museum, more to the dodo than to the rabbit.

Yalta was the splendid, select Nice of Imperial Russia – today it's become the rather tattered and decayed and vastly overcrowded Brighton of the Soviet Union. Of the two incarnations, the first interested me more than the second – and with an old pre-Revolutionary Russian Baedeker that I'd brought with me, I was able to lay the map of Yalta now against that of the past. I knew a little about the spirit of that old Yalta too, mostly from Chekhov's letters and some short stories written here at his villa on the hills where he'd spent the last four years of his life. Here he'd entertained Tolstoy, down for a long cure in 1901, and the young Maxim Gorky as well. Chaliapin had sung for him in the drawing room; Rachmaninov had played his piano and Stanislavsky had brought the Moscow Art Theatre down to perform *Uncle Vanya* in front of its ailing author.

As I moved about the town on my long walks, beneath the tired cedars and palm trees in the public gardens, pushing my way through the queues for Luna Park and the crowds round the ten kopeck fortune tellers, I tried to hear these other, older voices and look for the places where they'd met and spent their days – eating, drinking or taking the cure; where they'd read the Moscow papers two days late or brought Gorky's new work from Sinani's famous bookshop. I tried to set up and illuminate this past – like a stage with the original characters – and put it against just the same backdrops of lilac-coloured bay and sumptuously ornate, Edwardian Grand Hotels on the other side of the promenade; the Villa Helena, the Bristol, the Metropole and the Hotel Tavrida where Chekhov had first lived. I listened through the roar of the dodgems, trying to hear the echo of Strauss waltzes, to eavesdrop on those tea dances and tactful assignations amidst the potted palms eighty years before.

I looked for an image, listened for a murmur of all this intelligent and passionately individual civilisation. And I found not the slightest answering call. Lines of washing hung from every bedroom terrace of the old Hotel Tavrida, where now whole families were camped in one room, and what had once been Sinani's bookshop had become a dollar shop, with cheap trinkets and shiny tin samovars, strictly for Western tourists.

Yalta's mood is completely changed today – and I don't so much complain about that. The old life here was shallow as well as civilised. What I do complain of is that for today's inhabitants the dodgems and the uncomfortable pebble beach form the limits of their expectations, whereas for Chekhov and his circle, Yalta offered such very different, more stimulating horizons. Chekhov wrote to a friend in Moscow: 'My villa in Yalta turns out to be snug and warm, with a fine view. The orchard will be an unusual one. I plant with my own hands. I've planted a hundred roses – all the best and most cultivated varieties: fifty pyramidal acacias, many camellias, lilies, tuberoses, etc, etc.'

That afternoon in the drowsy autumn heat I climbed the hill to visit this house, now a well kept museum, where nearly everything remains exactly as it was when Chekhov left here in May 1904. There is an unfinished manuscript page from one of his last stories *The Bride* on his study desk, an antiquated telephone on the wall, a merry snap of Chekhov among the actors of the Moscow Art Theatre – and a very sombre, signed photograph of Tolstoy in his mighty bird's nest beard, looking as tall and old and wise as three prophets laid end to end. . . .

I went out into the gardens and the remains of the orchard in front, walking among the shrubs and trees which Chekhov himself had planted here, now heavily overgrown, but where you can still easily distinguish the pyramidal rose bushes and the precious silver birch trees which he'd specially brought down from the north to remind him of his real roots, the real Russia. Butterflies danced in the sunbeams falling through the Italian stone pines and cypresses. But nothing else moved and even the ghosts were asleep in the strong sunlight: Chaliapin, Rachmaninov and Gorki's tough peasant voice among the tuberoses, declaiming his dreams of a new Russia.

But suddenly, just beyond a bush of feathery flowers, something flashed in the light. I moved down a pathway and there, just ahead of me, was the woman in gold-rimmed spectacles I'd seen on the promenade that morning. She had the big folio on her knees. Of course, she was an artist, not a doctor. And when I came up behind her I saw she was doing a fine, delicately realised pen and ink sketch of the crowded rose gardens with Chekhov's villa rising up from the cypresses behind.

'That's lovely,' I said to her, risking my English.

She looked up. 'Is it? Thank you.' Her English was nearly as good. 'It's for a new illustrated edition of Chekhov's short stories we're doing in Moscow.'

'Oh, which story?' I asked.

'*The Lady with the Little Dog*,' she said, looking up at me again with her candid, intelligent eyes, brushing a strand of lovely blonde hair away from her spectacles.

It was too late for any tactful assignation, I was taking the boat for Sochi that evening. Still, it was a happy enough meeting, among the late roses and the butterflies. I'd been wrong about the entirely dead spirit of the old Yalta. Something of Chekhov's oblique style, his acute observation and sensitivity lived on in the new Russia; something in a woman with gold-rimmed spectacles sitting right there in front of me – and in her subtle drawing of Chekhov's garden.

5
Duck Soup in the Black Sea
(June 1982)

The first thing I saw when I got on board the Soviet cruise liner was the typewriter in the purser's office: a big sturdy machine with an even sturdier man behind it, pumping away at the Cyrillic characters, getting out that evening's menus and the next day's 'Programme of Events, Film Shows and Activities'.

There was something reassuring in the clattering noise, the steady 'thunk-thunk' of the keys – something I sensed I'd missed during my first two weeks in Russia, in and out of a dozen offices and hotel receptions. What was it exactly? It suddenly struck me: of course – it was the typewriter itself, the first typewriter I'd seen in Russia since my arrival.

Yes indeed, I thought: a typewriter is a rare thing in the Soviet Union, not because of any real difficulties in manufacture or cost, but because anything printed or typed immediately becomes evidence of some formal and exalted authority. So a typewriter, in the wrong hands, can be made to forge laws, demands, orders. Worse, the machine can turn out carbon copies, repeating all sorts of inflammatory material, spreading subversion. Thus typewriters in the Soviet Union are kept under lock and key and are only less potentially dangerous than duplicating or Xerox machines, which are kept under three *separate* locks and keys, like nuclear missiles.

But there are exceptions. This purser's typewriter was publicly allowed because we were all very nearly 'abroad' at that moment, about to move out into the middle of the Black Sea, where any seditious carbon copies could never wing it back to shore and were in any case unlikely to disturb the good Communist Party members – who form only about five per cent of the total population – and who, almost uniquely, are allowed to indulge in this much prized form of Soviet holiday making.

I'd joined the ship, the 16,000 ton *Kasakstan*, as a latecomer myself, out of Yalta bound only for Sochi, just an overnight journey. But the other five or six hundred Soviet passengers were nearly halfway through their week's romantic adventure. And that's what this cruise was really all about: ersatz foreign travel for these earnest Soviet citizens who are not allowed to travel overseas – an illusion of far-away places, while keeping them all the while confined in the Soviet pool of the Black Sea.

The boat itself, though, was a splendid modern ship, built in Finland only a few years ago. Things were very shipshape on the *Kasakstan*: meticulously clean, well run – everything *worked*. In these respects it was quite unlike any land-bound version of Soviet life and this refreshing efficiency was very much part of the holiday for the Soviet passengers.

Instead of ignoring you, or growling at you, the staff here answered any queries promptly and politely; the light and hot water in my small cabin actually appeared when I touched the appropriate taps and switches; the bunks were comfy, there was a cut glass water decanter by my pillow, a pair of brand new life jackets in the wardrobe and a radio loudspeaker, given over to brusque commands and medleys from 'My Fair Lady', which you could very nearly turn off.

As part of the essentially vicarious nature of this cruise, a line of brass clocks on 'A' deck next to the purser's office told you the exact time in London, New York and Tokyo, while various announcements beneath promised exotic entertainments in the 'Nite Club' after dinner. A belly dancer was the principal feature here, I noticed, along with some form of Russian bingo (not roulette, I was glad to see), assorted singers, comedians and an 'electric' band. The casino on the promenade deck was closed though, as was the tax-free liquor shop. These ultimate holiday sophistications, I discovered, were only available when the ship was turned over for cruises entirely in Western waters, with Western tourists.

All the same, the pleasures on offer seemed a very fair effort and there was an air of impending joy among the passengers as we stood at the rails and watched Yalta disappear behind us: Yalta, now that we were leaving it, looking magnificent in the pink and pearl sunset, a wine-dark twilight creeping in over the sea ahead of us. The passengers started to twitter and laugh at the rails, and mild practical jokes were played. They were no longer dour or sad like land-bound Russians; they were all children now, released at last from the Soviet Institution.

I had a Turkish coffee at the Neptune bar by the open pool on the after deck, where sunburnt Russian youths were limbering up, in Italian macho style, playing muscular lads, prior to their dinner and a seat well to the front for the belly dancer. And I suddenly felt an extraordinary sense of release myself, safely wombed in this great ship, sliding away into the night, after two very hard weeks spent fighting the system. I, too, was now on holiday, and didn't have to worry about my hotel bedroom pass or the grim ladies; the Gorgons guarding the aproaches on each floor of every hotel. Yes, I thought, when the Russians do something well, they can do it very well indeed – like going to the moon. And this cruise, as we set out, seemed about to be comparably exciting, fantastic, unreal. In the event, it surely was.

I first noticed the belly dancer with her husband and the two ill-behaved children, during the lifeboat drill before dinner. They were one boat ahead of me on the port bow and I was glad of that, since in the event of any emergency, I could see at once that the woman and children, at least, would prove awkward customers. Even at a distance they were, quite obviously, the least likely candidates to spend even a minute in an open boat with. The woman – of Caucasian gypsy stock, I thought: a big, tossy, dramatically dark-coloured creature – fussed impossibly with her lifejacket, first refusing to put it on at all and then pretending total ignorance about tying the straps when she finally got it over her great bosom. Her two girls meanwhile – gross brats in foreign jeans and jokey T-shirts – blew the whistles loudly on their lifejackets and would have thrown them overboard had not an officer intervened.

These were a trio, I thought, where hatchets would be required if we sank in the briny – to chop their fingers off as they reached for the lifeboat gunwales. The husband, on the other hand, seemed a gentle creature, put upon and anxious to please everyone, especially his wretched brood. He was a big, slumberous, middle-aged man in a dark business suit, balding, with a sad, long-suffering Armenian face. He had the air of an old-fashioned stockbroker; he might, indeed, have been a stay-at-home cousin of Nubar Gulbenkian's. All the same, I made a note to steer well clear of lifeboat number three on the port bow in the event of any nautical mishap that night.

It was during dinner, over a thimbleful of caviar and a shot of pepper vodka, that I first realised that all might not go exactly according to plan on my cruise over the Black Sea. Since I wasn't part of any group, I was sitting at a table by myself in the Orchid Saloon, when who should join me but Gulbenkian's cousin, the weary old Armenian, though minus his family, thank God.

He grunted sourly several times before asking me, in Russian, to pass him something or other. I misunderstood, replying in English – and it was at this point that his eyes lit up, as if he recognised in me the fulfilment of a great hope, I knew not what. His own English was minimal, but he overdrew wildly on the account at once, before mortgaging every Anglo-Saxon word and syllable he had ever possessed.

'I want you – help,' he finally managed to explain ominously as we were served a pimento goulash. I finished my pepper vodka, girding my loins.

'Yes?'

'Ve havs is *much* chilrun. Too many. And vivs,' he added.

'Vivs?'

'Womans,' he explained dismissively. 'I need you plis.'

I thought I knew at once what he was after. He wanted out to the West, he and his dreadful wife and children, all of them: the backing for a visa; a letter of recommendation from London; an invitation to stay with me in England; an introduction for his children to an Oxford College . . . I knew the sort of problem he had in mind for me to solve from years of travelling off the beaten track, where even a herdsman coming round a peak in the Himalayas had immediately expected me to provide him with a free English lesson or an entrée to Balliol College. Such beginnings, if encouraged in the slightest, always end badly, so that though I pitied the man's predicament – whatever it was – I quickly tried to change the topic.

'Well,' I said brightly. 'What are you doing on this boat? A working holiday?'

'I have too much vivs and chilrun,' he replied, returning doggedly to his original theme. 'I need you plis. Am *crushed*.' He brought his hands together slowly, like a vice closing, and I was truly sorry for the man. But I was determined to be firm. A helping hand in this kind of situation could land you in all sorts of trouble.

'I'm sorry, I can't help – about your wife and children,' I said. 'I'd like to, but – '

'Is not help,' he interrupted. 'I want you plis, your cabine, zimmer.'

'I see. You want my *place*, my *cabin*.'

The man nodded happily. We understood each other at last.

'Well, I'm sorry, but I'm afraid not,' I shook my head. 'I need it myself.'

He got out a lot of ticket stubs then and a pile of old roubles and I thought he was going to bribe me. I shook my head again and he let the lot fall among the debris of his pimento goulash. I offered him a pepper vodka to buck him up, but he lifted his eyes to heaven in a totally exhausted fashion as if only God could give him any strength now. I was truly sorry for him, but hoped all the same to avoid him thereafter. I was not successful in this.

I watched the cabaret that night – and his wife the belly dancer – though keeping well to the back of the packed saloon. She, of course, was top of the bill. It was a performance of little refinement but great vigour. The huge lady, heavily sequined now, and thankfully well clad in all sorts of heavy silks and satins, gave a suitably prudish, proletarian version of 'Cairo Nights', making up in thumps and thwacks and shuddering gyrations what she lacked in erotic finesse. Her husband, in an imitation dress suit and dancing pumps, sat in the front row near the captain and half a dozen of his senior officers – all of them sipping crème de menthe through straws – and all of them got up in identical braid caps and snow white naval uniforms, exactly like a chorus from 'HMS Pinafore'.

Behind, in crushed ogling ranks, the rest of the passengers craned their necks forward. It was a steamy sort of evening, especially when the 'electric' band got going, and I retired early, locking my cabin door firmly behind me.

Imagine my surprise, when several hours later I woke in my top bunk and, looking down to the one beneath, saw a pair of shiny black dancing pumps attached to some hairy legs leading up to a pair of flower-patterned underpants. It was the old Armenian about to get into bed. God knows how he ever got in – a pass key perhaps – I never found out, but I was out of my own bunk quick enough, remonstrating with him.

'Now look here,' I said. . . .

But his English, now that he'd achieved his aim of taking over my cabin, had quite deserted him and he merely smiled at me happily. His luggage, imitation dress suit and wash bag were already in place. He was home and dry.

I heard scufflings in the passageway outside then, and a moment later the cabin door opened. And, yes – it was the belly dancer, semi-clad, and the two children, together with their extensive baggage. I tried to keep them out, but might as well have stopped three frisky bullocks on the run. First the big woman forced entry, then the two gross brats.

'Listen,' I shouted. 'This is ridiculous!'

But none of them listened or apparently spoke any English except the old man, still sitting on the bunk in his flower-patterned underpants, repeating merrily to himself, 'This is our plis. *Our* plis!'

There were now five of us in various states of undress, pushing and shoving in the confined space.

'Come on!' I yelled. 'You'll have to move.'

But the party was settling in now, a triumphant gathering after a long journey, and there was an exotic, animal smell in the air, a mix of grease-paint, sweat – and crème de menthe, I thought, as I lurched about trying to find the bell for the cabin steward.

Some minutes later another large, swarthy woman, in a sort of nurse's uniform, squeezed into the cabin with us. That made it six. It was getting difficult to breathe and quite impossible to move. I panicked and tried to make for the lifejackets in the wardrobe. One of the gross brats yelped underfoot.

Then suddenly I knew that all this had happened somewhere before. It was a joke. It would be all right in the end. Of course – the Marx Brothers, that was it. It was all from that scene in the liner cabin in *A Night at the Opera*.

I turned to the company, smiling. 'All right,' I said. 'It's all right: come right on in and enjoy yourselves. Like the Marx Brothers – why not? Ask the captain and the first mate and the plumber and the ship's doctor – and let's ring for room service and get some hard-boiled eggs.'

The assembled company smiled on me then, recognising the word 'Marx' in my spiel, I suppose, and believing that for the greater glory of Karl, I was giving over my accommodation.

I slunk off the boat next morning at Sochi, a tired and wiser man. The typewriter was clattering away in the purser's office. He was writing another script for the Marx Brothers. It would be 'Duck Soup' that evening.

6

Georgia:
Champagne in the Morning
(June 1982)

The vast, snow-capped chain of mountains rose up to my left from the aeroplane window as we flew eastwards from the Black Sea: the Caucasus mountains, a pearly pink in the gathering sunlight of dawn, where Jason once sought the golden Fleece and Prometheus was bound to his rock, but which today, much more prosaically, divide Russia proper from the southern Soviet Republics of Georgia, Armenia and Azerbaijan.

I was on my way to Georgia that morning. And when we landed at Tbilisi the capital, an hour later, I knew I'd definitely left Russia behind. My guide was already out on the tarmac with a car to meet me, the bar was miraculously open in the arrival lounge, and the first thing she did was to offer me a glass of Georgian champagne before we set off for the city.

Yes, there was something immediately efficient, yet wayward and lightheaded about Georgia and the Georgians. The sun was out, a bright crisp autumn day, and a trellis of lush flowering bougainvillaea climbed up over the end of the counter, where some other lively Georgians were half way through a feast of pickled peppers and a few large bottles of the local product, the purple-coloured bubbly, which was seemingly standard issue in this part of the world. There was no doubt about it; I'd come in from the Russian cold at last.

The men down the far end of the bar all looked like stand-ins for

Omar Sharif – curly dark hair, piercing black eyes, bushy brows, outrageously handsome. Another bottle or two and they'd be dancing on the tables I thought, singing wild folk-songs and unsheathing secret daggers before storming out to conquer something or someone – a woman or a country.

I knew the dashing reputation of the Georgians – this vital, gifted race: the romantic people *par excellence*. And here, right at the airport, it seemed as if I'd stumbled straight into the middle of some happy propaganda movie about them. It all seemed too good to be true. And I remembered then: apart from the romance, I knew also some of the earlier history of this always threatened nation.

Georgia, originally an Orthodox outpost constantly attacked by its Moslem neighbours, had willingly sought the protection of Tzarist Russia back in 1801. But now, after a brief period and much bloodshed as an independent state just after the first world war, it was an unwilling part of the Soviet Union. Thus the Georgians today were far from being simply a merry race of people with a liking for champagne at ten in the morning. And there were other, even grimmer, more recent events which had been left out altogether in that propaganda movie in the airport lounge.

Stalin had been a Georgian. Yet because of his early career as a bank robber, Georgian society had rejected him. But Stalin lived to take his revenge. His policies in Georgia during the last war were aimed at nothing less than the total destruction of that State. First of all, cynically promoting his own Georgian background as a come-on, he recruited over half a million of his compatriots, not to defend the homeland, but to die on the worst sectors of the German front, where 350,000 of them perished. After the war, just to make sure of things, he exiled another 100,000 Georgians to the camps of Siberia. Few ever returned. Grim recent times indeed, for a population of barely three-and-a-half million.

The Georgians survived all that bloodletting. But how do these very individualistic people survive amidst all the conformities of today's Soviet regime? That was the real question for me. I finished my champagne and we headed off into the city. Tbilisi – 'Little Paris' as it's known – is set on the banks of the Kura river, nestling in a long, dramatic gorge in the foothills of the Caucasus.

The first thing I noticed when we got into town were the open public telephones on every street corner, each of them furiously occupied with chattering, gesticulating citizens – an entirely fresh sight for me in the Soviet Union – scores of telephones that actually worked and were constantly being used. And I remembered again then: the Georgians are intensely proud of their language. It's quite different from Russian, one of the oldest in the world, and obviously, I could see now, they were the sort of voluble, vivacious people who loved their words and wanted to use them at every opportunity. So they ensured that their telephones worked and were everywhere available.

One up to the Georgians, I thought. They *communicated* – in an unwilling union of Soviet people where most real communication is discouraged by Moscow, when it is not being vigorously repressed.

Of course, the highly nationalistic Georgians particularly resent Soviet domination, just as they resented the Tzarist view that theirs was a barbaric country fit only for political and other exiles. The facts are that Georgia was Christianised and had an alphabet 500 years before the Russians, with a vivid culture going back a thousand years before that – particularly an unbroken oral tradition: stories and epic poems, which, nearly always against Soviet will, they have retained in every way they can today. The Georgians never discard old words in their language, even as they evolve new ones. In short, against the oppressor – like the Irish and the Hungarians – they've made a stand on their words, words the only weapons of the vanquished. And this is the first way they fight for their identity today – not so much with guns, though they do that too, but with language. The Georgians, more than any other of the dozen or so minority Republics in the Soviet Union, pose a continuous political threat to Moscow: a clever, fearless, adaptable people. And the Russians don't like them for it.

In Moscow I was never done hearing stories of their wily, avaricious nature; how they did nothing but line their own pockets by taking suitcases of tangerines by air to the capital and selling them in midwinter. Yet the Georgians – rightly I think – will deny that they are merchants. They say it's their neighbours, the Armenians or more the Moslem Azerbaijanis, who, as middle men, hump the tangerines and profit from them in the big northern cities. No, the Georgians are much more obviously concerned with maintaining their own national identity: with music, dancing, poetry, argument, food and champagne – with things of the mind and the body rather than with financial gain, an important but secondary consideration for them.

It's the individual spirit that counts most in Georgia – and that's what I wanted to taste. Were the flavours surviving? A visit to the local champagne factory might offer an answer here. I'd heard there was good horse racing in Tbilisi as well and perhaps at the end of the day there'd be a little Georgian sword dancing and philosophy . . . I left with my guide for the champagne factory on the outskirts of town straight after lunch.

The long, grey, forbidding building had a Stalinist air about it. And though the huge marble-columned hall inside didn't anywhere commemorate this local celebrity, it was extremely liberal with the memory of his compatriot Lenin, that unlikely champagne drinker, whose thoughts were loudly proclaimed all round the walls, in a dominant Russian rather than Georgian script. 'Forward with the Workers' was the least severe of the exhortations and that red marble hall had a distinctly chilly air – the last place on earth, it seemed, where anyone was ever likely to make or get a drink.

But then a splendid, twinkly-eyed old man met us at the foot of the marble staircase: white pufsky hair and lop-sided spectacles, a veritable Professor Brainstorm, and the whole mood changed. The Marxist airs softened. For here was someone essentially human: Paul Mamaladze, Chief Technologist at the factory, a Georgian of the old school, as I found out later, who'd long before become top dog in this vital national industry, the grey men from Moscow taking a back seat. Together we set off on a tour of the cellars beneath, inspecting one musty, bottle-crammed vault after another, yet where interestingly, each dark cavern still proposed its own little Marxist admonishment on the cobwebby walls.

'What's that say?' I asked, looking at one such notice set above a great stack of magnums in the gloom.

My guide pondered the sign for a moment, for of course it was again in Cyrillic, not Georgian, characters – another, ever present reminder, even in these darkest recesses, of Moscow's dictates 1500 miles away.

'It says: "The duties of every worker in the Great Proletariat demand that he be constantly, vigilant, honest and – um, sober".'

'Quite so,' I added. 'Quite so.'

We all trooped upstairs to a vast marble conference room on the first floor and sat under a huge bust of Lenin at the end of the longest table I've ever seen, while Mr Mamaladze embarked on a history of the factory and all its works: 'Started in 1937, the champagne made from

Tsiska and Tesinuri grapes, 650 workers, unit costs of two roubles fifty kopecks, exports to all the other fraternal socialist nations. . . .'

Half an hour later the sun had come to slant directly in through the huge windows. It was very hot and I was getting genuinely thirsty. But the severe bust of Lenin gazed down on us all unpityingly and I began to fear that this sour-faced old ghost had put a jinx on the drinks. I was mistaken. A woman suddenly appeared, like a French maid in a farce, in a tight black bombasine dress with a small frilly apron and a well charged tray. From then on it was plain sailing. We sampled the Brut champagne – the best, with a huge, startlingly fruity bouquet – then the dry, the semi-dry and finally the semi-sweet. Each was extremely good – equal to all but the best French varieties. After half-a-dozen glasses I broached the question of 'outside interference' in the champagne business.

'No,' said Paul Mamaladze. 'Certainly not. There is none. Only we Georgians know how to make it suitably. The only interference is in trying to get more from us. We could sell five or ten times as much as we produce.'

He refilled our glasses and Lenin looked down on us all from his plinth with undisguised disapproval as the long afternoon waned. And despite Moscow's graffiti, all the injunctions and admonishments on the walls, it was obvious that the Georgians maintained their freedom and ascendancy in the champagne business at least.

The following day at the races in Tbilisi I found myself sitting next to a well dressed, prosperous-looking much younger Georgian. Again he was called Paul. But he was not as carefree as his namesake in the champagne factory. I'd asked him to explain the race card to me and afterwards, since his English was remarkably good, we got talking.

The horses – or rather the thin Arab ponies – scampered delicately and rather slowly round the sand track in front of us. The racing in Tbilisi wasn't as good as I'd heard. I asked Paul about having a bet, for I could see no tote and of course there were no bookies anywhere. But he was discouraging.

'Don't bother. All real gambling is done privately. Back in town. Anything good in Georgia is done privately, not with the State.'

Later we had a tremendous Georgian lunch: chicken *satsiri*, served in a delicious walnut sauce, *shaslik* and more champagne on the terrace of the racecourse restaurant. The whole place was strangely empty. Yet behind us long tables had been prepared for at least a hundred people.

41

'They're having a big function here today,' Paul told me. 'The local party bosses – and people from Moscow. But I know the restaurant manager, so it's all right.'

Paul was an engineer, a skilled motor mechanic. He was lucky, he said, because of this. Soviet cars rarely worked after the first few thousand miles. Official servicing was normally impossible and spare parts more impossible still. So Paul, as a moonlighter, had all the work, and had already earned all the money he wanted. He was a rich man.

'But actual money means nothing here,' he explained. 'There's nothing to buy. It's like what you call Monopoly money – no value. So we work for each other in Georgia now. Exchange work, barter. I fix one man's car; he takes photographs of my wife and family. For instance, we have hardly any private gasoline down here now. So we take it off the drivers of the State cars and trucks – outside town, with syphons – in exchange for some other service. We work for each other. It's the only way to survive. And we do.'

He cracked another bottle of champagne. 'You see, this is how we've always survived in Georgia – against the Turks, Mongols, Tartars – by beating the system. And so with Moscow. We accept their rules in the game. But *we* win,' he added sharply.

The ponies, dulled by the heat, ambled round the perimeter on their last race of the afternoon. The crowds had already left.

'No, we're not so good with horses any more,' Paul said. 'Most of that old Georgian life has gone. It's in the *mind* now.' He tapped his head. 'That's where we fight our battles today. Most of the best professors, the best actors, singers, movie makers in the Soviet Union today – they're all Georgian. And so is the ladies' world chess champion. That's where we win now.'

Later, as we left the restaurant, the big party men were starting to arrive for their meal. Several huge black Zil limousines drew up carefully by the doorway – ponderous, old-fashioned, curtained vehicles.

'All the way from Moscow, those cars,' Paul pointed at the number plates – and he smiled now. 'They need us more than we need them.'

'What do you mean?'

'They don't trust us – and they fear us. So today, now that Stalin has gone, they have to – how do you say? – please us?'

'Placate us,' I told him.

'Yes, that's it! That's the word!' Paul laughed. And we stepped into his souped-up, custom-styled Russian Fiat and drove off like a bomb.

7
Baku:
Commissars and Caravanserais

It was in Baku airport – 300 miles east of Tbilisi and nearly 2000 miles from Moscow – that I first realised what great colonisers the Russians have always been. For here in Baku, for the first time in my long journey, I had travelled far enough east to be able immediately to distinguish the minority *Russian* faces from those of the locals; the Azerbaijanis, a vastly mixed race of Persians, Tartars, Armenians and a dozen other ancient peoples who have settled over the centuries on the shores of the Caspian Sea, this gateway to Asia and the Far East.

I could spot all the Russians at once in the mad scramble to collect our bags. They held back: big, serious, chunky people, officials for the most part, in little, brimless leather hats, short polyester macs, carrying cheap briefcases, while the raggedly dressed Azerbaijanis moved about in confused hordes, like Mohammed's troops routed outside the gates of Vienna: small, nervous men, unshaven, with cadaverous gypsy faces and immense flat berets on their heads. The Russians were behaving like dowagers at some rough agricultural show, sure in the long run of both their bags and their position. Whereas the Azerbaijanis scuttled here and there in that insecure and despairing manner which all dependent, unsophisticated peoples show when confronted with the trappings of the coloniser's civilisation – in this case the automatic baggage conveyor belt which, in its bizarre service, suggested some awful mischief to them, as it did to me.

In that airport bedlam one thing at least was clear: I had arrived with the rulers amongst the ruled – just as I might have landed in Bombay 100 years before, taking up the white man's burden, before meting out good government to a recalcitrant race beyond the law.

It was late at night before I eventually got my own bags and drove into the city of Baku. But long before, I could see the livid orange flames all over the horizon and smell the acrid, sulphurous fumes, the residue of the oil and burnt-off natural gas that has sprouted from these parts for thousands of years. And when I finally got to the top of a rise, the city lay there beneath me, circled by plumes of slowly burning fire, a vision straight out of Dante's *Inferno*.

Baku, quite literally, is an underworld, lying fifty-six feet below sea level on the oily shores of the tideless Caspian, beneath the utterly barren foothills of the eastern Caucasus. It is a place of high, humid temperatures, with a few trees and less shade, and with a traditional violent wind like a roaring dragon's breath from the north. Baku struck me next morning as being just about the most uncomfortable and unpleasant place I'd ever been in, and I held an eau de cologne handkerchief to my forehead and nose as I walked along the seafront, the Oilworker's Boulevard, wondering what on earth I was doing here.

Well, there was one reason. My grandfather had come here in 1910. He'd written a chapter about Baku in a Persian travel book and I wanted to compare notes seventy years later. At the time of his visit, before the Revolution, Baku had been an underworld of another sort as well – a booming oil town, created by Alfred Nobel and the Rothschilds, the Gulch City of Imperial Russia, which had thus become a mecca for criminals, robber barons and adventurers of every sort.

'Filled with the flotsam and jetsam of the whole Middle East,' my grandfather had written. 'A town where an enemy may be disposed of at a cost of five roubles and where the average number of murders is said to be five per day. Here,' he went on, reflecting on the contemporary socialist agitation, 'Here there is no feature of the Tzar's police system that is not represented . . . a city as well of gamblers, brigands and blackmailers where the passions are crude and violent, where every nerve is highly strung.'

Having read his account of Baku, when I got there myself, I'd been tempted to put my money in my shoe. But I soon thought better of it. It was pretty obvious from my first few hours in the city that things had changed a great deal: the communist millennium had arrived in Baku some time before. The brigands, blackmailers and gamblers had all been put away and the contemporary citizens looked about as dangerous as spent cartridges. There was a glazed, heat-struck air about them, like people toasted on a spit for too long – people incapable of killing you even for a hundred roubles, I thought.

It's a remarkable feature of Soviet life, this conformity of spirit which in the space of just two generations, the Russians have managed to impose on the most opposite sorts of people in the wildest of places. The British in their colonial days ruled by division: a strict separation between them and the locals and a further great divide, if possible, between the local tribes and races; while only their missionaries ever expected the natives to accept the one true God. But the Russians – lacking this social apartheid – are far more thorough, uncompromising and successful in their colonisation, and in their minority Republics, Lenin is the one God whom each official expects absolutely everyone – black, white or indifferent – to obey, if not believe in.

I wandered along the seafront in Baku that morning in the boiling damp heat and made for an empty café at the end of a very long pier set right out in the Caspian. The heat was killing, there were no cool drinks and I was lucky to get a coffee before the staff closed everything up for their mid-morning break. An immense Russian woman in a headscarf, a real Babushka type from the kitchen, came out and sat at a table nearby with the other Russian waitresses. They had a samovar going somewhere inside and they started out on endless glasses of tea. And then the huge woman, relaxing like a ton of bricks, opened a pot of raspberry jam and ladled two great spoonfuls into her glass. Of course, I thought: jam in your tea, a traditional sweetener among Russians, the sort of old-fashioned detail one finds in Tolstoy's novels – and I'd never seen it done before on my trip. But here it was, 1500 miles away from Moscow, a quintessential Russian gesture, as typical as a whisky soda sundowner among the old British Raj in India, made and taken here in just the same relaxed manner: a manner of unquestioned, unconscious authority.

Of course, long before the oil, it was a need to secure their southern boundaries that brought the Russians to the Caspian in the early nineteenth century. But, just as much as political necessity, there's an emotional reason, I think, for their colonisations. The Russians, without much sea to play with, are tremendous land sailors. They love travelling their vast continent – on foot, camel, horseback, and down their great rivers in the old days, or by air and rail today. They love scouring their endless flat horizons, until they come to those final barriers, the Himalayas or the Pacific. And it's more the spur of *lebensraum* than Lenin, a need to seek space on the margins of their world, that takes them to settle in places like Baku and way beyond that in Samarkand, Alma Ata and Vladivostock. Like the Americans a hundred and more years ago, the Russians have a land fever, a longing for all the blue beyonds. But unlike the Americans, they can still more than satisfy themselves in this. Indeed, they've only recently begun properly to open up their vast territories between the Urals and the Pacific. 'Go east, young man', is a constant call – and a genuine promise – in the Soviet Union today.

But I wasn't going further east, not yet anyway. In fact I was spending that morning with a group of package tourists from Britain – an obligatory tour of the city – with the afternoon option of a coach trip twenty miles north to the thirteenth-century Temple of the fire worshippers at the old oil village of Surakhani. The great thing, I knew, was not to get depressed by the heat and the horrors in Baku – to keep reasonably active, hope that lunch wouldn't be more than an hour late and that the dollar bar in the hotel *might* just possibly be open for a cold beer later in the evening. Such mild ambitions, I'd long since discovered, become obsessive, mirage-like objectives when travelling in the Soviet Union.

The British package group back at the hotel, turned out to be as mixed as the Azerbaijani race. There were several dour retired miners from Yorkshire with their more spirited wives; some enthusiastic Scots communists; a very traditional ex-naval commander and his delicate daughter from Bexhill-on-Sea; a brace of Home-Counties maiden ladies with an enquiring archaeological bent and a heavy load of obscure guides and two young men, civil servants from Belfast, whose interests, I later found out, ran more towards other young men in the city than to ancient monuments.

I wondered how our Russian guide would handle the group,

particularly since Baku, for the communists, has most unfortunate British associations. It was from here, during the White Russian counter-revolution in 1920, that the twenty-six commissars of the city escaped by boat, only to be betrayed by the captain of their ship and taken south to British-held territory at the foot of the Caspian where they were all then summarily executed. Their bodies were eventually returned to Baku and buried beneath a martyr's memorial in the centre of town. And that in fact turned out to be our first stop – a vast, circular marble plaza with the figure of a mourning worker in the centre holding an eternal flame in his hands.

In the event – for reasons of tact, I suppose – the guide didn't mention the British involvement in this outrage, until one of the Scots communists brought the matter up squarely.

'Yes,' she admitted. 'It was the British.'

Our Bexhill naval commander chipped in at once. 'It was really the Turkish captain's doing,' he insisted. 'He betrayed them all.'

'Ah, yes!' interrupted one of the Yorkshire miners angrily. 'But who *bribed* the Turkish captain in the first place? The British commander in the south.'

'Oh, I don't know about that!' Bexhill was rising, purple, to the bait. 'The Turks were fighting the Communists then, too.'

It was quite apparent that our group knew a good deal more about the twenty-six Baku Commissars than the guide, and there seemed to be all the makings of an ugly little scene by the martyr's memorial – a most undiplomatic incident. The guide moved us on pretty smartly.

But later, on our way out to the Fire Worshipper's Temple, I was brooding on this sort of murderous interference in other people's affairs which powerful nations take for granted – now, just as much as in the past. The British in 1920 had had the brazen clout to execute all those Commissars. Yet the Russian Commissars themselves had used just the same sort of brutality in subduing the local non-communist Azerbaijanis. And there were no memorials to them. I was just about to bring up this point with our guide when, luckily perhaps, the Fire Worshippers' Temple hove in sight.

It lay behind a sun-baked wall at the edge of the sea – a small square pavilion with darkened chimneys at each corner, where flames of natural gas spiralled up into the lead-blue dome of sky. We got out of the coach and the heat nearly felled us all there and then. The village and the land beyond was deserted. Nothing moved except the stiff arms and elbows of ancient oil pumps, hissing and gurgling all about us, like the legs of an advancing plague of great black locusts. Here, for 700 years before the oilmen came, an isolated settlement of Persian Zoroastrians had lived in this monastery, in this cauldron, worshipping the flames, toasting their souls and torturing their bodies in an ecstasy of fire. It took our group but ten minutes to suffer the same effects, before heading for the shade in the monastic cells all round the walls, each of which had been turned into a museum piece, with startlingly lifelike figures depicting the self-mutilation of the original inmates. One naked, emaciated fakir lay on a bed of nails; another raised his hand high in perpetual salute so that his whole shoulder was deformed; others lay in eternal chains.

'So this is how it was,' one of the Yorkshire miners remarked, contemplating a life even more punishing than his own.

'Yes,' the guide nodded. 'In the old days things were *very* bad here. But all that's changed now of course.'

We murmured full agreement – anything to get back to Baku and the chance of a cold drink. But the old naval commander took me to one side as we left the museum. 'I've never seen such perfect representations of *present* conditions in this country,' he said rather loudly.

'Well, er, yes,' I muttered, hurrying on – not wishing for another political contretemps and the chance of being abandoned in this eerie, parched landscape, where only the oil pumps creaked and the flames blew forever in the furnace of the wind. But back at our hotel by evening, tongues literally hanging out, we found the dollar bar closed and not a hope in hell of a cold beer. It wasn't until much later that evening that the miracle happened.

I'd walked down into the old town of Baku, and then up a hill, along a warren of dark lanes, finding myself at last among the original Persian fortifications of the city: a great tower looking out to sea, old mosques, minarets, broken masonry, a vast serpentine wall. And behind this wall, beyond a great arched doorway firmly locked against the night, I heard a lot of squeaky Arab music, fiddles and tambourines, the sound of voices, laughter. Fatigue and thirst made me rash. I knocked hard on the great doors. Almost at once they opened a fraction and a tiny man in a white shirt and cummerbund peered out. I would have fallen on my knees, invoking the prophet. But I was let in anyway – through a long dark archway with a great brass gong in the middle and beyond I saw a palm tree and a fountain, and beyond that, all round the open courtyard, little lantern-lit rooms where people were eating with their fingers on great cushions with hubbly-bubblys at their side.

'Come along,' the man said in Russian. And then in English: 'This is the Caravanserai.'

I'd stumbled on a new restaurant, I later discovered, created in the buildings of an original mediaeval caravanserai and only recently excavated by the Russians from beneath the centuries of rubbish lying over the old Persian town; excavated complete in almost every detail, including the great gong above the doorway, put there as an alarm to wake the innkeeper as the silk-road camels pushed against it, finding succour at last after their long journeys from Samarkand and further east. The rest of my evening was pure delight.

I was given a small, cell-like, room to myself, the walls covered in sumptuous Azerbaijani carpets, where I sat on a pile of cushions looking straight out onto the glistening fountain and beyond that, to a trio of Azerbaijani gypsy musicians, in loose sheepskin jackets wearing their great black mushroom berets, and squeaking away beneath the velvet sky now filled with stars. I didn't need a beer. Before the astonishingly long meal began, I went out to the fountain and washed all the heat of the day away, splashing my hands and face in the crystal cool water and then letting the liquid luxury run down my throat, right to the bottom of my gut, a wild thirst slaked with a feeling of perfect wellbeing.

Afterwards I tossed back a tiny decanter of ice-cold vodka before moving on to a dozen spicy dishes and salads, including the local treat, *Na Kurma*, a kebab garnished with pomegranates. Apart from the musicians I could see no other Azerbaijanis in the place, only Russians, including large groups all the way from Moscow. But perhaps this was fair enough: we were all travellers after all, finding appropriate sanctuary from the desert in this magnificent old caravanserai.

And I reflected once more on the specifically Russian efforts here, the good side to their colonial coin. For it was they who had resurrected this place, this hidden balm lying deep in the sand and rubble of the old city, land sailors all of them, Russians who

'. . . travel not for trafficking alone;
By hotter winds our fiery hearts are fanned:
For lust of knowing what should not be known,
We take the Golden Road to Samarkand.'

Under the stars, by the fountain, I was cool at last in Baku – and tomorrow I too was leaving for Samarkand.

8

The Truths of Samarkand
(June 1982)

For some extraordinary reason – it wasn't Christmas and I was nearly a thousand miles from the nearest Christian country – the old taxi radio was playing a medley of carols as we crept into Samarkand from the airport, in the very midst of a star-filled, almost frosty night. I should have arrived by camel, of course, but this musical accompaniment – 'Holy Night', 'Away in a Manger' – was almost as good and certainly it seemed appropriate. As we bumped along a back road past moon-bathed orchards, palm shadows and little mud-walled, white-washed huts – I might well have been coming into Bethlehem 2000 years ago, a time traveller if not one of the Three Wise Men.

I opened the car window and suddenly there was a faintly musky, acrid, vegetable smell in the air: burnt dung, something spicy, crushed clover, some kind of herb? – the rumour of an ancient countryside where things had not yet started to go wrong.

I have some of those herbs with me still – wrapped in a cone of newspaper torn from *Pravda* – which I bought in the market before I left Samarkand: thyme and mint, certainly, and tarragon, I think – that acrid smell – a very distinctive, slightly bitter leaf that they sprinkled all over the soup in my hotel there. I've only to open the packet and I'm back in Tamerlane's Babylon in the desert. Samarkand – Maracanda to Alexander the Great when he rushed through the place in 328 BC and afterwards Sa-mo-kien, the westernmost outpost of the Celestial Empire.

Today, of course, the town is in the Soviet Republic of Uzbekistan, just north of Afghanistan: a great cotton, tea and wine producing centre on the newly irrigated Kyzyl Kum desert. Once the ultimate journey for prophets, pilgrims, merchants, intrepid British explorers and Edwardian poets, today you can reach Samarkand in a five-hour flight from Moscow, via Intourist in Regent Street. And where Tamerlane held court in vast, silk-tented pavilions with stupendous feasts lasting a month or more, now equally huge billboards of Lenin keep a duller, but no less stern eye on things.

This city – the centre of a Mongol Empire that so excited Elizabethan England, whose brutality, wealth, luxury and art were the fantastic rumours behind Marlowe's *Tamburlaine the Great* – is today a shadow of its old self. And yet the reality was so formidable, composed of such glittering and extensive artefacts, that even the shadows take your breath away, 500 years later.

Samarkand, first of all, is a city of endless natural and man-made colour; a reflecting jewel caught between the snow-topped, Heavenly Mountains of Tien-Shan on one side, with the deserts running away forever to the north. It takes its pale lilac and gold first from the hills and then from the burning sands. And after this natural shading there is the brilliant surge of mosaic and tile reaching up above all the buildings – the mosques, minarets and mausoleums of Tamerlane's city – picked out in every shade of blue – madonna, duck egg, navy, turquoise, ultramarine. Coming to Samarkand, after the weeks of grey uniformity I'd experienced elsewhere in the Soviet Union, was like swimming in over a tropical reef, gazing down at a coral city, where the doves were the fishes, circling the minarets in endless shoals.

Samarkand is still a true caravanserai, a resting place, a real consolation for the spirit. Set midway between Soviet austerity and Chinese clamour, it remains a place apart, still more past than present; a place where you can set aside contemporary ideology – at least in the evenings or at first light when the whole town dissolves or wakes in all its limpid colours.

For on closer inspection, out on the streets in the keen blue midday light, you can't forget Lenin, since in the first instance, without him and his successors, the glittering mediaeval city would have crumbled into dust by now. The intricate filigree wood carvings in the mausoleums, the many coloured glazes on the tiles and terracottas, the fabulously patterned mosaics – most of all this is new or has been painstakingly restored by the Soviets in the past fifty years, so that Tamerlane's fading Moslem dream has become a communist-restored reality now. It's a strange feeling, when you gaze on all this resurrected and essentially religious splendour and realise that you are looking at the handiwork of the October Revolution, the product of a world without God, yet which here has been made over again exactly in the Prophet's images.

Strange. But then the Russians, so insecure and mistrustful abroad, make up for this through some staggering technical achievements at home and restored Samarkand is definitely one of them. And it doesn't matter at all that the inspiration they are perpetuating here is religious, not communist. They lovingly resuscitate Samarkand as an example of their 'civilising mission', as a means of showing the Uzbek people, recently no more than a nomadic horde, that they are now part of an admirable Soviet Union: Soviet citizen, not camel herders, who may thus share in all Moscow's fabulous imperial benefits. Restored Samarkand, in this context, is an incredibly accomplished public-relations exercise. But it's more than skin deep – the depth of a new mosaic tile – for the Russians have brought genuine economic and educational success as well, and these Soviet Central Asian Republics, unlike most of the dozen others in the Union, can be said to have benefited from Moscow's rule in the past fifty years.

Certainly on my first morning out and about I saw things on the streets impossible even to imagine elsewhere in Russia: a vivacity, colour and material plenty – images of people willingly embarked on the twentieth century who had not yet, at least, lost much of their national identity.

In Samarkand most of the Uzbeks still wear their traditional dress: the men in long cotton shirts and worsted jackets with tiny box-like, black and white striped skullcaps. And there was the old high fashion of the delicate, blackberry-eyed girls. They were maidens straight out of a Persian miniature – with raven-coloured pigtails, eyebrows in one dark slash straight across their foreheads and all wearing the *khalat*; the best in silk, a loose printed dress with billowy pantaloons, each a mix of brilliant neon colours, so that they hopped and skittered about the place in their gilt slippers, exotic birds freed from an aviary, illuminating the covered markets as they passed in flights between the stalls.

Here, on the long stone counters, and in the shops outside was provender enough to sustain one of Tamerlane's great month-long banquets: herbs, vegetables, fruit of every conceivable kind – and above all, meat and huge perch from the Aral Sea, freely available in a dozen butchers' shops, something I'd not seen so presented elsewhere in the Soviet Union at all. There were riches in these markets of Samarkand beyond the dreams of avarice for other Soviet citizens, though the Uzbeks took them for granted, just as the older men in from the country took their ease outside the markets in the sun, dreamers from a Thousand and One Nights, lying among the vast pyramids of melons like mediaeval relics. Unlike the embattled Georgians to the west, the Uzbeks don't have to beat the Soviet system. So far, materially at least, they simply benefit from it.

In the practice of their religion though, things are not so convenient for them. Moscow, as part of its 'civilising mission', placates Islam to various degrees in its annexed territories today. But it does so unwillingly, with many tacit curbs and some outright prohibition. The faith, for Moscow, must never become a growth product. Thus there are only a few hundred mosques for the seventeen million Moslems in these Soviet Central Asian Republics. And since the religious colleges are forced to maintain a minimum output, there are over 300 illegal Mullahs in the area, constantly on the move, serving their flocks in the most unlikely and out of the way places. And very few of the faithful ever manage the pilgrimage to Mecca. They must make do instead with journeys to the holy shrines in Samarkand, most notably to the tomb of Shah-Zinda, the Living King, a cousin of the prophet's, who brought the faith here in the seventh century, trying to convert the local fire worshippers and was duly beheaded for his efforts. The Russians, strenuously attempting their own conversions thirteen hundred years later, have had little success here while rarely meeting with the same fate: the Politburo offers no rewards in heaven but carries an even greater clout than the Prophet in the here and now.

The Russians came to Samarkand in 1868, to secure their southern frontiers. And one of the most revealing walks in the city, which the tourists are not told about and rarely take, is away to the west of Tamerlane's Imperial monuments and into the old Russian Imperial town, the Tzarist garrison quarter. Here the mediaeval lanes become great tree-lined, nineteenth-century boulevards, radiating out, Hausmann-like, into a fan of noble vistas. The mood is almost *belle époque* in these Imperial parks surrounded by grand villas and barracks. They are crumbling and festooned with vines, but still intact and still very much in use as the Soviet administrative centre, where the men from Moscow and their converted Uzbek colleagues walk the streets piously with their little brief cases dreaming of five-year plans.

And here Russian soldiers (not Uzbek, of course) from the cold northern wastes stroll through the heavy-leafed, ornamental parks in sturdy droves, queuing for bowls of spicy rice pilaff, enjoying a bit of Rest and Recreation from their 'civilising war' in Afghanistan only 200 miles to the south. In Samarkand, when you leave the lovely world of faience and majolica and come into the garrison town, you move into present Soviet reality; a sticks-and-carrots society where coercion and reward walk hand in hand, exactly as Lenin forecast. A system which one feels – since the sticks and carrots are more than sufficiently painful and tempting – will jog along indefinitely, for certainly, there is as much a feeling of permanence in Samarkand's nineteenth-century quarter as there is in Tamerlane's old mediaeval city.

The Soviet Union today, is essentially a nineteenth-century, Victorian society: a deeply conservative world where the official impulses are always sluggish, concerned everywhere with long-term developments, punishments, rewards – where behaviour is seen in the light of a communist eternity, an historic mission which in the end will justify every present mistake or sacrifice. Thus everything is publicly considered in the highest moral tones while privately all true feelings are repressed. The Victorian analogy is complete in almost every detail: from the sexual prudery and covert alcoholism to the continual accent on 'good works' both at home and abroad. It's a world that Gladstone would have easily recognised with its hand-written chits and the endless flow of printed propaganda – just like Victorian religious tracts – found in every hotel room, lobby or airport lounge.

This severely paternalistic and authoritarian world is not a communist invention – we tend to forget that. It's been a part of Russian life since the first of the Tzars and will be, barring a holocaust, long after Brezhnev's men have departed. And the Russian people will survive it, for they learnt long ago how to work the system, to keep their heads down, while remaining fully aware of the system's failures and completely cynical about its claims.

On the plus side of this Victorian account – and as a direct result of these traditional official prohibitions – there are marvellous qualities in Russian life today which we've largely lost in the West: an acute accent on the familial, for example, on very strong feelings and vibrant associations in families and between friends. Because of all their material difficulties, ordinary Russians have developed their charity, one with another, to an extraordinary extent and Russians are often horrified by the emotional wilderness which they sense or experience everywhere in the West.

But all in all, theirs is a firmly closed society, where only a very few things bloom in the mud heap – and one where we can expect few changes in the future. Life in the Soviet Union is like a very long run of a very bad play: the text is corrupt but there are no critics; the audience captive while the geriatric players strut the boards behind a lowered safety curtain – a farce in short, but without any laughter: theatre of the absurd. And so most Russians live in a daze, broken toys in the spoilt design, living in an empire as mighty and as cruel as Tamerlane's but quite lacking any of the redeeming artistry and faith which also characterised that Mongol Kingdom.

And that was the strongest, overall feeling I had in Russia – that though the Soviets had achieved all sorts of technical miracles since the war, they had failed entirely to produce any spiritual benefits: the people, alive in the body, were often dead from the neck up. It's a terrible indictment – and it's a condition which even Tamerlane, for all his other brutalities, would not have allowed or encouraged. His empire was built on what he saw as any number of holy premises, hence the glory of his remaining monuments, but Lenin was no such spiritual architect and his successors, so unlike Tamerlane, have been even less concerned with the grace of things in the here and now or in the hereafter.

Tamerlane is buried in Samarkand, in the most dramatically beautiful of all its old buildings, the Gur-Emir mausoleum. It is a wonderfully restored monument, with its vast turquoise dome, its walls filled with all the glittering mosaic texts and patterns of a Koranic paradise, where the old monster lies asleep beneath the largest single piece of pure jade ever quarried, a slab like a billiard table. I visited him alone, late on my last afternoon in Samarkand, when the tourists had all left and the doves were flapping in overhead, coming to rest everywhere out of the lilac evening sky. The tomb, unlike those of his relations and cronies all round him, is simple, completely unadorned. Yet Tamerlane had a motto, which he might well have had inscribed on it: 'Rasti, Rusti' – 'Truth is Safety'. And this is the one vital message from the past which the Soviets have not restored in Samarkand – perhaps it lies above the city still, floating in its limpid, golden airs, waiting for its time to come? I wonder. I doubt it. Tamerlane saw safety in the truth. But Soviet leaders today see only danger there.

AFRICA:
COAST TO COAST

1

Zaïre:
A Low Profile
(April 1983)

The taxi lurched violently on its side and I saw one of our rear wheels – smoking, flaming – spinning away towards the suburban mud huts and cassava shops, where the African crowds, intent on their immemorial business, seemed only vaguely surprised by this wondrous wheel of fire, looking at it haughtily, dodging it neatly, before it flew among them, on its way into a storm drain where it ended up, in a cloud of smoke.

Meanwhile we had literally ground to a halt, a great hole in the floor of the car, the road visible inches beneath my feet. The driver untied a piece of string which he'd been using as a seat belt – one of the many pieces of string which had held his taxi together.

'Ça va,' he said.

'It's not "Ça va" at all!' I shouted, shaking with nerves, breaking into bitter English at last – provoked almost beyond endurance. 'I'm supposed to be crossing this damn great continent – coast to coast. I've been here more than a week already and I've not even begun at the *first* coast yet.'

The driver looked at me happily, uncomprehendingly. 'Ça va,' he said again.

We'd been coming into Boma at that point, the old capital of what was once the Belgian Congo, at the mouth of the Congo river, now in the Republic of Zaïre. But there was still another fifty miles to go down the huge estuary before we reached the sea, before I could turn round and properly start my journey back, west to east, across the whole continent. Earlier that morning, a previous taxi which I'd had to take from the big port of Matadi further up-river, had come to a halt in an almost identical fashion.

'Hot brakes!' that driver had said, dancing round the old Peugeot van, glorying in his little English, while I and the fifteen other bulky African passengers sweated it out, crammed in the back of the van, stuck together like warm corpses among a mountain of bananas. We'd been stranded for several hours on the deserted road, hedged in on either side by the vast, threatening shadows of a tropical rainforest. A gaggle of small naked children chewing cassava roots had suddenly emerged from the jungle and laughed at us, particularly at me; vastly surprised by this grim, marooned white man and equally pleased by my impatient discomfiture.

And before that, very first thing that day in Matadi, the riverboat on which I'd booked a seat to take me downstream to the Atlantic had never left – conked out, no fuel, no something anyway – and thus I'd lost my own car and driver from Kinshasa who by then had gone ahead, intending to meet me that evening at Boma, when I'd made my trip down-river.

As it was I was keeled over, not in a boat but in an old taxi, sunk with all hands, one foot through the floor, several miles short of my objective. The driver's transistor suddenly came up with 'Blue Skies are smiling at me', while the driver himself disappeared among the African crowds, embarked already, no doubt, on a lengthy palaver in the matter of his truant wheel.

'Travel broadens the mind,' I thought, as I sat there in the humid coastal heat. This was just the sort of cliché Dr Chillerjam would have introduced as a text, in one of his chattery attempts to cadge a free English lesson off me, back in the Memling Hotel bar in Kinshasa, during one of the many sessions I'd shared with him and his other friends: Harry Jupiter, the garrulous American language specialist; Eleanor in her pirate pants; the Reverend Mustard from his Church of All Sinners and Naxos – known as 'Noxious' – the exiled Albanian dentist. Dr Chillerjam and these others, already old hands in the country, never left Kinshasa. They knew better. How they would have enjoyed my predicament now.

'Another Primus all round,' would have been the call then, as the long beer-laden afternoon waned. . . .

'You should know perfectly well by now,' Harry Jupiter would have said. 'There's no such *thing* as travel in Zaïre today.' And Dr Chillerjam would have interrupted in his piping, sing-song manner – his voice another cliché: 'Hot brakes, no fuel, no seats, no permits – reasons are long as transport is short!'

And certainly I'd proved them all right. This vast, blank space that I'd entered, like a great green balloon tied to the Atlantic by the river's thread, this Congo, Zaïre, with its tempting serpent of a river, this holy grail for every Victorian missionary and explorer – all this is now almost as inaccessible as it was before Stanley first opened the country up a hundred years ago.

'Since the Belgians left, the jungle is coming back, creeping in: the green things – every day a little more . . .' I remembered the Reverend Mustard's soft accent in the Memling bar a few days before. He was speaking with relish, his big spade beard jumping about, contemplating it seemed, in all this encroaching greenery, some really hard-won conversions now in his proposed ministries up-river. He was hearing the tom-toms already. 'Up-river,' he'd murmured confidentially to me then. 'In parts, you know, some of them have started eating each other again.' And I'd laughed.

'What, missionaries in the pot? You're joking. Have you even *been* up-river?'

'No,' he admitted. 'I've enough on hand in Kinshasa for the moment. But we've heard the rumours and you'll see for yourself, if you ever do get up-river, or down for that matter.' And he'd looked at me hungrily, already a likely candidate for his Church of All Sinners.

Eleanor at least had commiserated with me. Ah, Eleanor, that tall, dizzy, Home-Counties girl, in one of her startlingly unsuitable pieces of leg wear: knickerbockers, Bermuda shorts, cropped jeans, old-fashioned golfing slacks, jodhpurs – she was like a clothes horse gone mad, a trousered dream of a girl. Eleanor, smiling sweetly beneath her great helmet of blonde curls, that rather sad and empty smile of hers, as if she'd lost something vital in her life minutes before, but had quite forgotten what it was. I haven't yet hinted at her business in Kinshasa, for the good reason that I don't think she – and certainly none of us – ever quite knew what it was. It was rumoured that she had a fiancé or boyfriend somewhere far up river, a Belgian engineer on some mobile project who she wished to join if she could ever find out exactly where he was, or if any of the impossible river boats ever left Kinshasa to take her up there.

Meanwhile she was permanently stalled in the capital, at the Memling bar or café, or in the dubious little hotel by the Grand Marché where, on my own researches, I had sometimes seen her picking over the fantastic goods – usually the dried snake skins, chicken feathers, the evil-smelling roots and herbs and old teeth on the witch doctors' stalls. And twice I'd seen her carrying back great empty metal trunks from the market, balancing them on her head, practising with them, these boxes which she would one day fill for that long journey she planned – to find her lover in the heart of darkness.

But for the moment all of us were stranded exiles in Kinshasa, all anxious to get somewhere else. Dr Chillerjam wanted to practise in Britain of course – Coventry in particular – and was waiting on some necessary letter, visa – or qualification more likely, a document in any case which he never elaborated on, confirming my suspicion that his medicine contained more fiction than fact.

The Reverend Mustard strained at the traces of his vision, sensing some glorious martyrdom among the revived cannibals in the distant rainforests. And Harry Jupiter too, was always thinking of moving on as he had to I suspect, given the doubtful nature of his credentials and of his 'Academy'. This was little more than a crammer, I gathered, but set up in some smart downtown offices and received with all the excitement of a circus in this disadvantaged spot, where many of the locals craved passage to an English-speaking haven and could thus be persuaded, if only for a year or two, to buy his strange version of the English tongue.

Naxos, the elderly morose dentist, dreamt of change too. Fondly remembering King Zog of Albania and listening to the World Service round the clock, he hoped for that most unlikely of events: news of a successful Royalist coup in his homeland.

We were all exiles even where we stood, unable or unwilling to travel into the fulfilling hinterlands of the country and separated, in our common English tongue, from all the French or native-speaking Africans and Belgians of Kinshasa. The Belgians of the city – the new Belgians, at least, who had been asked back in strength some five years ago by President Mobutu when the whole country had come to a full economic stop – congregated every day in a rival bar-restaurant on the other side of the main boulevard, a swanky velvet-chaired place called

the Kins Inn, where, in a heavy baronial setting of fumed hardwood
and eccentric plastering, these neo-colonialists fed their faces on
'steack tartare' and fresh salads flown in from Brussels that morning
and filled their cups, before falling into them, with cases of Beaujolais
off the same flight.

They never deigned to appear in the Memling opposite. The
Memling was for the few poor whites left over from the old regime: for
Greek and Lebanese traders; for uncertain Anglo-Saxon transients
like me; for visiting Africans – those who couldn't afford the Inter
Continental Hotel three miles up town – and for the odd, the very odd
tourist who, since the demise of the Ministry of Tourism two years
before, braved this heart of the dark continent.

In the ten days since my arrival, I'd found Kinshasa more
depressingly strange each morning. It was a divided city, cut clean
down the middle by its great four-mile boulevard, which separated
the old Belgian and native quarters; the luxurious bougainvillaea-
shrouded villas neatly laid out on the one side and the vast, crammed,
poverty-stricken African 'cité' of tin or breeze-block shacks and mud
huts on the other. And, among all the de-tribalised blacks and whites
of the city, our equally disparate little group at the Memling, more
distant still from all the bizarre human mechanics of a place which
Stanley, with the uncomplicated tools of gunpowder, gin and
coloured beads, had carved out of the bush here exactly a hundred
years ago.

I, in my attempt to reverse and retrace his great journey across the
continent, carried no such Victorian certainties with me. Guns, in this
erratic military dictatorship were definitely out. And though I had a
bottle of duty-free gin with me, the rest of my kit was, on reflection
now, totally inadequate: my son's Christmas present compass; some
tinned salmon and water biscuits; a lot of malaria and dysentery pills;
a map of equatorial Africa on far too small a scale and a few hundred
dollar notes secreted in a money belt.

I'd mentioned these provisions to Harry Jupiter when I met him on
my first morning having breakfast on the café terrace of the Memling.

'My God,' he'd said. 'That's hardly enough to see you out of the
suburbs of Kinshasa. I'd rearrange your itinerary – or cancel it. Hang
around the city here a bit. You'll probably have to anyway. They don't
much care for inquisitive foreigners nosing about out of town.
Besides, Kinshasa's a country in itself and all you need is money to

discover it. Money is a very interesting thing here,' he was speaking with gravitas now, a gleam in his eye. 'With inflation recently, it's just like it must have been in the old Weimar Republic: you have to carry a lot of it around, in a wheelbarrow ideally. There's no coin now at all. It's all in small old notes, five-Zaïre notes mostly. That used to buy you a whole night on the town; now it won't even get you a beer.'

Harry was right. I'd gone to the bank that same morning and in exchange for a hundred and fifty pounds sterling had emerged with a whole briefcase full of five-Zaïre notes. I'd shown it to Harry later that day in the bar.

'Oh, that's nothing,' he said. 'If you'd changed your money on the parallel rate you wouldn't be able to stand upright now.'

'The parallel rate?'

'The unofficial rate. You get three or four times as much. And *that's* when you really start to lead the life of Reilly here.' He was beginning to get enthusiastic. 'Puts a whole different complexion on things: fresh radishes and sole *bonne femme* from Brussels every day; a Mercedes, two chauffeurs, a dozen servants and a big villa in the old Belgian town by the river. That's when you really start to move here – on the parallel rate. And of course, you can build yourself a wall then.'

'A wall?'

'Yeah. A big wall, round your property. You'll see when you get around town – they're all building walls now, furiously. It's the smartest thing of the season. The bigger the better.'

Harry suddenly looked up. A large, fat, middle-aged African in a dazzling, multi-coloured nightgown affair was making royal progress through the lobby, followed by a scatter of supplicants, attendants and hangers-on.

'That's General n'Gongo,' Harry whispered. 'A minister last year, but temporarily in eclipse right now. *He's* building a wall – the biggest in Kinshasa, I'd say.'

'On the parallel rate?' I suggested.

'I wouldn't speak too loudly. In the good old days the general had people like you for breakfast. And that's another thing to bear in mind here, if you're white – keep a low profile, and don't talk French if you can help it. They might think you're Belgian, and that's not so good. The Belgians caused some "trouble" here over the years, to put it mildly. The old King Leopold and his friends especially – when they ran the whole place as his private estate – used to chop all the slaves' hands off up-river if the rubber wasn't coming in fast enough. Yeah, talk English,' Harry said. 'They like that. They all want to learn English. That's why *I'm* here.'

So that was one reason why, ten days later, wrecked in my old taxi, I'd shouted at the driver in English. And certainly my profile was low enough at that point, only feet from the ground. And I thought – stalled once more – how the hell was I ever going to get across 3,000 miles of the *rest* of Africa?

2

Kinshasa:
A Little Local Election
(April 1983)

Almost as soon as I arrived in Kinshasa I was trying to get out of the place; down to the Atlantic coast 300 miles away, where I could properly start my journey back across the whole continent. But getting out of the city wasn't proving so easy. The tall, elegantly dressed counsellor at the Press Centre had even confirmed official policy in the matter of such travel.

'We're holding local government elections everywhere now,' he told me suavely, fingering a moist red rose at the throat of his Kaunda jacket, then added most pleasantly – the one thing obviously following quite naturally on the other – 'No foreigners are allowed out of town for the time being.' I mused on what form this local democracy took. It must have been of an obligatory nature, I decided, where the voters were rounded up and packed off in lorries to support a single candidate. But I said nothing. I'd surely find a way out of Kinshasa – once I'd seen a bit of this capital of Zaïre. Besides, I'd met that clutch of congenial English-speaking expatriates at the Memling Hotel bar downtown. And there were several lively Kinois – citizens of Kinshasa – whom I'd got to know too: boisterous students of the world, resident bar-philosophers whose joy it was to pontificate every afternoon, in passionate French, each outdoing the other in condemning political mischief and corruption in countries everywhere except their own. So to begin with, among such disparate new-found friends,

I thought I could happily bear with Kinshasa until these elections were over, when I could then set off on my own lengthy travels.

But Harry Jupiter, as he had from the start, maintained doubts about my itinerary through Zaïre. I saw him one day among a crowd of glazed-eyed people, gazing into the Sabena airways window just off the main boulevard. They were all absorbed in a notice which had just been set up inside. It gave the latest details of flights to and from Europe. Harry, always uneasy about the future of his American-language Academy, was no doubt studying the departure times.

He looked up rather guiltily when he saw me . . . 'I was expecting some textbooks,' he blustered. 'There are so few damn flights in or out of here these days.'

But later, feeding his great bulk yet another beer at the Memling, he admitted the real problem. 'It gets you, this place. It traps you – a sort of mental coast-fever. You find yourself haunting the Sabena window – that's the first symptom. The drink comes next, or a woman you don't need, along with the prickly heat, followed by a punch-up at some diplomatic party and then you're on a stretcher to the airport for that Sunday midday flight. Red hot Caesar,' he murmured, shaking his head, sweating now. 'Heap big mischief.' Harry seemed in for a bad dose of mental coast-fever at that very moment. 'The fact is, Mr Hone,' he went on. 'Unless they carry you out, you're not likely to get out of here any other way.'

I was sure Harry was exaggerating, though I had to admit I was finding Kinshasa a pretty depressing place myself. I'd arrived in the middle of the dry season in Zaïre, the three months of Congo winter when the cleansing tropical rains and brilliant blue skies disappear completely, replaced by a permanent grey: when lowering, dust-filled, dirty clouds come to crouch over the city, day in, day out, so that everyone, native and white, becomes restless, edgy, congregating outside airline offices, in bars or in bed.

Harry had told me that some people in Kinshasa never got up at all for these three months of the year. I often felt that way myself when I drew the curtains back each morning in my hotel bedroom to be confronted with so unexpected a vision of tropical Africa. The view from my window, high up, was as grim as something from the old English Black Country. It was a drab, messy landscape, a half-built, half-decayed city of monstrous grey high-rises and tin shacks; a shabby, broken-down place, oppressed by this continual sullen blanket of cloud, hedged in by the malign Congo river on one side, the jungle of the huge African cité on the other.

There was nothing to suggest the vast liberating spaces of Africa here, no fierce sun, rampant fruits or vivid-coloured blossom. In that winter world the city was besieged by the grey weather, feeding on what little it possessed itself, so that all its flaws stood out. The native poverty was all the more evident, while the trappings of Western 'civilisation' – the few smart bars and hotels, French restaurants, pizza shops, airline offices, Belgian delicatessens – these had less point than ever now in the all-embracing gloom. Usually deserted, they were like forgotten way-stations in an old colonial march, memoirs of so much discredited European adventure in these parts. It was the dry season indeed, the juices of the city everywhere squeezed out by the crushing weather.

Yet as the grey days went by and I still failed to make any exits from Kinshasa, I began to find a certain crazy charm in the place, a mood of the permanently unexpected and eccentric. I had a clear sense here – without mail, newspapers, radio or television, where the telephone never worked and there were no roads out – of living in a fantastic quarantine, where all previous notions of health and efficiency had no meaning whatsoever.

Here, among the sumptuous colonial villas by the river and the tin huts of the African cité, in the bars, casinos, night clubs and beer shops, in all the people and places, there was just the same kind of late sleeping, little doing, chatter-filled, utterly inconsequential dolce vita that I'd last tasted twenty-five years before in Cairo, as a young schoolteacher, after Suez, when all the British had been chucked out.

It was life in a decrepit, shoddy, poverty-stricken world certainly, but one in which, freed from its colonial ambitions and restraints, the human character, black or white, could emerge unfettered, glorying in every sort of nutty excess, each bizarre whim. So that Kinshasa when I was there, without its Belgian straitjacket, its old European ties, had become a circus of every sort of human folly and delusion, a honey pot for misfits. Here, I soon saw, a man could live with the person he really was; freely expressing the dark or light sides, no longer having to put up with his boring, indeterminate shadow.

'You remember I told you about General n'Gongo,' Harry said to me on my first weekend morning, when he was free from his Academy and had offered to show me round town in his vast peach-coloured Cadillac.

'Yes. The ex-Minister, temporarily in eclipse. The man who was building a wall round his house?'

'That's him,' Harry said. 'Well he's trying to get into the sun again, by standing in these local elections. He's giving a party. Shall we take a look-see?'

'Splendid.' I was delighted by this unexpected opportunity to observe the vital democratic processes in Zaïre which the counsellor at the Press Centre had tried to deny me. 'But a party?' I asked. 'At ten in the morning?'

'Why certainly. The General's parties usually last a week. This one only started yesterday.'

Harry sped off down the main boulevard. I was surprised, since we were going pretty fast already, when he suddenly put his foot down and the great candy-coloured car, hesitating for an instant, literally shot forward, all two tons of it, with a great 'Wrumph!' I found myself pinned against the seat back like an astronaut taking off. We were doing over seventy in seconds.

'Don't the police? – ' I ventured.

'No – they don't.' Harry grinned. 'I got this car off them. They "sequestrated" it, from some poor old Belge. I bought it from them – and I'm still paying for it. If they stop me, the payments stop. It's very simple. Life's amazingly simple here, as long as you have the money first and *they* have it afterwards.' Harry laughed and even the big car shook.

A mile down the boulevard we turned off into the old Belgian residential quarter; a grid of gracious tree-filled avenues and over-grown cross streets, where the grand, pre-war colonial villas nestled in their half-acre plots, all variously shrouded in bougainvillaea and mimosa and surrounded beyond that by frangipani and flamboyant trees. The trees were in their dull winter plumage but they still arched right over the long roads, so that the huge car glided beneath them, soundlessly, a magic barque floating through a tropical wood-land.

'Mostly embassies and residencies are here now,' Harry said. 'And some of the local fellows making good, of course. You can spot their houses: they're the ones with the new walls.'

And I could indeed. Half the elegant villas here had ugly walls round them, each competing with the next in height and grandeur, built in every shape and material, from cut stone to breeze block – many of them in the process of construction.

'There were no walls here in the old days,' Harry explained. 'Now it's the only sort of construction work you see in the city. They're all at it. It's not for robbers, just for status. A new Mercedes used to fill that bill. But now you need a wall as well.'

We came to a great open space, with an overgrown meadow in the middle and a splendid empty plinth in the centre of that. 'The Place de la République,' Harry gestured, circling it in a leisurely arc. 'And that used to be old King Leopold out there riding in the middle: government buildings all round and the Parliament on the far side by the river. The Belgians got it all together twenty years ago, just before they took fright here and beat it. But nothing much has happened since, as you'll notice.'

I looked round the huge plaza. It was totally deserted. A long, concrete, bunker-like building lay half complete down one side. 'That was to have been the Mint, or the Treasury,' Harry explained. 'But the government likes to keep its money closer to hand these days – in their pockets,' he added and laughed again, another belly-ripping laugh, like Orson Welles being tickled. We passed a soldier dozing on a chair inside the gates of the Parliament. He was dressed in a perfect Ruritanian military outfit, a chocolate soldier, in colour and uniform, wearing a green double-breasted jacket crossed in lines of glittering braid, hung with red shoulder-tassels, with puffy pantaloons below that tucked into *Beau Geste* boots at the bottom and a plumed, dove-grey pillbox cap askew at the top.

'A member of the Presidential Guard,' Harry advised me in hushed tones. I gazed round the great meadow again at this splendid empty space which the Belgians must have seen as the crowning glory of their civilising mission in the Congo; a legacy that would last a thousand years. But the natives had found no use for these Western beads and trinkets. The King, had been rudely unhorsed, long since, the plaza gone to grass, the buildings empty. Only the sleeping chocolate soldier remained as living evidence of Europe's sartorial hand: a man appropriately dressed as if for some *opera comique*; for this, much more, is the true Belgian legacy in Zaïre, the real form of life in these parts.

General n'Gongo's house must have been the biggest in Kinshasa. It was a vast, slate-grey colonial building by the river, much more like a Victorian railway terminus than a villa. His wall was a superb creation, an easy winner in these wall games of the city – a veritable Maginot Line in dark granite topped with spiky railings. On the street side the mansion was fronted by a miniature Versailles garden: formal borders, gravel paths, clipped lawns, though little of all this was visible that morning. The General's party was gathering momentum. Long tables and benches covered most of the ground, interspersed with little cook-houses, charcoal braziers and mobile bars. Excitable servants moved with crates of Primus beer in wheelbarrows among an even more excited multitude of convivial electors, whole families camped about the ground for the duration. It all seemed very like a high moment in the miracle of the loaves and fishes.

We'd parked our car at the end of a long line of other equally exotic autos outside in the street and moved among the throng, disciples ourselves at the feast. It was the very merriest of occasions, the crowd en fête, in dazzling cotton print mammy cloths and togas, swaying about, some joined together dancing, snaking along the paths in an absolutely authentic version of the Conga. The smell of burnt kebabs and the bitter aroma of stewed cassava roots lay heavy on the air. Palm wine moved rapidly down many gullets, along with yams, sweet potatoes, steamed bananas and telapia, that tasty Congo-river hogfish.

Harry ran through the menu. 'But it's the beer they like best,' he added. I could see the truth in this: the big green litre-bottles were being drained on a no-tomorrow basis.

'Isn't this all rather dubious? Buying votes? Or has the election already taken place?'

Harry snorted. 'Votes here are counted in empties. I'm told the present rate runs at somewhere between two and three bottles a vote – just like Tammany Hall in old New York.'

'Where's the General?' I wondered, after half an hour. It was only then that we learnt that the poor man had suffered a stroke and died during the night. But the merry-making had continued unabated, indeed had increased: we'd not attended General n'Gongo's election party that morning, but his wake. And that was only the start of the *comédie*. On my return from the coast, a week later, Harry told me that the General, shortly after his funeral, had been elected to the City Council – by an overwhelming majority.

3
Zaïre:
Wild Extremes
(April 1983)

The African was dressed in a tattered lounge suit and jaunty trilby – like some down-at-heel 'forties spiv – an unusual outfit in Zaïre, where everyone ten years ago was forced to be 'authentic' in native dress and names. But what really caught my attention as we stopped by the roadside shop was the monkey the man was holding up. Its tail was arched back and tied to its neck and he held it up by the tail, like a handbag, its arms forked out in front, so that it appeared about to spring forward, struggling free of its captor. It was then I realised that it was dead.

'Bush meat,' my driver told me. 'Very nice, very happy, very expensive.' He looked at the monkey enviously.

A little further on groups of matchstick children were stalking up the banks on either side of the road. They would hover like birds of prey, before pouncing on something hidden in the tufts of dry grass. 'They looking for mice,' the driver explained.

'To eat – of course,' I said, beginning to get the hang of these rural food supplies. The driver nodded.

We stopped at the big mission hospital further on. The administrator showed me round. In the X-ray room a ragged African was writhing about on an operating table, groaning in some deep pain, a look of astounded outrage on his old face.. He was surrounded by numbed relatives and friends. One of these unhandy men was trying to take his blood pressure, pumping up a rubber band round his arm. Meanwhile the blood seeped from the rags which covered his stomach and dripped over the side of the table. The administrator closed the door.

'A hunting accident,' he told me easily.

'Looking for bush meat?' I asked. The man nodded.

One of the European doctors spoke to me afterwards. 'In this part of lower Zaïre, he said, 'there's terrible malnutrition, rickets – and tuberculosis. Half the children here never reach the age of ten. And the hospital wouldn't survive but for the six bags of rice we get every week from the Chinese farm down the road.' He told me how vital drugs and medical equipment, ordered from Europe, now never arrived intact. Most of them were nearly always stolen on the docks or in warehouses down river. 'The last crates we had,' he said, 'came filled with stones.'

Later, when we'd left the hospital, there was a splendid granite railway bridge over the road, Stanley Bridge, where the legend, cut in the side, loudly proclaimed how this railway, in 1898, had 'Opened up the Congo to Civilisation'.

I was going down to the Zaïre coast at that stage, driving through the tortuous passes of the Crystal mountains that lie between the capital of Kinshasa and the Atlantic. The road ran up and down the arid hills, twisting and turning, making supreme efforts to force a passage through the cruel geography.

Fifty miles away to the north, the Congo river fell much more directly from Kinshasa to the sea, but in a series of deep gorges and terrifying cataracts that had always denied navigation and had thus kept the world out of the Congo interior from 1482, when the Portuguese first discovered the river mouth, until 1877, when Stanley's great transcontinental expedition, coming from the east and discovering the dark heartlands, had dragged itself through these same jagged mountains to the sea.

A few years afterwards this road had been hacked out and then, as another by-pass to the rapids, the Belgians had built the railway, 250 miles up from the port of Matadi to Kinshasa. It took them eight years – and 'a black for every sleeper', as the likely rumour has it. That was the start of the long Congo tragedy, the start of King Leopold's so-called Congo Free State, the start of the rubber boom in all the virgin rainforests upstream and of the fearful atrocities committed by the

Belgian administrators and their brutal African 'Force Publique' – a situation which the Irishman, Roger Casement, then British Consul at Boma, finally exposed in his famous report of 1904. And now, in search of Stanley and Roger Casement and of the Atlantic itself, I was travelling these same rough paths.

Later that day, when it grew dark, passing through the mud-hut villages near Matadi, the driving became more difficult. Long lines of people walked on either side of the narrow strip of tarmac, women mostly, their heads bent low, carrying immense bundles of sticks in straps against their forehead, the men walking like lords, empty-handed, ahead of them. The huts were everywhere, running back into the darkness of the bush, a few with windows where a faint candle burnt inside. There was no electricity. It was all very strange somehow: the people were like dark ants emerging from these mud structures, walking endlessly in long lines with their great burdens, up and down the road. What goes on inside all these dark or barely lit huts, I wondered, during the long twelve-hour tropical night? I couldn't even imagine the form, the words, the style, the thoughts of the humanity that lived here.

This road, and the railway nearby, that the Belgians had cut through these formidable forests and mountains eighty years ago, had certainly brought me no closer to these people. Had they brought them 'civilisation'? It didn't look like it – and perhaps that was all for the best. But what was I doing here, more lordly than any of the local men, sweeping by in my fast car? My journey down that road seemed absurd then; and more absurd later in the Grand Metropole Hotel in Matadi, when I tucked into a pork dinner costing an average month's wages in Zaïre. They were eating mice further back up the road and killing themselves shooting monkeys.

A rugged, weather-beaten, middle-aged Belgian joined my table, an engineering contractor, down from Kinshasa – an *enfant du pays*, he told me later – involved in the huge power-line project, running from the Inga Dam above Matadi to the copper mines in the Shaba region a thousand miles away to the south east.

'This country's a paradise.' He lolled back, after a few beers. 'Europe's finished. Damn great cities and motorways, dirt, drugs, hippies. I hardly ever go there now. My boy looks after me here, he really does. Anything I want. A good cook; steak, whatever I want.'

'Where do you get the steak?'

'Oh, up from South Africa – there's plenty of it.'

'But the Africans round here are starving. Mice and monkeys . . .'.

'Rubbish,' the Belgian interrupted. 'No one's starving here. And they've always eaten monkeys – and mongoose too. They're great delicacies among the locals. You've heard too much mission and UN aid talk. And read too many lying articles about President Mobutu. What do you want them to eat here – *pâté de foie gras*? And you expect *democracy* here – your Houses of Parliament? They just need one strong man in Zaïre and they've got him. Anything less and there'd be real chaos, don't mind about mice and monkeys. I was *born* here. I know what it's all about.'

He called the waiter over, paid my bill too, before I could stop him, and tipped the man heavily. I frequently came across this Belgian's attitude in Zaïre; it was common to most Europeans I met. The few old or new colonialists left in the country condescended to it now, excusing their plunder here by praising the servants; calling Zaïre a 'paradise' allowed them to forget the hell they'd made it. And yet there was some truth in what the engineer had said. Democracy here was hardly the answer. The lies rested in what he and most other white people here always failed to say.

Next morning we crossed the river on the ferry and drove thirty miles to Inga Dam where, on a steep headland, we looked up-river on the mile or so of continuous, withering rapids. The dam immediately beneath us seemed insignificant by comparison – a garden wall on a slipstream off the main torrent. It was here in 1877 that Stanley lost his second-in-command and great friend, Frank Pollock, the Kentish fisherman who, incapacitated by blistered feet, had drowned along with several other Zanzibaris in one of these white-water whirlpools. Stanley's whole troupe had been on the point of death at this stage in any case. There was no food to be had in these cruel hills.

Beneath the dam the local workers made a living of sorts, trapping catfish and *crevettes* and selling them to visitors. I realised now why my driver had been so keen to take me here: we drove back with the car filled with slimy, wriggling goodies, smelling like a fish shop.

In fact I'd much more wanted to see Vivi, a small village near Matadi where Stanley, on his return to the Congo on behalf of King Leopold II in 1879, had created the first European settlement in the interior. Stanley's original wooden house, I'd been assured, was still there, kept as a museum. But no one knew where Vivi was now. The local people had never heard of the place. At last, a smartly dressed schoolmaster, to whom we'd given a lift, explained the position: Vivi was thirty miles away, along an impossible track. Besides, there was nothing there. Stanley's house had been burnt down a year before: some children, a cigarette end, a bush fire. No one quite knew. It had just disappeared.

'But anyway,' the schoolmaster went on, much more eagerly now, bearding me as a vital contact from the outside world, 'what I'm interested in is international affairs. I wish to be a diplomat. You could help me there.'

When I expressed doubts about this, the schoolteacher became indignant. 'But why are you interested in this man Stanley?' he demanded. 'This colonial robber.'

'I'm interested in the history here, that's why.'

'Well why not *our* history, then? Why yours? *Yours* was just one of murder and exploitation.'

He had a point and at that moment I felt further away than ever – from Zaïre, from the concerns and attitudes of both men I'd met; African schoolmaster and Belgian contractor, black and white. Here in Zaïre, I saw, there was no room for any middle ground, any objectivity. Black or white, you either loved or hated the place; as a native you furiously condemned the whole of the colonial past; as a European you conveniently forgot about it and tipped the waiters double. Enquiring strangers like me, vaguely archaeological, aiming for balance, had no place here at all. The Belgian would go on getting rump steaks from South Africa and the children would continue to eat mice. That was the condition of things in Zaïre today, as it had been in the Colonial State. Poverty and wealth was all that mattered then as now. History was irrelevant. All the same, I was determined to go on looking for it.

When I got to Boma, the old capital of the Belgian Congo, I felt I'd driven into a ghost town. The long line of ancient wooden-frame houses facing the stream were all deserted. Nothing moved on the dockside. A flotilla of ancient dredgers and steamboats rusted away in the smooth brown current that gave across to a mangrove-covered island and the flat alluvial delta land ran away for miles beyond that.

With a guide and my driver, I looked everywhere for Casement's house. And though there were half-a-dozen riverside buildings sufficiently old to qualify, no one knew anything about Casement here, this saviour of the Congolese eighty years before. Stanley they knew about. The great hollow baobab tree on the riverfront where he'd camped after his three year journey was still there – now used as a *pissoir* and behind it, a small brick hut with the word 'Archives' on the door. I went inside expectantly. But the place was used as an empty-bottle store now, except for one dusty corner with a small bookshelf containing half a dozen French 'tec novels, stamped inside with the words: 'Belgian Cultural Centre, Boma, 1947'.

Behind the riverfront was the wilderness of the old Belgian town, a grid of overgrown, tree-filled streets, once tidy boulevards where the remnants of imperial villas lurked in a tangled undergrowth of weeds, creeper and long grass, the jungle taking over again. No one lived here now. The African town lay behind on the hills. I found the old European cemetery, though only a few of the tallest headstones were still visible above the hungry vegetation: a Portuguese nun and a Danish officer, one of the many mercenaries from King Leopold's deathly army. Monkeys rustled out of the long grass, scratching their backsides on the broken graves.

No one came to Boma now – though eighty years before it had been the crowded gateway to a tremendous El Dorado up-river. And I had a strange feeling then: in other countries, tracing such European arrivals and adventures, one must go back hundreds, even thousands, of years. But here, right in front of me in Boma, was a European presence that had come and gone in little more than the last seventy years: a country which had been discovered, colonised, plundered and abandoned all in the space of a single lifetime. Where was Stanley's 'civilisation' now? It lay broken between an angry, de-tribalised schoolteacher who wanted to be a diplomat and a Belgian who praised the strong leader who allowed him to eat rumpsteak, while the real children of the country searched for mice.

I went back and looked out over the deserted river again, the Atlantic only a few miles away: Stanley's 'hateful, murderous river' and I wished I could have taken a boat home, just as Stanley had, there and then. Instead I had to turn back and cross the whole of Africa – on the very edge of it now, night falling – still the dark continent, where I had already seen the shadow of Conrad's Mr Kurtz and heard the echo of his words, 'The horror! The horror!' coming from somewhere far up this same river, in the heart of the darkness.

4
Zaïre:
Up the Congo
(April 1983)

The riverboat timetable was the most elaborate collection of promises I've ever seen. Its twenty large pages gave comprehensive details of every trip you could possibly take – up, down or off the Congo river. With its dozen routes and destinations throughout the great river basin, its hundreds of stopping places and its tempting collection of symbols denoting 'De Luxe Cabin', 'Dog Kennels' and 'First-Class Restaurant', it clearly offered the ultimate in African travel; particularly on the Onatra company's main line, the weekly service from the capital of Kinshasa one thousand miles upstream to Kisangani, the port on the great bend of the river in the heartlands of the continent.

Mbandaka, Mobeka, Lisala, Bumba, Isangi, Yangambi, Kisangani . . . The names of the provincial capitals and river stations en route made a dramatic litany, conjuring up a fabulous mix of African fact and fiction. The explorer Stanley had literally fought his way down this river 100 years ago, an astounding journey in commandeered war canoes, thirty-two ferocious battles, beating off an endless succession of local cannibal tribes. The Belgians had taken over shortly afterwards – with hippopotamus-hide whips, obscene brutalities, mutilations, mass executions. Conrad had come this way a few years later and long after, Graham Greene had followed him in search of his character Querry, the stricken architect, maimed by civilisation, finally placing him among the genuine lepers crawling along these forest paths in *A Burnt-out Case*. Savagery, mystery, primeval darkness – these were the real images, the real destinations hidden behind the bland facts and figures of the riverboat timetable. And now I was in Kinshasa myself, another traveller about to be named in this fantastic passenger list of men who had journeyed to Conrad's 'dark places of the earth'.

Long before, in England, I had planned this journey up-river. Why else come to Zaïre, I thought, unless to cross the country by these fabled waterways? I'd imagined myself on the steamer's foredeck: turning from a last sunset over the capital, looking grimly out into the darkness ahead, a bottle of Scotch waiting for me in the de luxe cabin below. Now I was here, all I had to do was buy my ticket.

'That'll be three thousand Zaires, first class, inclusive, for the ten-day trip.' The important African loomed over his huge, empty, glass-topped desk. We were in the vast Onatra building downtown, the biggest office block in Zaïre, air-conditioned, built by the Belgians just before they ran from the country twenty years ago. By comparison with any of the other offices I'd been to in Kinshasa, where little but numb incomprehension or blind panic was ever on view, there was an air of ponderous efficiency and necessarily so I thought, since river transport is often the only transport throughout Zaïre. I was just about to hand over the money (more than three hundred pounds on the official rate), when something made me hesitate.

'The boat still leaves on Monday?' I checked.

'No. Thursday. It's late coming downstream.'

I knew enough about bureaucratic life in Kinshasa by then to put my money away. 'I'll come back,' I said. 'Fix things up after the weekend.'

I walked away up the main boulevard, past the crippled beggars sliding about on trolleys and stumps outside the Post Office, the sky the usual suffocating blanket of grey above me. I was longing to get out of Kinshasa. But my friend Harry Jupiter at the Memling Hotel bar that lunchtime had, as usual, grave doubts about my ambitions.

'They're lying,' he said. 'Or else they're blind. The Kisangani steamer is here right now, in port. I saw the funnel this morning.'

'Maybe that's another steamer?'

'Listen, they're all the same now: they don't work, they break down, they can't repair them, there's no fuel. The local boys cannibalise the boats, then sell the stuff as spare parts. It's all a dream – travelling up-river now.'

I showed Harry the elaborate timetable. He was amazed. 'I've never seen one of these before.' He looked at it carefully handling it like a rare manuscript. 'Lisala, Bumba, Basoko, Lokutu, Yangambi,' he intoned. 'Just names,' he said finally. 'Words – not deeds. You haven't realised that yet, have you? In Zaïre, if they put something in writing – especially if they print it up like this – it stands for the deed. You don't actually have to *do* the thing then. It's a neat trick: timetables like this absolve them from taking any further action.' Harry laughed, a generous rumble.

On Monday I saw another, more junior man in the operations room of the Onatra building; short, portly, officious, he was sitting in front of a huge wall-plan of the whole river network, where little sliding coloured buttons represented all the Company's boats on stream at that moment.

'Ah yes,' he was confident. 'The Kisangani boat has been delayed, until the end of the week I think. Repairs. Come back tomorrow and I'll be able to tell you the position.'

The next day the fat man had disappeared. Instead a junior clerk looked at the wall-plan for me, mystified, considering it like the Rosetta Stone. He tried to move one of the little coloured buttons. But it was stuck fast. He consulted a big ledger. 'Kisangani?' he seemed equally perplexed here, thumbing nervously through the pages. But, finding nothing to suit his purposes in the book, he suddenly looked up and, grasping the words out of the air, said sharply: 'That boat is not leaving here until the seventeenth.' This was ten days away.

'What's the problem?' I asked.

'No problem.' He was affronted now. 'The Kisangani boat left here yesterday. The next one isn't until the seventeenth.'

Triumphantly he closed the ledger. I produced my timetable, pointing out that the Kisangani boat was supposed to leave not yesterday or on the seventeenth, but every Monday at nine o'clock. The clerk took the timetable from me gingerly – viewing it, like Harry, with amazement. He was speechless, turning all the wonderful pages, pondering the remote places, exciting destinations, the exotic symbols for dog kennels, de luxe cabins and first-class restaurants. He'd obviously never seen this fantastic document in his life before.

'Lisala, Bumba, Basoko,' he chanted reverently, 'Lokutu, Isangi, Yangambi . . .' He was spellbound by the majesty of it all. I left him at it.

Harry laughed again when I met him later that morning. He rolled
in the aisles. 'You're beginning to get the hang of things here,' he said.
'You see – and perhaps you can't blame them for it – the white man is
prey in Africa now. Fair game, to be stalked. They like to play you on
all sorts of hooks. It's their revenge – just as we preyed on them. They
do it very politely, you think they're playing straight. But what
they're actually doing is tying you up in knots – and they're pleased to!
It's our turn for the slavery now; we're at the sharp end and there's
nothing much you can do about it. Except money. You could try
hiring a private boat, or hitch a lift on a cargo barge.'

I went down to the port that afternoon, noticing how the city – the
old Belgian residential and commercial quarter – had been built *away*
from the river; it turned its back on it, as one would on a malign
presence. No one had ever really liked the river here, that was the
obvious, interesting thing. The waterfront quite lacked any happy
life, native or European. There was just a long run of dirty wharves,
crumbling warehouses, stalled cranes and endless lines of rusting or
sunken ships, odd bows and masts poking up through the vast brown
sheet of water, broken shards, remnants of a vibrant river-transport
system which had long since disappeared. The Congo had won this
anti-colonial battle hands down.

There was a ferry company here which Harry had told me about,
but making my way towards its office, I keeled over, slipping on the
years of congealed palm oil that lay everywhere on the dockside. I fell
across the two lines of a narrow gauge railway, so that when I finally
got to the office I was striped like a zebra, my smart linen tropicals
sharply patterned in black and white, with a taste in my mouth, where
I'd grazed my cheek, of rancid vegetable oil. Hair askew, blood on my
lip, cursing everything to do with the Congo, I was already beginning
to look and behave like Mr Kurtz without ever having even been out
on the river.

A woman was at the desk, dressed in high Parisian chic, her long
nails painted a bright vermilion. Her French was perfect – straight
from the Boulevard St Honoré, not this decrepit, flyblown riverside
hut. We surveyed each other in considerable surprise.

'A boat?' she said eventually. 'A private boat – up river? – Yes –
fifteen hundred Zaires for the day.'

'That's expensive – three hundred dollars? When would it be?
Now?'

'It depends. How far do you want to go?'

'Mbandaka,' I began. 'Lisala, Bumba, Basoko, Lokutu, Yangambi –'

'Stop!' the woman cried. She was horrified. 'I thought you just wanted to go across the pool. You want the big steamer for those places. It leaves here every Monday – at nine o'clock. Go to the Onatra building downtown –'

'I know,' I said. 'I know.'

'Bumba, Basoko, Lokutu indeed . . .' I heard the woman laugh after I'd left the office. 'Il est fou, cet homme. Il est vraiment fou.'

Later that evening, Harry sent a Zaïrean friend of his down to the docks to enquire about cargo boats for me. The man was promptly arrested.

'As a smuggler – or what?' I asked Harry next morning.

'No. He was just the wrong tribe. Not a river tribe. He's from the Shaba region. They're very fussy about who they let on the river these days.'

'Fussy? They don't seem to let *anybody* on it.'

'Yes. But I think you're going about the whole thing the wrong way. You're asking them "yes" or "no" questions. That's fatal here. You're sort of saying, "Does the boat leave for Kisangani today?" What you have to do is shout, "What have you *done* with the boat for Kisangani?" They'll understand you then.'

'I see.'

'Maybe I can still fix you something up,' Harry relented. 'If you insist.'

By the time I was tearing my hair out at the end of the week, Harry had fixed me up with a boat, but only for a long day-trip; forty miles up Stanley pool to the mouth of the river and back. It was a tiny old river-tug, nearly all engine, a vast great throbbing diesel, set behind a raised foredeck where I sat on a battered cane chair under a canvas awning in splendid isolation, while the crew of six lurked beneath me. One man tended the pistons, a second steered, the other four had just come for the ride – fascinated men who gazed at me wide-eyed, incredulous, wondering what possible mischief this great white Bwana was up to, sitting there above them, to no apparent purpose, in his freshly laundered linen tropicals.

We chugged off across the Pool – no Scotch, no dog kennels and no first-class restaurants. But at least, and at last, I was going up-river, up the Congo, the 'River that eats all rivers'.

It was a crashingly boring journey. Once out on the Pool there was almost nothing to see, just the vast flat expanse of pewter-coloured water all round us, with no horizons, for the sky was exactly the same grey shade. On one distant bank I could just make out the odd fisherman in a dugout, a few coffee-coloured cows browsing among the water hyacinth, with the little birds, the *pique-boeufs*, browsing off them. Besides this – nothing. The crew spoke no French. I was alone on this empty waterway, on this ridiculous voyage, going nowhere.

But perhaps I'm a lucky traveller. A few hours later, as if predestined, our trip suddenly took on a purpose. We were several miles up the river proper by then, pressing against a sharp current, between steep, real jungle-clad hills on either side, when we saw the other tug half a mile ahead of us, four heavily-laden pontoons tied all round it. The boats were broadside against the current, drifting helplessly towards us, the tug's engine obviously gone. A white man, on the nearest pontoon, was shouting, waving violently at us.

In half an hour, coming alongside and tying up, our own strong little tug had pulled all the boats round and dragged them very slowly to the river bank. We'd saved the day. The man – an Italian, many years in the Congo cargo business – proclaimed a miracle.

I've never seen anyone look so relieved. He asked me on board to share a Chianti and salami lunch with him, while they tried to repair his engine.

'But surely,' I said. 'With your radio, you could have called out some boat to help you?'

'*No* other boats now,' he said. 'None.' He was suddenly vehement, angry. 'I would have drifted right across the Pool for days, who knows where?'

'Where were you going?'

'Mbandaka,' he replied. 'Then Lisala, Bumba, Basoko –'

'Lokutu, Isangi, Yangambi,' I interrupted.

'That's right. How did you know?'

'Everyone's trying to get up there,' I said.

We finished the rest of the Chianti and that warmed me as I looked out on the grey, cold river. I saw its endless unexplained ripples and eddies and twirling patterns, little silent whirlpools where the clumps of hyacinth spun, suggesting great depths. This river was exactly as

Conrad had described it: 'An implacable force brooding over an inscrutable intention.'

'C'est malin,' the Italian shuddered, following my gaze. And he was dead right, too. It was evil. I hadn't been very far up the Congo, but I knew that much about it now. I had got nowhere as far as Stanley had, nor Graham Greene's Querry, let alone come to those ultimate regions away upstream in the interior where Mr Kurtz lurked. And I didn't want to get there now either. The heart of darkness? Just at this mouth of the river, I felt I'd arrived there already.

5
Eastern Zaïre:
The Real Thing
(May 1983)

I'd crossed half Africa that morning in the big jet; high above and far away from the endless carpet of green rainforest beneath me. But now my heart was in my mouth as the much smaller aeroplane dodged and spun between the two huge volcano cones, in this mountainous, lake-filled Kivu region of Eastern Zaïre, right in the heart of the continent. The pilot pointed up to the smoking summit on our left.

'That's Nyiragongo,' he shouted. 'It's erupting again. Maybe we'll get high enough to see it.' The plane lurched then in a sudden thermal. I could see almost enough of this belching volcano already, I thought: a great mushroom of red-flecked cloud rising up into the lead-blue sky from the 12,000-foot mountain.

'Four years ago it really exploded,' the pilot went on. 'Burst a great hole out of the side of the crater, ran down the valley into Goma. Hundreds were just buried.'

The little plane lifted steeply in another sudden up-draught, haphazardly buoyant now, tossing about like a kite between the great peaks. Yet I wasn't frightened any more. This was exhilarating; swooping about in the hot air above the lakes, dancing round the craters, the tawny flat savannah land to one side of us where the animals were, and beyond them the Pygmy tribes in the distant rainforests. Suddenly, after the weeks of grey weather in the ugly cities by the coast, this seemed the real Africa at last – wild, hot, menacing, touched with coming adventure, a country straight from an old *Boys' Own Paper* serial or a reel of *Raiders of the lost Ark*. Bouncing around in the thermals it all lay beneath me – Africa at my command, the way one had always expected, always secretly wanted it to be.

It was midday, the volcanoes above us, as we flew down over the stark blue, Italian-style lake, dropping onto the runway outside the little town of Goma. The heat on the tarmac lapped over my face; the sweat was already coursing down my chest. I took my bags over to the Karibu Hotel bus, the pretty Zaïrean hostess ready and waiting. Yes, this was more like it. Here I was, set down in this empty, fiery core of Africa, just in time for a cold beer, lunch, a nap, and a swim in the pool or lake before sunset.

Then I saw the lone Japanese at the head of a column of porters, boxes and camera equipment on their heads, with two armed askaris at the rear. They were moving up the road past the airport. The Japanese traveller – a tough, evil-faced young man in grimy leather shorts with days of stubble on his chin – looked at me and all the little aeroplanes contemptuously before striding away into the vast distances towards the volcanoes.

The real thing? Now, amazed, I had seen it. This man, not me, was straight out of that *Boys' Own Paper* serial. He was journeying through the dark continent in the proper way, on foot, with native porters and guns. I was just a cosseted tourist, fallen to earth now, the rough dream gone.

His was the journey I should like to have made across Africa, I knew, as I sat down to my splendid, napkined lunch: travelling with tea chests and bearers towards tents under the stars. When I slept in my well appointed cabin that afternoon, sweating on the crisp sheets, I dreamt of failure. And when I woke I thought what a long way I had come, to this heart of the continent, to no real purpose. I was seeing Africa as little more than a succession of picture post-cards, the sanitised view, from aeroplanes, hotel buses, Land Rovers. There were the odd discomforts, heats and hungers; but I was never far from the balm of a soft bed, a shower, a few cold beers. I resolved to stretch myself in some way, do something demanding, dramatic; to tear a chapter out of that *Boys' Own Paper* serial or go bust in the attempt.

Two or three hundred miles north of Goma, beyond the Virunga National Park, lie the Pygmy tribes, still lurking in the almost impenetrable Ituri Forest. I thought I might well further my ambitions in that direction. There were also very rare mountain gorillas in the dense bamboo forests of Mount Kahuzi, a hundred miles to the south. It was machete country here; a two or three day hike to see them, clearing the jungle as you went. And there were the 12,000-foot volcanoes, one of them erupting at that very moment. I could climb them. There was plenty to do, mastering the wilds, in this part of the world. But could you do it, or rather, could you even get to the starting blocks for any such muscular adventure? That was always the trouble in Zaïre. Mechanised transport, I knew already, had come to a full stop almost everywhere in the country.

The manager of the hotel confirmed my worst fears: 'You can get to Rwindi Game Lodge from here,' he told me. 'But the road north from there to the Pygmy forests is so bad now, no one will take you, not even in four-wheel drive. And the road south from here, round the lake to Bukavu to see the mountain gorillas is just the same.'

'What about the lake ferry?'

'No fuel. Sometimes it goes. Much more usually not.'

That left only the volcanoes. I could see the nearest one, Nyiragongo, from the lobby of the hotel – a great spew of dull steamy cloud lifting from the cone ten miles away.

'A two-day trip,' said the manager. 'I've never done it. But you take a guide at the bottom. There's a cabin near the crater rim to spend the night.'

'Can't you do it in one day?' I asked, anxious to stretch myself properly.

The manager smiled. 'Probably. But no one does. It's a forty-five degree angle up most of the way, I'm told. A seven or eight-thousand-foot climb from the bottom. And even when you get there, you often see nothing – just clouds, vapour!'

'Never mind,' I said firmly. 'Nothing venture . . .'

I set off first thing next morning in the hotel bus, travelling through the outskirts of Goma. It was lava country here already, even in the suburbs. The shanty town itself had been built from cut blocks of lava and beyond this lay a whole sea of grey stone, with lines of great black boulders, like a tide wrack, marking the end of the lava-run that had come here four years ago, burying the outlying villages. Now there was an open meat market on these ruined sites, the live animals being slaughtered with pangas as we passed. Rough country – adventurous country, I thought. Just the job.

At the bottom of the mountain I paid my seven pounds fee to the surly Park Ranger and after a lot of palaver and not sufficient a tip, I suspect, he gave me the smallest and youngest of the guides – a ragged, barefoot, consumptive-looking boy, equipped with nothing but a large panga. Looking up at the long stretch of thick rainforest and the steep slopes beyond that, neither he nor it seemed up to the tasks ahead. But there was no alternative.

'Back by five o'clock,' the Ranger warned. That gave us just over nine hours, up and down. And to begin with, for the first hour, walking across the sharp edges of an old lava bed, the going was easy enough: I had stout boots on. How the barefoot boy-guide managed I couldn't imagine. I asked him several times, only to discover that he spoke no French whatsoever, only syllables in some arcane local tongue.

But once into the thick rainforest on the middle slopes, things were very different. There was only a slippery, twisting, rising, foot-wide path to follow here, which often disappeared completely, so that we had to clamber over slimy, rotten tree trunks, struggle through snakes of hanging creeper and fantastically bearded branches, the boy forging ahead through the moist gloom, cutting great swathes out of the dense undergrowth, grappling with the creeper, felling the arm-thick stalks of vast sprouting weeds – rampant, exotic vegetation that rose ten feet in the air and showered us with water as it collapsed. There was no sound. The jungle seemed dead beyond our cleared path, except, every so often, for a high, eerie whine which came from the matted leaves above us: the noise of the telegraph bird as I came to call it, for the ear-splitting sound it made was almost exactly that of a big wind singing through wires.

Steam rose from evil marshy pools and faults in the volcanic rock now and then, clouding the grey with a damp, sulphurous mist. This, without doubt, was *Boys' Own Paper* stuff; the impenetrable African rainforest – full of all the fears, nightmares, the dreams of childhood.

After several hours we left the tree belt, emerging on open, rocky slopes. Now, as the manager had warned, the going was at forty-five degrees and I had to stop every few minutes, gasping, my legs withering with pain, as I pulled myself up, gripping the mossy lichens and glass-edged lava outcrop. The guide was never out of breath for one moment; this whole thing for him was no more than a walk to the shops and back.

Behind us great rain clouds had covered all the world beneath, swirling up the slopes, edging towards us. The guide called me on. We had to move up fast now or lose ourselves in the mists. One mistake here, I suddenly realised, and I would be far too much a part of that boys' adventure serial.

We stopped for a few minutes in a tin cabin just beneath the summit and though I could still see nothing of the eruption, I had the nasty smell now: a mix of Fourth-form chemistry and old socks on a bonfire. The last 500 feet to the top seemed like an almost sheer climb, so that when I got there, exhausted, blinded with sweat, I nearly fell over the rim. The guide grabbed my leg and I slithered back.

There was nothing but vast space beyond the lip of the crater. It gave right over, sheer down, in a half-mile-deep drop to an astonishing molten lake at the bottom. And we were lucky with the weather. There were no clouds in the huge grey cauldron. We could see right down to the spurting fountains of orange lava that rose and fell, in slow motion it seemed from this height; the liquid rock thundering up, jetting hundreds of feet in the air, with an inky, spitting column of smoke above that. The colours of the seething lake were a fantastic, changing mix: a dull silver white at the heart of the eruption, the fountains a ruddy orange flecked with blood, spreading to vermilion, then dark ochre and finally a pink-tinted lead at the edges. I gazed on it all for a quarter of an hour, spellbound, this seeming entrance to another childhood fable that had once brought Africa close to me – Rider Haggard's *King Solomon's Mines*. Here it was, right in front of me: the real thing.

The manager was surprised to see me back at the hotel that evening for a hot bath. But this time, at least, I felt I'd deserved it – and all the French cooking that followed. It struck me I was getting the hang of all this African adventure stuff now.

The next morning the Governor's fishing party arrived at the lakeside hotel. The advance guard came at first light, waking me, rattling along in two military jeeps just outside my cabin. And when I got across to the dining room the big men with shoulder holsters and dark glasses, the Governor's aides and bodyguards, were already halfway through breakfast – a bottle of Scotch nearly empty on the long table. Outside dozens of raggedy children were running amok in the bright African dawn, gathering up the hotel's chairs and parasols from the terrace and trying to cram them into the back of one of the jeeps, an impossible task given the other larger urchins already installed there, clinging onto the seats for dear life, trying to guarantee themselves a place for the day's sport.

I joined the men at the long table, wondering whether I might cadge a day's sport with them myself. But the toughest of the bodyguards gestured out of the window at the children. 'Look,' he said, 'there'll hardly be room for us.' He offered me a Scotch instead. 'The Governor likes to give the children a treat when he comes out here. What can you do?' He was a picture of innocence. I saw them all off later, the Governor in a huge gleaming Mercedes, leading the parade, the jeeps following, literally overflowing with children and half the hotel's furniture.

I suddenly thought then how I'd got this whole African adventure thing all wrong. Africa was something else, something more than volcanoes, mountain gorillas, Pygmies, *Boys' Own Paper* serials or clips from *Raiders of the Lost Ark*. The *real* Africa was disappearing in front of me at that very moment; in the jeeps. Reality was the stalk-thin children fighting for a day's outing, craving a share of the Governor's coke and crisps, stuffed in like chaff among the gross, whisky-slugging bodyguards.

And they, too, were very much the real thing, these vicious players in the African tribal power games, dark-glassed shock troops, Presidential fat cats, propping up corrupt and brutal regimes, one after the other, ever since the white men had cleared out of Zaïre and the other countries. 'Africa for the Africans' since Independence of course. But only for some of them, a very few. In that little aeroplane, dodging the craters, and afterwards climbing the volcano dreaming of *King Solomon's Mines*, I'd been indulging in all the splendid fictions of Africa, avoiding the reality at all costs, which of course was everywhere at hand, just waiting to strike.

Two days later, on the lush valley road up to the Virunga National Park, the drunken soldiers jumped the Lodge van, the bullets spitting a neat line across the dust right in front of us. It was a hidden checkpoint. I'd been stopped many times like this on the roads in Zaïre, though without the guns going off. This was how the army earned their money, especially in these remote areas, where they were rarely paid – they simply held cars and lorries to ransom, at gunpoint.

The driver paid up – thirty Zaires, three pounds at the official rate – without a murmur. It was a regular toll, nothing unusual in this part of Africa these days, where everyone who didn't starve paid up – with their money, or their lives. This was the real thing.

6

Rwanda:
Living and Dying
(May 1983)

'When the man says ya gotta go, ya gotta go,' the laconic Texan pilot intoned, repeating this grim injunction just in front of me, as he began to set the Twin Otter down, flying in low over the bare brown hills, on his final approach to Kigali airport.

Dear me, I thought, not at all relishing this Humphrey Bogart commentary and its implications. After four hard weeks in Zaïre, I was hoping for a little rest and recreation in the tiny central African republic of Rwanda, not some dumping on a hill a mile short of the tarmac.

In the event I needn't have worried. When we landed we seemed to go on taxiing forever towards the big airport buildings. And when I finally got out of the plane, I looked back on the longest, widest, grandest runway I'd ever seen; an immense concrete strip disappearing into the hazy distances. So what was it for? – that was the strange thing. There wasn't a single other plane at the airport – nor any other passengers either – and when we got to the splendid glass-boxed terminal building, there were no travellers, no mechanics, baggage handlers, hostesses, no officials of any kind. The place was deserted. It was as if some magic hand had set down the whole vast airport overnight, while all the locals were asleep. It brooded there now in the sun like a huge, dazzling space toy that some bleary-eyed African official would soon discover, out from the capital, getting the hell of a surprise in a few minutes.

In fact some people had already been to this great new airport.

Outside a dozen smart cars with UN and other diplomatic number plates, Volvos and Mercedes, were neatly parked and locked and beyond them, a few local men hovered, one of whom told me he drove the hotel minibus. He didn't, of course. He was moonlighting with someone else's bus. But we set off all the same, at a vastly inflated rate in every sense, for the capital, Kigali, some ten miles away.

And now there was an even greater surprise – for we were immediately out onto an equally new, four-lane, black-top highway, a splendid racing circuit that snaked up and down the dry, razed hills, with flyovers, underpasses and spaghetti junctions. Roads in Africa usually vie with one another in offering you the toughest section of a rally course. There are quagmires, pot-holes, dream-stunned pedestrians and whole families camped at every bend. But here was something on the smoothest, grandest, emptiest scale – a million-pounds-a-mile motorway with no other traffic on it bar the odd foot-slogging peasant, a scrawny beast in tow, both bent double with vast loads of dry sticks.

The Mille Collines hotel, situated on one of Rwanda's thousand hills, was as sumptuous a creation as the road and the airport had been: glass, marble, aluminium, a smooth blue pool, a top-floor terrace restaurant, white painted pine and bamboo Habitat-style furniture in the bedrooms, shops of all sorts in the lobby, airline offices, telex machines humming. But there was one marked difference. The hotel was full as a boot, bursting at the seams. They were white visitors mostly: not tourists, but businessmen, salesmen, a hive of executives, pushing and shoving, eating, drinking, swimming, making endless self-important promenades up and down the lobby. The Mille Collines Hotel was really buzzing, a complete little First-World city on its own.

Was I really in Rwanda, one of the poorest and certainly most crowded countries in Africa? Nothing so far – not in the magnificent approaches nor this grand hotel – smacked of Africa at all. There was a mistake somewhere. I wondered what it was. And then, down from my room with time before dinner, I had the beginings of an answer. It lay in all the well heeled guests around me. I could hear their voices now, eavesdrop on their conversations – in the bar, the lobby. I could see them more clearly.

Of course they were Western business and salesmen. But above all they were those readily identifiable Third-World 'experts' – bilateral and multilateral 'aid' people, loan officers from the UN and other government development agencies. I spent several years in this same business myself so I could identify these gentlemen fairly easily.

Though far too well dressed and manicured, with tax-free jowls and pot bellies, they did their best, with elegant gravitas, to suggest a missionary air, one of concern and high purpose and such grand hotels, I knew, all over the Third World, were their churches. The plain businessmen on the other hand, unrestrained by even the vaguest notions of charity, oozed a blunt confidence. They were men bent on all sorts of immediate and practical good works on behalf of the African poor: aspirin, video games, naughty nighties, grand cars, skin-whitening lotions – there was no sophisticated Western development, from tractor to trinket, which you couldn't unload either on the unsuspecting locals or on the rich fat cats in the government.

And where would most of the hard currency come from, to pay for all these unsuitable goodies? Why, from the aid men, of course, with their various development grants, dollar or deutschmark cheques to be drawn on the UN agencies or on banks in Washington, Tokyo, Paris or Bonn: a hard currency grant or loan would be arranged and another new and quite unnecessary motorway, airport or hotel would be put in train. Thus the circle of content would be complete: aid given, sales made, with a ten per cent cut off the top of both transactions for the African fat cat involved and his cronies. All the aid and sales men in the lobby that evening certainly saw the flaw in these financial bargains; the fact that ninety-nine per cent of the local people were unlikely ever to benefit from their generous arrangements. But what could you do about that? Very little. It wasn't your country. You'd made the effort, the gesture towards Third-World development. It was better now to order up a vodka martini and think about that South African steak, the choice tenderloin, imported for your dinner . . .

All this was the old sad story of aid and trade in the Third World. I'd experienced it myself fifteen years before, traipsing round the barren places of the earth on behalf of several international development agencies. What surprised me now was the obvious intensity of Western aid and salesmanship in the minute, impoverished and politically insignificant country of Rwanda, this Liechtenstein of Africa, the size of Wales, yet crammed with people, a population of over seven million, rising desperately all the time, the highest human density in Africa. Aid? They certainly needed it. But how was it operating – what had they got?

At first hand, I never properly found out, since that same evening a Congo stomach bug finally caught up with me and I spent most of the next few days in bed, with some considerable sprinting between there and the bathroom. And when I did recover I was very much in the limp rag department, able for little else but weak perambulations about the hotel: mornings in the lobby, afternoons by the pool, omelettes in the evening.

And yet, by this enforced immobility, striking up odd acquaintances on my travels through the great glass and aluminium jungle of the hotel, I was able to get some picture of the stricken world outside – in the shape of these aid and businessmen, returning each evening from their various engagements, bringing me news direct from the battlefront.

The damp-haired, little jockey-like Irishman in dark glasses was the first of these scouts to get through to me. I met him one morning in the bar, both of us beginning to recover (though from different ills I think), I with a tonic water, Patrick with something a little stronger. He was with his local 'Fixer', a tall, talky, pushy young man, revelling in his present important Western connections; on a permanent 'high', in a track suit, he jogged even at the bar, dancing with joy over his collection of cold beers. Patrick was a good deal less merry. He'd been trying for several weeks now to see the Minister of Agriculture and the only constant in his life was his complete lack of success in this direction. I asked him what he was doing here anyway, on his own, so far from home, which was in the rich racing country of County Kildare.

'Turf,' he said, so that I thought at first he was involved with horses and I was surprised at this equestrian element in Rwandan development.

'Breeding?' I asked.

'No. Digging. There's a damp valley a hundred miles south. Irish Government aid. We're helping organise a turf-cutting machine. You see, they've burnt all their trees, all the sticks here. Turf would be an ideal replacement. Trouble is I can't get to see the Minister, let alone get down to the place.'

'You never mind that,' the Fixer put in. 'This country is the pearl of Africa. You'll see the Minister this very morning and no mistake.'

Patrick was not convinced. 'Holy Mother and all the Saints,' he mumbled.

'But why a turf-cutting *machine*?' I enquired. 'With so much local labour at hand, needing the work.'

'Not down there apparently. There's hardly anyone. It's a damp place, I told you.' Patrick shook his damp head. The two of them left a few minutes later, like the end of a Morecambe and Wise show, the Fixer skipping, dancing out of the bar, Patrick following with less attack. 'The pearl of Africa . . .' 'Holy Mother of God . . .' They were appropriately paired – there was all the makings of a fine comic duo there. As for the turf-cutting machine in the damp wilds – well, that was certainly on a par with the grand airport and the motorway: exactly what Rwanda needed – apart from a racecourse, I suddenly thought. Now that wouldn't be a bad idea . . .

The man who really gave me a proper field report on Rwandan development was an American Agronomist, a soil specialist, who'd been studying the land here for the past few months. He was a dry and independent academic, not given, I felt, to exaggeration or a tax-free salary.

We had lunch high up in the hotel's top-floor restaurant, looking out over the raw brown hills that ran away to the horizon. The American waved his hand at them. 'That's Rwanda's food supply,' he said. 'All over those thousand hills. Trouble is there isn't any food on them now. It won't grow. The Belgians – in their own interests of course – developed a stepped, terraced cultivation here, with all sorts of conduits and careful drainage for the rains. But all that has been tramped down by the land-hungry farmers; flattened, ruined, so that when the rains come, the water just flows straight off the hills taking all the top-soil with it. And they use the scrub, the trees – whatever wind-breaks there might be – for firewood. Result? Total erosion – and no food. In five or ten years' time? Famine, complete famine, nothing less.'

'But what about all the aid programmes?' I asked.

The man smiled. 'Listen,' he said. 'This country gets more aid per square hectare than any other in Africa. But it's bags of flour, rice, dried milk and so on, and not bags of soil – that's the point. How do you replace the soil? – billions of tons of it. There's the problem. Aid, or the Belgians, should have taught them about soil conservation years ago. Now it's too late. You can't conserve what's not there. I've seen it so often in so many Third-World countries. They all wanted to be free twenty years ago – and that was surely right. They talked about *their* 'land' – and that was just too. Trouble was they talked about it in the abstract and never got to manage it properly, so that it would feed *them* at least, when they had it.

I could see the hills perfectly from this high vantage point, shimmering in the afternoon heat haze, deserted, the blackened stumps of trees running up the razed valleys. The view reminded me of the Kingdom of the Elephants in the first 'Babar' book, after the rhinoceros battle, when the whole landscape has been devastated by Rataxes and his evil cohorts.

Walter tapped his fingers gently on the table. 'Africa since independence – well, it's become a shambles, I'm afraid, utter and complete. I remember colonial times out here. It certainly wasn't good. But it was better than this, and not many ever actually starved. Everyone admits this now, including most Africans – privately. But we pretend otherwise. That's called diplomacy, because what *we* really want is power and political influence in all these new countries, before the Russians or Cubans stick *their* noses in. We're diplomatic, the local officials live in clover and the rest usually starve, that's the basic equation. Aid will always save a handful of people. But it won't give them long-term good land-husbandry habits. You have to stay here, to *live* in a country if you want to teach or induce that – have a stake in it.'

Walter had become almost roused. 'Independence is fine,' he said, waving his hand out over the bare hills. 'But it hasn't fed them. They're free out there now,' he said. 'And they're dying.'

7

Nairobi:
Railways and Racing
(May 1983)

In Zaïre it's strictly cash in advance before they let you near any hotel bedroom; in the very few Rwandan hotels the staff haunt you like jailers, expecting you to break for the streets without paying at any moment. So it was good to be back in the old Norfolk Hotel in Nairobi which, though physically changed by a bomb since I was last there fifteen years ago, still has all the right notions about comfort and service. It must be one of the best hotels in Africa – discreetly efficient, touched with a little hauteur and a deft style, where the receptionists have fresh red rosebuds in their lapels each morning and the waiters parade like Coronation attendants, in scarlet and dazzling white.

I felt I'd earned the Norfolk after the mad farce of a month in Zaïre and the fracas leaving Kigali airport in Rwanda where I'd been, literally, trampled underfoot by hundreds of Indians and other local passengers, stampeding the big DC10, desperate for seats on this single means of once-weekly transport between Tanzania and Kenya, with their closed frontiers.

Now I was recovering in the Norfolk dining room. The big mural was still there, over the whole of one end wall, and I'd been long enough away from home to gaze on it now with some nostalgia. It showed an idealised England of fifty, sixty years ago: the local hunt meeting outside an inn, in some comfy half-timbered market town in the shires. A genial bobby looks on among the jolly farmers and tweedy women, all is benign, reassuring; the town filled with winter cosiness. The painting is so literal, in that snowy, coach-and-horses Christmas-card style, that you can very nearly hear the hounds yelping, the horses champing at the bit, both straining to be off out among the bare December oaks and elms that lie beyond the gabled roofs. England, their England – so firm, so sure. Yet this mural, and one in the same vein above the Norfolk bar showing the arrival of the Mombasa train among red-faced, sola-topeed white highlanders, is almost the only evidence left in Nairobi of the old British East African Raj.

Nairobi itself is a soulless, glass-and-aluminium high-rise place these days, a city light-years away from the original rail-head camp it was only eighty years ago and nearly the same distance from its subsequent colonial settlement of Home-Counties bungalows, Indian shopping arcades, Kikuyu and Somali quarters. Since Independence, with Kenya taking on the accolade of being the only place that 'works' in black Africa, Nairobi has become a vast concrete money box, a haven for Western capital, where the big multinationals have deposited their cash and their staff, creating ugly headquarters from which they can make trading forays into the less secure parts of the dark continent.

What you immediately ask yourself when you get to Nairobi is, 'Where is Africa here – and the Africans?' and then, as an afterthought, you wonder whatever happened to the British and their influence, for better or worse, in a place which they built and dominated for sixty years. Beyond the busy bankers and the ubiquitous tourists from Tokyo or Rio there's not even a mirage of an old gin sling, the ghost of a Happy Valley remittance man. And the Africans no longer seem 'African' here. If Zaïre and Rwanda had been sad, inefficient holes, at least there'd been the real smack of devil-may-care 'authenticity' in the air: unavoidable collisions with the vast folly, spirit and character of the local people.

But in Nairobi the Kikuyu clerks walked the streets in proud imitation of their Western counterparts. They were like uncertain actors, self-consciously dignified in just the same neat, dark suits, with little briefcases and brollies; men who had passed from the colonial chit system to computer accounting without ever having known a life of their own.

It's fair to add that this new Kenyan bourgeoisie have never much *wanted* to know their own authentic life. As Kikuyu for the most part, this sharply ambitious majority race favours a comfortable, reticent, well heeled existence. And with these aims, they found in the old British colonial administrators, men with just the same status-conscious attitudes – the image of their own ambitions. And so now, filled with Western beliefs and addictions, these Kenyans have taken happily to their mimic lives, living in surburban bungalows or in one of the many smart new council estates that ring south Nairobi, catching the early bus to their glass-boxed offices like any London commuter.

But there is of course the obvious problem. I could see it clearly enough on my first day in Nairobi, looking at the shanty towns beyond the National Museum on the Nakuru road. The dispossessed live there, a good 100,000 and more of them clinging to the outskirts of the city, without land, and with no chance of a downtown office or a red rose in their lapel: people without a stake now in their own rural, tribal world but who would never handle a smart computer for a multinational company on Kenyatta Avenue.

It was the usual sad story of post-independence African migration to cities. Only a few can ever successfully thrive in an urban manner, while the rest – the landless, the rural Johnnies-come-to-town – are inevitably headed for the corrugated iron or paper shacks.

All the same, at the time I got to Nairobi – and despite this shanty town shadow – there was a formidably successful air about the city. It was still, demonstrably, the one place in black Africa that 'worked'. You could dial London direct from here: telegrams and railways still existed, leaving and arriving sometimes on the dot. The Indian shops did their usual canny business in everything under the sun. The smart, haute couture safari outfitters were still in business, with names like 'Sir Henry', where rich gross Germans and Americans kitted themselves out, disguising their pot bellies and round shoulders, and promoting their preposterous illusions, in well cut and padded beige safari suits, falling over themselves in their eagerness to play Hemingway up-country.

The other, poorer, package tourists made a fevered, rapacious show everywhere else; battalions in a permanent big push, constantly embarking in their zebra-striped animal assault wagons. The new young set of British Kenyans and the other smart-Alec short-term contract boys, together with their mindless girls, filled the Norfolk bar every sundown, dripping with Tusker lager, yelping loudly in grating suburban voices about 'the Yewkay', about planned car rallies and how they would 'bomb the coast' next weekend. Shaw's *Candida* was playing at the Donovan Maule theatre; 'Glittering Nights' were offered at the International Casino and the last meeting of the season was coming up at the Ngong racecourse that Sunday. Yes, Nairobi worked all right, in business and pleasure, and it was all infinitely depressing, a place without heart, without history.

Then, on my second morning, running for my life across the speed track of Haile Selassie Avenue, I suddenly saw a great black railway engine stalled in a marshy back-lot beyond the lines of shimmering traffic. On closer inspection, I found half a dozen other vast old steam engines with cow catchers, parked alongside a number of small, wooden, maroon and cream carriages. I'd stumbled on the Kenya Railways Museum and with it, at last, a key to some real continuity in the country, the past living properly in the present, for it's the Kenyans, not the tourists or the old British Raj, who use the railways these days. The tourist brochures don't mention the rail museum and the building was deserted except for one grey-haired old African, a real stationmaster type, in a crumpled peak cap, sitting by the door at a table organised just like the booking office of Adlestrop Station sixty years ago, with an ancient telephone and ticket punch.

He issued me with a passenger ticket in the traditional form, heavily printed on stout cardboard and then clipped it with a resounding 'snip!' that pierced the silence of the big room.

All about me, crammed in glass cabinets and covering every foot of wall space, was a marvellous, quirky collection of railway photographs and models, together with other railway bits and pieces, taken from every stage in the development of the old Uganda Railway, started in 1896, which ran (as it still does) from Mombasa to Lake Victoria and beyond. Nothing was missing. You could have reconstructed an early station, complete with rolling stock and half a mile of the original track, without any trouble at all. There were detailed engineering and contour maps and sepia-tinted photographs of turbanned Indian station-wallahs, leisurely Edwardians on safari and Teddy Roosevelt in a hurry, American calendar clocks, clear line tablets, Dâk boxes, engine models and splendid cast-iron coloured railway crests rescued from defunct companies all over East Africa.

Best of all perhaps, was the equipment taken complete from a 1930s dining car: wood stove, sensible pre-war commercial hotel cutlery, wine and bottled Bass glasses, silver-plated cruets, dented Birmingham teapots, Bombay cane chairs and the actual five-course luncheon menu, featuring 'Brown Windsor Soup', 'Baked Lake Fish – au gratin' and 'Sherry-cream Trifle', dated 19 December 1935, and priced at three shillings inclusive. It was all so real you could have stepped straight into the display there and then, and taken straight off for Happy Valley.

Outside, the vast engines loomed in the air, hiding all the ugly city beyond and you could climb all over these monsters, ringing bells, turning brakes and pulling ghostly whistle wires. In a nearby shed there were half a dozen of the original tiny metre-gauge carriages, including the one in which – in 1900 – Superintendent Ryall had met with a grim fate. He was dragged from his bunk and devoured by a man-eating lion as they built the line through what became Tsaro Game Park.

Here was a good deal of Kenya's recent history in miniature; solid evidence of some genuine life lived in the country, not just a trade in ever-increasing tourists and diminishing wildlife. And the Kenyans had preserved all this pioneering endeavour and adventure, these artefacts forged in iron, with rosewood panelling, which were now supplanted by the plastic veneers and ugly concrete of the disposable city beyond, a city geared almost entirely to the financial ambitions and pleasures of transient foreigners, barely an African city at all. The British at least worked whole lifetimes here, and I wondered whether the end of their paternalism and the arrival of the rapacious international money men and the tourists had given ordinary Kenyans any greater stake in their country? I doubted it. White domination in Africa has naturally been replaced by black, but in Kenya this control is largely financed by outsiders with only the slightest real knowledge of, or interest in, the country. Or it's paid for by the millions of goggle-eyed tourists, who experience the country only through their cameras as they are whisked from one animal 'event' to another, ever-renewable locusts feeding on ever-wasting assets. The world of the Railway Museum smacked of colonialism, no doubt. But it had been a world based, for the most part, on a deep knowledge and understanding of the country and on a long-term commitment to it.

The world of the Ngong racecourse stirred the same thoughts in me when I got out there for the last meeting of the season that Sunday. There were few, if any, tourists or foreign businessmen among the leisurely crowds strolling in the sunshine around this sensationally beautiful park. Ringed with tall, glitter-leafed trees, the white rails tracing brilliant lines against the shamrock-green sward, one might at first sight – like the mural in the Norfolk dining room – have been in an England of fifty years ago. The paddock and the reserved stand, apart from several groups of Wabenzi, the richest of the Kenyan tribes, were filled with the remnants of the old white highlanders come to town for a last spree before the rains. There were elderly, hawk-eyed grandes dames, bulky in tweeds; younger women, Happy Valley reincarnate, in Gucci scarves; others more formal, nearly at Ascot in flowery dresses and floppy hats and all with their cavalry-twill or pinstripe-and-trilby escorts, ramrod men, thinly moustached, choked by Guards' ties. The bars were awash with a rougher white element, among them the Norfolk-terrace cowboys, still shouting about 'the Yewkay' and 'bombing the coast'.

But outside, in the betting tent and behind the paddock, this very English picture suddenly took on a different colour: the bookies were all Indian and the stables boys all black. Looking around, I thought how in one way this careful class and colour structure simply reinforced the pre-war feeling of the racecourse: here, it seemed, was an exact reproduction of former British times, at home and overseas, when everyone had known their place . . .

The horses thundered round the curves, some white jockeys, just as many black. The sun sank into the trees, dipping towards the hills. Hints of a violet velvet twilight leaked into the air. Of course, many would say the whole thing was indefensible, this colonial ethos lovingly preserved at Ngong racecourse, but the fact is the black Africans themselves – the ones outside the shanty towns at least – defend it all, allow it, involve themselves in it. And why not, I thought? For all the wrongness, the arrogance and stupidity of most of the old colonial system in Kenya, there seemed more vibrant life in its legacy here, than in any of the glass and concrete monstrosities which the new colonialists had built downtown.

And the Kenyans at Ngong racecourse – black, brown and white – reflected a knowledge, an involvement in the life of their country that few of the tourists would ever gain on their frenetic safaris. There had been a real past in the Railway Museum and there was a real present out here among the racehorses, though no doubt the Kenyan future lurked somewhere down in the shanty towns, already stirring itself: men with a famished envy and violence for land and food – food from the grand tourist hotels and land from out here. Then this lovely green pasture would be cut up into pocket-handkerchief plots, the trees felled with pangas that had already cut down the rich – white, brown and black.

8

Kenya:
The Mara Flight
(May 1983)

One morning in Nairobi, I took coffee with Petal – a friend of a friend of mine in England and an oldtimer from better days in Kenya – in her room almost at the top of the thirty-storey Hilton Hotel where, up from the coast and holidaying, she was staying for a few days.

I picked up a pair of binoculars by the window and, casually focusing them on what I thought would be the suburbs of the city, I saw instead an old silver DC3 rising into the blue from a country runway that seemed just at the end of the street.

'That's Wilson – the original airport,' Petal said. 'Even now Nairobi is much smaller than one thinks, stuck down on the streets beneath all these phoney skyscrapers. In the old days, with field glasses, you could see the animals in Nairobi Park from the top of most buildings here. Not now. Fewer animals, more poaching, more skyscrapers, more tourists.'

'Where's the best place to see the animals then?'

'Maasai Mara,' Petal said at once. 'Game reserve, 200 miles south-west of here, on the Tanzanian border. We always went there hunting in the old days: best lion in East Africa. And I was there ten years ago, for a last look. Still pretty unbelievable – the package tourists haven't got into it, costs too much. It's really a continuation of the Serengeti. You can take a plane from Wilson, right there, just down the road. Or a car, do it in about a day. You'd be just in time for the wildebeest migration. That's quite breathtaking – sausages-and-mash! They start to cross over the border about now, hundreds of thousands of them, going north looking for the fresher grass. Never seen anything like it.'

'You take a truck out after them, do you?'

'No,' Petal said firmly. 'You take a balloon out *over* them. They run one every morning from Keekorok Lodge now. That's how I did it – utterly extraordinary.'

'Costly,' I ventured.

Petal nodded. 'Worth every penny, though. Worth a week's safari pushing about on the ground. Once you've done it – well, I couldn't believe it: really the only way to see game. And Maasai Mara is the last place for that out here anyway. All the other parks are overrun – with tourists and poachers, of course, not animals.'

I took the glasses up again. The DC3 was rising high now, a silver fish in the sun above the N'gong hills, moving south-west toward an armada of little puffy clouds that ran across the sky, all suspended in a perfect line, at exactly the same height, like dazzling meringues seen from beneath on a transparent oven tray.

'That must be the Mara flight now.' Petal looked out the window with me. 'The one I got. Leaves every morning and there's nothing else in that direction, just Maasailand, and beyond that the last really wild plainslands left in Kenya. They're like it all was a hundred years ago before we came out here, shot most of the animals and put the rest in parks. Out there in Mara it's like it was,' she added abruptly, turning away suddenly with a couldn't-care-less look, lighting a cigarette. I recognised the form of Petal's emotion now, for things she really felt about in Africa: it emerged in a clipped shorthand, the voice of a bored and irascible telephone operator conveying the words of a marvellous sonnet. Only in such dull telegraphese could Petal accept the content of the message.

I hadn't really wanted to see the animals this time in Kenya; I didn't want to be part of any frenzied safari groups in zebra-striped minibuses. But something moved quickly in my stomach as I watched the silver DC3 and I experienced that magic moment in travel when a plan not even dreamed of a minute before suddenly comes to you fully formed – kicking you, beckoning irresistibly. Suddenly I had to be out there in the sky, among the puffball clouds, on the way to Mara and a hot-air balloon, no matter what the cost. I told Petal; she nodded. 'I'd come with you, come again. But enough is enough. Besides, I'm cured – there's nothing like Mara for sorting oneself out. We all went down there for that in the old days. Little tiffs, hangovers, even deaths – whatever awful things – we all made off for a few weeks' safari in Mara. That was the greatest cure of all out here.'

Twenty-four hours later I was in the same silver DC3, the great wings bumping over the N'gong hills, pushing up into just the same little blobs of cotton wool, about to launch out over the vast brown depths of the Rift Valley. 'Sausages and mash,' I thought to myself, looking down on the stupendous view. The passengers with me were straight out of an updated Grand Hotel-type movie. A fashion-plated, real blonde in tight designer cords and an almost diaphanous silk shirt sat right behind; on the other side of the aisle was a cultured American genealogist from Maine. Right in front a chic Parisian family, parents and two teenage children, commented on the sensational view in the purest, money-laden tones of the *Seizième*. The others in the plane were similarly varied, individual and well heeled. This was no cheap package tour certainly. The cost of staying at Keekorok Lodge, if you included the balloon flight, worked out at more than a hundred pounds a day. The manager at my Norfolk Hotel had fixed the trip for me. 'Trouble is there are no rooms at the Lodge right now,' he said. 'But I've fixed you up to stay with the balloon pilot and his wife for a night or two, so you'll be all right.'

And I was. The plane shivered and bounced continuously in the hot thermals over the great rift valley. A sudden delicate rumour of eau de cologne and the rustle of a sick bag came through the air of the cabin. The very rich, slightly out of bounds on this escapade, were being mildly punished for their temerity. They gazed nervously down at the blazing desert wastes far below us; red-brown, endless, empty except for a few Maasai *manyattas*, circular *bomas*, portable thorn-bush camps, which from this height appeared as mysterious human patterns on the floor of the red valley, archaeological remains of some long lost tribe.

But twenty minutes later, the tawny slopes of the western escarpment rose up on the other side of the great valley, then yellow-streaked hills and ten minutes after that, the desert was all gone and we swooped down over a very different world skimming in just above a line of lush green river-trees, startling an ostrich that gangled away before the engines roared again and we powered in to Keekorok airstrip.

As soon as my feet sank into the springy yellow meadow grass I knew

I'd come somewhere special: grass, I thought, nothing but gently undulating grass – twenty or thirty miles of it disappearing away toward the thin purple hills on the horizon – not the clapped-out, eroded soils and gloomy rainforest that I'd seen everywhere else on this African journey. Here was real land at last, untouched, singing in the wind beneath a huge sky in the blade-keen light. The equator was just a hundred miles to the north, but at over 5000 feet, high up on this great plateau, the air was only warm, not hot – it cooled you in little eddies as you looked into the great distances through the light that was clear and blue as old Mediterranean water. And now I knew the truth of Karen Blixen's words, from her classic memoirs *Out of Africa*: 'Up here in this high air you breathed easily, drawing in a vital assurance and lightness of heart. In the highlands you woke up in the morning and thought: Here I am, where I ought to be.'

We stood together on the grass airstrip. The plane left again at once, engines roaring as it turned at the end of the grass strip and hammered away, up like a heavy bird, toward the north. The French woman said, 'Alors . . .' Even she was speechless, the warm wind flickering at her silk Gucci scarf as we stood there, amazed swimmers about to dip into a limitless green-gold sea.

Dudley Chignall, the balloon pilot, came to meet me in his new Toyota jeep – a small, fair-haired, delicate-featured man, whose eyes saw everything and whose mouth said only what needed to be said. He was young, with a milky tan, but already had that sunswept, wind-weathered face, the narrowed eyelids, the easy gait that every white frame must take on here in time: toasted, enriched, relaxed, by the limelight intensity of these high plainslands. He'd made a life here floating over this rippling sea, a young old-timer already. We left straight away for his little bungalow where he and his wife Vicki lived on the very edge of the Keekorok settlement. At the end of their small back garden there was nothing but a bamboo fence between them and all the rest of empty Africa beyond, the vast, rolling plain running away forever.

'Buffalo and zebra – and sometimes lion – they come right up to us here all the time,' Vicki told me, looking out over her gardenias and geraniums. 'And we have an elephant that leans in over the fence too – trying to get at the flowers or the washing. And if you go down to the Lodge after dark, keep to the lighted path. Else there's a chance of unexpected meetings.'

'Ending up as, not at, dinner?'

'Well, not quite – I hope.'

It was late afternoon now, the silver-ringed sun beginning to dip into the violet light over Lake Victoria a hundred miles to the west. 'The sunsets here are unbelievable,' Vicki said. 'Reflections from all that water, I suppose – with the clouds above it. You'd think the sun might go down the same way once in a while out here. But it never does, each night's different. You'd go mad trying to paint it. But come on before the light goes. We'll go out in the wagon, see what's to be seen down by the river.'

I offered a present of gin I'd brought from Nairobi and Dudley took it away to the kitchen where we heard the clunk of ice, the clatter of a blender. 'Sundowners – I expect,' Vicki said. A few minutes later, Dudley was back with a pair of binoculars and a big thermos flask, and then we were out in the Toyota, moving off into the creamy yellow evening light.

Moving south-west out of the settlement we left the dirt track almost at once, speeding through the long grass, swerving round thorn bushes, missing hidden logs and tree stumps by inches at the last moment: real land cruising, using land just like water, like the sea this great space was, avoiding the reefs. Soon we came to a twisting line of shaggy, green-topped trees, where the ground fell abruptly, and suddenly we were hanging over the steep, forty-five-degree angle of a sandbank above the river, before tobogganing down it, bumping through the shallow water and climbing straight up the far side like an airplane coming out of a dive. The leaves of the trees above us exploded as we passed and a lot of small, stork-like birds which we'd woken, flapped away, crying, long-legged, long-beaked heraldic devices against the pearl-blue sky.

Finally we stopped half a mile beyond the river, facing the sunset, and Dudley got out the thermos-flask cocktail. I raised my glass to the dwindling sun, the horizon now a violent, sweeping mass of colours. But so far there were no animals, or none that I'd seen. Then Dudley pointed ahead. What was it? A lot of dark, motionless shapes: thorn bushes, rotten branches. But no, they moved minutely here and there, and then I smelled something heavy and rancid on the air, a mix of old goat's cheese and socks, and then I saw them. It was a large herd of wildebeest, grazing quietly, barely more than a hundred yards from us, these black, high-shouldered, tousle-headed animals that I simply hadn't noticed against the darkening plains.

'The beesties,' Dudley said. 'They're beginning to move again. They might really get going tomorrow, cross the river here, so we should get a good look at them from the balloon.'

There comes a moment, like the acceptance of a drug, when Africa finally 'takes', when after weeks of incomprehension or distaste, stumbling across the continent, you finally discover its special quality, what all the old-timers like Petal loved about it. A mix of extraordinary space, air, light, potent sundowners perhaps and animals moving like silent armies through the dusk – all that. But there's something more to this sudden revelation: it's when intellect, worry, fate all die in you and all your senses correspondingly sharpen, when you become at once more human and more animal, too, living miraculously in the best of both worlds. Like a drug, it's a sort of 'high', an elation you know you could come to crave, so that you'd want to stay here forever, just as Petal had. Africa 'took' for me at last that evening by the river.

A hot-air balloon ideally travels in the cool, calm airs of dawn. So I was up at six with Dudley and Vicki and down to the take-off strip half an hour later, where the big wicker basket was on its side and there was the sound like a jet engine coming from it as the huge flames, both gas burners full on, spouted into the vast nylon canopy. Dudley took over, crouching inside the wicker basket now and manning the burners like a machine gunner. The balloon gradually inflated, then slowly rose into the vertical, where it finally stood up against the brilliant dawn: a pear upside down, striped in vivid red and orange, ten storeys high.

With the three other passengers from the Lodge we stood there mesmerised. But there was no time for dreams or faint hearts now. The basket, held by half-a-dozen sliding, dangling Africans, was straining upward. Dudley, already inside, had his hands on the brass control knobs above him – and then, tumbling in with him, we were lifting off, imperceptibly at first, still earthbound, but suddenly free, moving straight up into the air, but so smoothly that there was no sense of the gathering distances beneath. I'd expected the feeling to be like going up in a lift. It wasn't. Once airborne, we were entirely part of space, quite unrestricted, not part of any mechanical contrivance. Beneath us, as we rose, the tawny yellow-gold plains gradually lengthened, unrolled in front of us, displaying their real size now, and their intimacies. You could see all the secrets of the land hidden from the ground, the shade from the low sun behind us outlined the contours of the small hills, uncovered the hidden twists of the animal trails like a railway layout, traced the gunmetal shine of the Mara river away to our right, explained all its hidden snake turns as it ran down from the escarpment.

And there were the animals now, of every sort, displayed below us as if we were players leaning over a Noah's Ark game: the striped white flanks of leaping gazelle; pairs of topi standing head to tail on anthills, canny lookouts gazing in opposite directions; a herd of elephant like overloaded trucks out of control in slow motion, crashing through thick scrub by the river and a group of boot-black buffalo beyond them, who rushed for cover when the shadow of the great balloon passed over them – nervous, dangerous-looking animals which, like all the others, never looked up at us, unaware of where the threat of noise and shadow came from. But most of all there were the wildebeest and their outlying runners of zebra. They were on the move this morning as Dudley had thought, vast black herds of them, 100,000 strong, massing along the southern horizon and ambling forward in the dawn. From a height, they moved like thick rivulets of treacle down a window pane, but then, the burners off, the balloon dropped, gliding down in the morning breeze right over them – a hundred, fifty feet above them, so that the rancid, cowey smell was everywhere in the air again and I thought we must crash into the herds, before Dudley gave another long blast on the gas and we sailed away above the animals at the last moment. The tousle-maned, big-shouldered, crooked-horned, small-assed beasts galloped madly, swerving and charging, spurred on by the noise, dancing and kicking like bucking broncos, over the Tanzanian border, prancing in their holiday excitement some with all four feet off the ground, these comics of the plains.

'Designed by committee,' Dudley said, watching them stream away. 'But the buffalo are quite different. No joke at all. See that one there? That male – gone in behind the bushes, right next to the river? There, turning outward now, back to the water. If you stumbled on him – and that's exactly what you would do, walking along the banks – well, you'd meet the charge at about zero feet. Almost no chance. Most dangerous of the big five. The others will try to avoid you. The buff, in that position, is just looking for trouble.'

'But he doesn't see us up here,' I said.

'No. But he knows something is up. Good smell, hearing, sight, and can turn on a sixpence. One of them got in amongst a walking safari here some time ago, by the river down there. Havoc. Gored and tossed one woman, tried to shake another down from a tree. The warden grabbed his tail and the ranger got a shot at him. But he galloped off. It was flying doctor stuff afterwards.'

The balloon was coming down while Dudley was talking, sinking toward the dark shape hiding in the bushes by the water. 'I wonder . . .' I said nervously, looking up at the silent gas jets. Dudley gave the brass knob another pull.

The sun had risen as we rose again, up into the sky where the night-blue of dawn was beginning to whiten out, dissolving into the light blues of morning, the sky seeming to expand above us, a great milk-streaked arc running away into the universe. And the early chill was beginning to fall from the air as well; a frail zephyr warmth replacing it, pushing us imperceptibly westward: higher up now, then higher still, to a thousand feet when Dudley cut the burners and one was barely conscious of any movement across the earth far below. In the absolute silence I could hear Dudley breathing beside me. An Egyptian vulture, a great white-headed bird with finger feathers at the end of each wing, sailed slowly past beneath us, floating on an early thermal, moving away to the east. That was the strange thing: to be up here, above the birds – they quite unaware of us – yet sharing the same medium, free as they were. I couldn't get over the feeling that this mysterious buoyancy had given me; an overwhelming confidence. I had left my human frame and mind behind and had entered every other natural dimension: air and space, animal and bird, sunlight, sky and landscape, they were all mine, gliding through this vast aerial ballroom which was home to me now, inexplicably home.

The balloon was sinking again, dropping towards a thick tree-covered ridge, a shoulder that rose from the plateau with a huge shadow beyond, so that the hill was spotlit by the rising sun in brilliant greens and golds set against a background of night. 'We saw a leopard with her cubs a week ago here, hiding out on the top somewhere,' Dudley said, and we all craned round to look. The balloon was sinking fast, in a long sloping glide, straight toward the treetops. Again, I couldn't see how we could miss them, I crouched over the edge of the basket, trance-like, waiting for the crash. But there was no crash, I'd misjudged the distances – not long enough a gliding bird, as Dudley was. The top branches rubbed gently along the bottom of the basket. I reached out and touched a leaf and suddenly we were over the top of the ridge, looking down into the valley again, leaping over it, the ground falling sheer away for hundreds of feet. As we swung away from the trees, launched into air again, gravity-free, it was the stuff of dreams, gliding above woods, where you will: the classic dream of repression, they say, of lost sex. But here I felt what nonsense this was – how such night thoughts, earthbound, were but a longing to slough off mortality and re-enter the thoughtless kingdoms which we sprang from. There was no question: we were all of us allowed to play God for two hours that morning. And when finally we fell to earth, sitting on the padded gas canisters over a champagne breakfast – the chilled bottle corks exploding, the only gunshots in this vast, spectacular Eden all round us – I had to pinch myself to know it was all really true. Champagne, chicken, mango chutney, brown bread, fresh rolls and orange juice, coffee, cold beer if you needed it; basking in the middle of Eden.

This was Africa of the beautiful people, of course: the rich, silk-shirted blonde in the designer jeans; the money-cultured genealogist from Maine; the chic family from the *seizième*. Africa on a 'high', without cares in the world. It had nothing to do with the real, contemporary Africa at all. Yet for all that it offered another reality: living history – a look into the past of the continent, this empty world where everything was just as it had been a hundred, a thousand or a million years before. Though this reality was now under threat.

'Only last week,' Dudley said, 'they found two rhinoceroses, dead, with machine-gun holes spattered all over them, minus the horns. There are probably only half a dozen left in the whole park now, with fifty or sixty a few years ago. The Arabs will pay up to twenty thousand dollars for a good specimen, a dagger handle.'

Later in the two trucks that had followed our flight from Keekorok, we went down to the banks of the Mara river and watched the crocodiles lazing in the sun. They stared, malevolently beady-eyed, before sloping off like card sharpers into the water. Beyond them, in a wide pool, hippos wallowed and snuffled, big-snouted, toothy burblers, tiny baby eyes set out in orbs from punch-bag faces in car-sized bodies. Their glistening black skins looked like islands erupting slowly in the stream: first a water spout, then a nasal promontory following in line ahead, with liquid eyes emerging for hills, then the great backbone rising over a parish of flesh, the island complete for a minute, before the whole cumbersome geography disappeared like Atlantis beneath the waves.

Afterwards there was a long game run, back among the beesties. We stood up in the balloon's wicker basket in the back of the truck and ran right in among the herds, swerving round them, as they swerved in ever bigger circles round us, so that it became giddy-making, the truck a spinning carousel, the dust rising now, the sharply acrid cheesey smell churning in the air. It was wild-westish, with these thousands of dark-maned beasts drumming, thundering over the earth, colossal rhythms where the world danced.

Back at the Lodge we had coffee and biscuits on the sun-filled terrace and exchanged names and addresses. We'd never really write to each other or meet again, but that didn't matter. We were friends for life after what we'd shared. And if we did happen to meet, on a street corner in Paris or in Maine, we would immediately shine for each other, in the secret we'd been part of, like miraculous survivors of a wreck, in the knowledge that we had seen Eden together and lived to tell the tale.

9
Kenya:
The Jade Sea
(May 1983)

'Katey' was a seven-ton Bedford truck and we were belting along the tarmac, out of Nairobi, on our way north to the Jade Sea of Lake Turkana, 500 miles and three days' drive away. Apart from John, the New Zealand driver and two merry African cooks, there were sixteen passengers. Half were a group of clannish, childish British Kenyans who laughed irritatingly all the time; the rest (who I could see already as an opposing team), consisted of two nervous Milanese spinster teachers; an absolutely authentic hippy from the sixties; a studious-looking, reserved New York couple, of the sandals, rimless specs and rampant-beard type (harbouring anthropological interests, I suspected); a pale waif of a cheese-clothed Scandinavian woman, unassuming to the point of invisibility, who looked ill at the outset; Walter, an amiably handsome, slightly rogueish Italian computer-specialist who might just have escaped from a Fellini movie and me, bringing up the rear, as it were, someone as old as God by comparison with everyone else in the party. A mixed bunch all right, with our rucksacks, sitting on tents and the rest of the gear, in the back of this once-weekly 'Turkana Bus' where, for a hundred-and-twenty pounds all in, we were, we hoped, set fair for seven days camping out in the very wildest parts of Kenya, driving up to the lake and then back round via the deserts of the Northern Frontier District.

The trip had been advertised as 'A Safari into Vanishing Africa'.

And the truth of this was obvious soon enough, even on the new dull carriageway up to Nakuru, where the land-famished locals were busily digging up the central reservations and both grass shoulders of the road, planting out maize and potatoes on endless little strips. An hour later we stopped at the edge of the escarpment, looking down 5000 feet into the Great Rift Valley, where the white dish of the Longonot Satellite Communication Station was clearly visible fifteen miles away. Yes, you could dial Nairobi direct these days. Distance and delay had gone for us tourists – on these new roads, or for phone calls we might make home. But the locals had little food and no land, and thus the Africa most of us had come so far and paid so much to see was vanishing indeed, before our very eyes. 'Progress' was in the van that morning in the Kenyan highlands, no doubt about it . . .

At the same time the whole point of the 'Turkana Bus' was that we were getting out of progress, going far north, dropping off the end of the escarpment, where the maps, the tarmac and the cultivated land ran out and there was nothing but a punishing track across the baking lava fields, through the red deserts and the warring, nomadic tribes: a bare blazing land where no one would ever grow potatoes or dial London direct. Thumping along in the big truck we were going into Africa before the fall – and even further back in time, moving up to the fossil-strewn shores of the great lake where man was born.

It wasn't until we got to Maralal first thing next morning – the last town on the edge of the escarpment where the road runs out – that contemporary Kenya suddenly caught up with us, taking violent shape, exploding in the capital a few hundred miles behind us. There was that sure sign of impending Third-World disaster as we drove down the one dusty main street of the town: they were starting to close and lock up the shutters of all the tin shops. A few minutes later, some of us heard the news from the locals. There had been a coup in Nairobi hours earlier. A new revolutionary government had apparently taken over the country. Everyone was to stay indoors, or stay put, wherever they were. All movement was prohibited, since neither the army nor the police would now accept any responsibility for public order.

We were poised on the very end of the escarpment at that point – a revolution running up behind us; an empty, pristine world ahead. The continentals still in the truck understood nothing of the news, while the others down the street buying curios, hadn't heard it. I looked round at the flyblown tin huts of Maralal – a week stuck here would be like two weeks in Belfast. And John, our driver, obviously had the same thought. We called the others back, the big engine revving urgently, and left the little frontier town, clattering north down the stony mountainside like the hammers of hell.

'Mama mia!' One of the Italian teachers exclaimed, when Walter, who understood some English, explained matters to her. John had told me we'd be safe enough as far as the police and the army were concerned, since there weren't any ahead of us, apart from the small police post at Loyalgalani, our destination on the lake. The only trouble might come from the *shifta*, the brigands, the armed cow- and camel-raiding gangs that roamed this lake and desert area. If they had heard the news from Nairobi, they might well take advantage of it, seeing a truck load of camera-toting travellers, ripe for the picking in these completely isolated parts, where our own Turkana Bus was often the only vehicle seen in a week on this wild track.

'I banditi!' Walter leered, flourishing his arms at the Italian women. 'Garibaldi!' one of them replied, blessing herself, mopping her face, for we were down four, five thousand feet now, nearing the bottom of the escarpment, and it was suddenly very hot, the land turned red, streaked with sharp, slate-grey lava fields, nothing but the long raw scrubby desert ahead.

And yet the razed landscape, we soon saw, wasn't entirely empty or without movement. An ostrich loped away from us behind a stunted acacia tree; dik-diks skipped delicately through the odd thorn bushes; hornbills flapped up into the searing light on one side of the track, while dust devils gathered force, darkening the sky on the other, spinning up malevolently from the horizon. A priest in a Land Rover and two soldiers in a jeep rushed past in the opposite direction, taking no notice of us – making for safety, we wondered? Was there more danger ahead than behind us? The desert, we could see, contained all sorts of unexpected life.

We scanned the hills around nervously, waiting for the brigands . . . Walter was enjoying himself. But the two Italian women, crouching down, had hidden their cameras, while the laughter died at last among the juvenile Brits. Normally we'd have paused for breaks and meals, but we drove all that day to our evening camp-site without stopping. It was a thumpingly slow journey, manœuvring round the sharp rocks on the lava track, groaning down across dried out riverbeds or moving through sudden vicious winds that blew the sand up from the wheels, covering us, caking us from head to foot in a yellow choking mist. The jokes died then all right. It was genuinely tough going. And because of this we soon stopped thinking about the bandits and quite forgot the revolution behind. Instead a sort of silent, desert-dry exaltation dawned on us.

That day, we all became completely absorbed in, awed by, the gigantic, ferocious landscape unfolding in front of us. Revolution meant nothing here – and man himself very little either. This was true wilderness, where you could put away all earthly things. And next morning, still driving through it, still punching our way up between the rising lava hills at five miles an hour, I began to think we'd be stuck here for the full forty days.

But just before noon, getting to the top of the jagged pass and rounding a shoulder of black rock, we saw a line of faint blue in the huge valley beyond, not the lead blue sky, but the white-flecked, sapphire tint of water, which gradually expanded as we ran down the mountain, until finally we got to the shore and there was nothing in front of us then but the great lake.

It wasn't jade that morning, but lilac blue – the colour changes from one to the other, depending on the strength and direction of the wind which moves all the green algae in the lake up or down in the water. A hundred and eighty miles long and up to thirty-five miles wide, the lake is surrounded by malignant old volcanoes, filled with crocodiles and scorched, almost year round, with a really fierce, dragon's breath wind which was out in strength when we arrived and tossed the water up into big white-capped waves in the distance. An Austrian, Count Teleki, was the first European here in 1888 and named the lake after the suicidal Hapsburg Crown Prince Rudolph. But now it takes its title from the powerful, warring Turkana tribe who live on its western shores. On our side, to the east, only a few hundred remaining El Molo fishermen are indigenous to the area. They are the 'Wretched Ones' in translation, a dying tribe, literally, whose bones and teeth bend and rot before they're thirty; debilitated, over centuries, by their vast chlorine intake from the lake water.

That morning, on the treeless, burnt-black volcanic shoreline, we had only the migrant birds for company, a huge array and variety of them: pelicans, ibises, spoonbills, Egyptian geese, waders of all sorts. Shimmering a mile away in the distance was the raised plateau of a large volcanic island, with sheer cliffs: an inaccessible, mysterious landfall. We were all Professor Challengers just then, gazing out onto a lost world. Yes, we'd vanished into Africa all right – a brutal, radiant landscape that had been here a million, two million years before. We were standing now where man himself, down from the trees, had first stood upright and set out on his long trail of two-footed destruction.

Later that afternoon we set our tents up ten miles north, at the palm-fringed oasis of Loyalgalani. It was an airstrip and a smart fishing lodge, where rich people like Prince Charles and Gregory Peck stay, flying up from Nairobi to have a go at the 300 and 400 pound Nile perch lurking in the deeper waters of the lake. Our accommodation was less salubrious and the little Indian in the camp bar, running short of fizz and beer in this wild spot, was mean with the cooling beverages. It was hot, an oven-damp heat, with flies that tortured you quickly, so that soon we were all down to the lava-pebble beach, where the crocs had been frightened away (we'd been told) and were swimming out into the hot bath water. It was turning jade now, as the wind died down, so that your legs were bottle green in the rising algae and you swam like Jeremy Fisher – fast, toes well up – frightened of all sorts of potential nips, or much worse, from beneath you.

Because of bad radio static from the magnetic hills, the people here had barely heard the news from Nairobi. But the curfews and mayhem 500 miles behind us couldn't have mattered less in any case. The only thing the local Samburu and Rendille tribes feared here was the fierce Turkana, raiding their way round the southern end of the lake for the last few years, pushing all the other tribes north where, as refugees, they'd settled in this oasis. Refugees? That's much too modern a word in what was really a very ancient business. What was happening was what had happened in these parts for several million years: since man had first triumphed over the other animals around this lake. And he continued to do so, among his own kind now, the strong forever lording it over the weak.

The next morning there was a photo-call out among the remnants of the 'Wretched Ones' at El Molo Bay ten miles further north, where they lived on a scorched lava beach in several dozen leaf and stick huts, surviving on fish, but supplementing this now with a small income from allowing the few tourists like us to photograph them.

In fact, and perhaps as a result of this recent cash flow, they didn't look very wretched at all – rather a plump, marvellously dusky lot: the young child-brides ogling us, laden down with their foot-deep necklace collars, each strand representing a conquest, while their elders did business in curios and trinkets; hippo teeth, bead bangles and harpoon heads.

Apart from their palm-log rafts they had a real boat now as well, in fibre glass, with an outboard motor. And another deal was soon made, among half of us at least, for a trip around the island in the bay. The El Molo headman came with us, a splendidly piratical gent in a red bandana choker, sitting up in the bows with two harpoons, brought purely as a tourist show, I thought, until we neared the island and I saw the crocodiles basking along the shoreline.

Then the helmsman suddenly accelerated, driving the boat towards them and it all happened in a flash. The headman was on his feet in the bow, the harpoon raised. A huge beast lolloped into the water ten yards in front of him with a great splash. At the same moment the boat tipped in a shower of spray and the harpoon flew downwards, deep into the green swirl. By then we were all gasping, the Italian women frantic, shrieking in alarm, the 'Mama Mias!' and 'Madonnas!' coming thick and fast. Another crocodile followed into the water, its great green shadow diving quickly down, and a second harpoon followed it. Both narrowly missed.

We pursued the crocs round the island for the rest of the morning – without success and I have to admit that I came to enjoy it. The old bloodlusts rose all too easily in me and civilisation was only varnish thick in this kill-or-be-killed world. So that when we got back to Nairobi a few days later, the shop fronts everywhere smashed in, the glass crepitating beneath our feet, the abortive Air Force coup there seemed very small beer. My eyes were still glazed, sun-shot, with a vision of jade and sapphire; bones aching, skin desert-burnt and caked, with a half-inch-deep beard – I had returned from man's first world, that scorching wilderness where the real revolution had once taken place.

10

Lamu:
Gathering of the Tribes
(June 1983)

After nearly three months crossing Africa from the Congo coast, I was rolling off the Kenyan plateau in the Mombasa train, getting near the other coast at last, the Indian ocean. However, it wasn't until next morning, when I was airborne from Mombasa in the small plane, that I finally saw it, for I was making for the island of Lamu, 150 miles north, as my last stop on this journey.

And there the ocean was at last, suddenly making up the whole world as we rose: the blue water creaming against the endless coral reefs, the jade shadows inshore moving like vast shoals of fish, then the dazzling white beaches and the mud-green mangrove swamps – all spread out beneath me. I'd made it coast to coast. And when I crossed on the ferry from the airstrip to Lamu – bouncing about on the hot waves, blinded by the sea dazzle – when I got to Petley's Inn, right on Lamu waterfront and opened my first-floor terrace window, I knew – as the guide books had promised – that I'd arrived in a tropical paradise. But more than that, as other older wiser books had told me, I'd come to a place which people, not just climate, had made rich and strange.

Lamu, geographically, has never been more than a speck on the map, a tiny island oasis just south of the Somali deserts, but its history makes it far more significant – a jewel at the base of this scorched horn of Africa. For it was here, in and around Lamu, somewhere in the tenth century, that the Swahili culture was born, a vitalising mix of Arab and African traditions, which first of all resulted in the distinct Kiswahali language, and then, from about 1500 onwards, in an elaborately decorative Afro-Arab civilisation. Lamu became a tiny glittering world on the edge of a vast darkness, kept alight, fed by dhows on the monsoon winds by all the riches of India and Arabia. It was an elegant stone-and-mortar town, filled with a mixed race of sailors, merchants, craftsmen, poets, with wonderfully carved doorways, metal and plaster work and inlaid furniture. A town pouched in silk and held together with gold and silver thread, complete with harems, hookahs, powerful sheiks, booming cannon and delicate mosques, where nothing lacked in the arts of pleasure, faith or war. Lamu, for 100 years and more, was a vigorous, dominant City State, in fact a sort of Venice on the edge of the mangrove swamps, which reached its heights in the eighteenth century and then, with the consolidation of Mombasan and Zanzibari power in the south, embarked on its long decline – an indolent pursuit, which it has followed ever since.

But as I could see at once that afternoon from my first-floor balcony, the great trick, the miracle of Lamu – which makes it unique on this African coast – is that not very much has been changed here since the eighteenth century. The jewel is still almost intact. The layout, the fabric, the décor of that golden age lay all about me, to either side and rising up the slopes behind the hotel, a seeming hodge-podge of buildings, at first, yet with a secret order, where the raw coral-walled, or whitewashed or mortar-blackened, flat-roofed, largely windowless houses – crammed together at all angles and heights across the yard-wide alleys – gave the place the air of a three-dimensional cubist painting.

In front of me, unfolding graciously like some old Arabian maritime scroll beyond the sea wall, was a collection of lateen-sailed dhows of every shape and size – not a modern boat among them – from vast, high-transomed ocean-going boats to the much more numerous local *jahazis*, little arrogantly shaped craft with sharp perpendicular bows and 'eyes' to either side, painted as stars and crescent moons. Equally arrogant-looking Afro-Arabs, iron-faced, hook-nosed loungers in faded red *kekoi* skirts and white embroidered skull caps, squatted on the sea wall, legs akimbo, letting the faint breeze aerate them, their skirts flapping adventurously. Three donkeys, Indian file, dead set on some mysterious purpose, made down the middle of the sand track road.

Well, it wasn't actually a road, for there are no cars, no wheeled vehicles apart from a few wooden wheelbarrows, on Lamu island. No, there was nothing in front of me just then which might not have been there 100, even 200, years before – except, as I soon saw, the hippies. Bleach-haired, sun-struck northerners, eyes fixed like sleepwalkers, they moved up and down the seafront, dressed in just the same native *kekois*, but from there up kitted out in the standard uniform of beads, beards and leather begging bags.

The hippies, I knew, like some of the jet setters, rich remittance men and richer widows, had discovered Lamu some ten years before. The latter were still taking their siesta no doubt, in their refurbished thousand-and-one-night holiday homes. But these ageing flower children had to keep on their long march, in every weather, permanently on the look out for a potential 'crash', the cheap pad or kip, the rice bowl and the unsweetened yoghurt. The aristocratic loungers on the sea wall, mostly local guides and conmen, as I'd already discovered when I got off the ferry, looked at these equally brazen freeloaders with dumb distaste. Neither could take advantage of the other. There could be no financial exchange or gain between them, no expensive trips in a *jahazi* to see the Arab ruins on Manda island opposite. The hippies, with tuppence on them, were looking for the sun – while the conmen, among the rich visitors here, were hoping for the moon.

I wasn't rich or hippy, but I was a single foreigner all the same. So that when I went out and about later that afternoon and had again been offered, and had again refused, all sorts of decent and indecent proposals right along the sea front, I soon recognised a tension in the air between the black and white tribes here: envy, avarice, a mix of all kinds of vivid expectations; sexual and commercial, hopes repulsed on their side and a growing disappointment and ill humour rising in me. There were snakes in this Eden.

Later that day an old acquaintance of mine in Lamu, an ex-white hunter who I'd met years before in Kenya, confirmed my uneasy feelings. 'Bum boys, hippies, trendies, superannuated jet setters, riff-raff of every sort – that's the only problem here now.' We were talking – as we sank a few Tusker beers – in the open under a palm-leaf awning, right on top of his splendid old nineteenth-century sheik's house, halfway up the slope behind Petley's Inn. The channel below us had turned royal blue in the short twilight, an evening breeze frisking the waves and the palm leaves above us.

'The whites, I'm afraid to say, these newcomers, are well on their way to ruining this place,' he went on. 'Mind you, the locals have always been smarter than the Europeans here. I won't say these new folk have corrupted them. No. Just antagonised them – turning Lamu into an unpleasant sort of permanent holiday camp. These frightful people live here mostly. Not tourists, you see. Just either very rich or very poor whites – but both on the make, out for anything they can get.'

He eased his cravat and we broached another Tusker. 'The rich come to buy the old seafront houses and when they do, they tart 'em up like Turkish brothels. The youngsters are laid out in some squalid room smoking grass or whatever. Of course both these pursuits annoy the locals, and naturally they begin to want to take advantage of the situation in any way they can.

'But then it's *their* island and they reckon, quite rightly, that they should be first in line for any pickings going. Net result – undeclared war between everyone involved. The rich hate the hippies and the feeling's mutual, and the locals secretly despise them both. My response is simple. I keep well clear of the lot. And that suits me fine. Even cut off way up the coast here, miles from anywhere, I'm still in East Africa and that's where I've always wanted to be. I'd like to see more of the plains, of course. Oh yes, I miss that badly – the old shag, the deserts up country; love to get a look at a dik-dik even, now and then. All the same, you won't ever find me in Croydon or South Ken, that's for sure!'

Before it got dark, Dougie showed me over the rest of the old house, which looked nothing much at all from the outside, but where the interior was an elaborately conceived and decorated rabbit warren. The little narrow, whitewashed rooms, with their black mangrove pole ceilings on the first and second floors, had been inset, built as part of the very thick walls – with open stone staircases winding up to them inside from a courtyard beneath, which in turn was built not on the ground, but on the *roof* of the ground floor, where, in the old days, servants must have lived in a windowless gloom.

The house was like a big squat funnel, opening out to the world above, where you lived on the rim, slept in the wall just beneath, with your other needs and fancies – your harem, Chinese porcelain latrine, kitchens and servants' quarters – all tucked into little stone rooms, shelves, drawers and embrasures below. It was an extraordinarily well designed place, precisely adapted both to Lamu's steamy climate and all its old social and domestic conventions. And my friend Dougie, 150 years later, had kept the place exactly as it had been. This was why he lived here, why he'd always lived in East Africa, I was sure: not to change or 'civilise' the place, upset the balance, lay down the concrete, not to gain, to take things *out* of it, to set himself in any way apart from it. His ambition was just the opposite; to be one with the country, as he was in this old house now and had been, for forty-five years previously, up on the plains and in the deserts.

We went down to Petley's later on and had lobster salad on the terrace looking over the seafront, the tides running fast now, pitch dark, with just a few lamps splashing yellow pools along the sand track. It was the hour of release for all the local women of the town, strolling in groups of six or a dozen; laughing, tittering, shawled from head to foot in black cotton, like long cigars, just the white flash around their eyes showing through the dark letterboxes in their robes. The rich were having gimlets and martinis in their silk-cushioned seraglios. The hippies had gone to ground, too, pondering their rice bowls. The town, at last, in this slight coolness of the evening, had been returned to its rightful owners. The pirate-faced men, joined now by the elders of the town, gossiped all along the sea wall, eyeing their invisible wives or potential brides. Now that there were no foreigners about, all the tension had left the air.

Yet as I looked at these finally contented people, remembering their mix of very different Arab and African blood, I could well imagine the awful tensions – the bloodshed, the slaughter – in this very same place 500 or 1000 years earlier, when the Omani raiders had come in successive waves to rape these shores. The tribal antagonisms had eventually died between them as the two races had mixed, married, settled down together. In time, a rich new Swahili culture had emerged and after that, an indolent little paradise, which everyone enjoyed until 100 years ago, when the British in their turn came to pillage along this same coast. First to impose a military, then a political and now an economic domination.

These Europeans, unlike the Arabs, hadn't, and never would, mix or intermarry with the local people. Apart from a few old-timers like my friend Dougie, very few of these whites really knew Africa now, or would get to know it as a loved and lived-in place, though they might come to know it well enough through fixing the African commodity markets or in other ways which favoured them financially.

The white tribes in the continent, unlike the coast Arabs here, never learnt how to resolve the tensions they created in Africa. They leave no culture behind them, other than, at best, that of 'O' levels; an irrelevant package of exported Lake Poets and basic computer manuals, presenting images of daffodils and word processors, to a people who had never seen such flowers, whose fingers would never touch those alien keyboards. Was there – as in the Afro-Arab combinations of Lamu – a decorative, intelligent mix of white and African tradition in any person, or in any town or city in this whole continent? Certainly not in Nairobi – least of all in Johannesburg. Would there ever be? I doubt it. The white tribes have had their day. We have discovered, plundered and abandoned most of Africa, in little more than a single lifetime, leaving only the most ugly memorials behind us: harsh colonial brick, rusting corrugated iron.

The following afternoon – my last day – walking along the vast, deserted ten-mile beach at the ocean end of Lamu island, I suddenly saw a lone figure coming slowly towards me, dancing above the sand, a mirage I thought, in the shimmering heat haze. As the figure came nearer I could see that it was an African, a tall, well built Kikuyu highlander, I thought, certainly not a Lamuite, out jogging in a pair of smart silk shorts. He trotted straight past, without looking at me, without either of us speaking. What was there to say? We both knew too well already the arid, suspicious black–white dialogue in Africa – I was sure of that. And so there was nothing for it but for him to run past me and for me to go home.

TREASURE ISLANDS

1

Barbados:
Looking for an Angle
(February 1985)

Every day, for lunch and dinner, the old lady took her separate table on the terrace of the sedate Ocean View Hotel in Hastings. She ate, as I did, from the excellent set menu: cold consommé, a fish entrée, pork or lamb chops, fresh vegetables and fresh fruit salad, a glass of water, then coffee, as the two of us, among the other off-season guests, gazed out at the deep blue sea, waves gently caressing the little beach below.

I sometimes saw her sitting alone in Marine Gardens in the afternoon, when I returned to the hotel to hear the muted cricket commentary on the radio above Miss Macleod's desk in reception, before going on for a gin sling served up by Mr Lynch in the antique-furnished bar with its Quorn hunting prints. I would then sit down to another traditional supper in the twilit blue-and-white dining room with its cane chairs and dainty table bouquets in little silver-plated chalices, while Braithwaite, the head waiter, tactfully hovered about, master-minding the breaded veal cutlets, or a half bottle of Mateus Rosé for some of the more daring among the few guests. None of us were sufficiently aroused to stay up much beyond nine when the grandfather clock on the stairs chimed the hours of bedtime, bringing a virtuous silence over the old hotel.

A somnolent, Terence Rattigan mood: a quintessential English south-coast resort – the early 'fifties perhaps – a lost time-capsule here at the Ocean View Hotel, complete in every respect, except for the potted palms.

There was no need for them, for the beach outside had splendidly real palm trees leaning over the water, and it was a coral beach at that, while Miss Macleod and Messrs Braithwaite and Lynch were dusky dark and this Hastings was a suburb of Bridgetown, Barbados, 3000 miles away from its original counterpart.

Barbados has always been a tropical mirror image of England; a black and white negative of the old 'homeland', a Caribbean Isle of Wight. It is a geographical, geological and historical anomaly among the rest of the West Indian islands: a coral island where the others are volcanic; acquired by accident and without conquest (for it was deserted) by the English in 1625 and never attacked by the fierce local Caribs, the French, Portuguese or Spanish. It lies too far windward, out in the Atlantic and the marauding war canoes and square-rigged galleons from the other islands could rarely reach it. 'Bimshire' they call Barbados, no one quite knows why, though the name perfectly reflects the cosy slightly self-satisfied Home-Counties air of the whole place.

Barbados is a happy anachronism at the edge of varying doubts and difficulties in the rest of the Caribbean basin: pith-helmeted, unarmed, Empire-style police move traffic round a tiny Admiral Nelson in Bridgetown's Trafalgar Square; there is the aggressively signed 'John Bull' rum shop on Tudor Street and the dart-boarded Windsor Arms full of Royal-Family photos out in Worthing. It is tropical but never too hot, with a climate which the Encyclopaedia Britannica described, seventy years ago, as being 'remarkable in arresting the decay of vital power consequent upon age' and with a local black population which it graciously went on to say was 'more intelligent than in other West Indian islands'. Yes, Barbados is the comfy little island in the sun par excellence.

I had something rather more dashing in mind when I first thought of touring the West Indies. I wasn't interested in the sun, sand, sea, surf and sex bit. There must be – there had been certainly – a lot more to these 'sun-kissed' Carib isles than this. Tourism here is largely a post-war, package, jumbo-jet development after all. Most of these islands have a 350-year-old European history at least, with Arawak and Carib Indian settlements for a thousand years before that. And we know more of the island Africans here than we do of their luckier cousins, hidden from the slavers back in the dark continent during most of the same period. Above all the Caribbean was the start of Columbus's New World; the crucible of an age of miracles and horrors, of earth-changing discovery, exploration and exploitation, where half-a-dozen European nations fought for the spoils of supremacy over two centuries – with all that rich legacy, as I thought, in fact and fiction.

Here is Stevenson's *Treasure Island* for example, for us the *locus classicus* of this old Caribbean, a world unforgettably introduced by the menacing 'tap-tap' of Blind Pew's stick as he makes his way to the Admiral Benbow Inn and all the subsequent heart-stopping adventure. Here is the real derring-do, equal to any fiction, of the naval commanders, Nelson and Rodney, and of the buccaneers, Captain Morgan, Francis Drake and others, with their freebooting life in the sun under the Jolly Roger, sacking the Spanish galleons. A world dominated by pieces of eight, by secret maps where 'X' always marks the spot, by mayhem, murder and treasure of every sort – gold, sugar, rum, sunken caskets of jewels beyond price – as well as the awful human treasure of African slaves.

Here in the West Indies, it always seemed to me, was a history of unparalleled colour and evil, where there must still be sharp reminders of all those unprincipled Europeans, let loose among these paradise islands, using them as no more than dice, with the slaves as coin, in one long debauched gambling game. It struck me, in short, that here was a tremendous cache for any traveller, that there ought to be much more to do and see in the West Indies than lie on a coral beach or look for double top on the dart board of the Windsor Arms in Worthing.

Well, there was and there wasn't. The fact is that mass tourism in the West Indies in the last twenty years has softened all the edges of these islands, dulled individual temper, eased out the quirky marks of history and rubbed away topographical, architectural and social character in the Caribbean. The West Indies has become one vast rum-and-sun spot, dedicated to satisfying the idlest pleasures, which all the local Tourist Boards and hoteliers do remarkably well. But as a consequence of this imported dolce vita, there is something dull, flaccid and banal now in the spirit of the islands and islanders themselves. The natives, now that they are no longer dominated and oppressed – have lost a lot of their vital, idiosyncratic response: rough diamond has become dull paste, strong rum replaced by frothy Pina Coladas.

Since independence, history, one feels, has ceased to be made or properly remembered in the West Indies. It appears, where it shows itself at all, as an antiseptic packaged commodity, half-heartedly offered to the tourists on their one day off from the beach: the morning at an old sugar plantation, afternoon looking round the Great House, limbo dancing at a so-called pirate's cove that evening. The past doesn't really seem to matter any more; it has been over-printed by every tropical tourist cliché there is. This is understandable when you consider that history, for the local people, was not a pleasant thing; it wasn't made by them, they simply suffered it. So that now, the islanders make the most of each rich cargo that arrives, the white slaves to pleasure, packaged head to toe, manacled almost, in the big jets.

The West Indies, prostrate at this altar of tourism, has become a world of aeroplanes, from jumbos and Twin Otters to small five-seaters and consequently, one of the obvious, lovely things about a pattern of islands has been lost almost completely. It is no longer possible to take passage by boat between the islands, watch a pink coral shore disappear with the sunset, wake next morning in a volcanic harbour beneath a towering peak, green clad, head in the clouds.

Island-hopping, which the long and varied necklace of the Lesser Antilles so perfectly allows for, is unavailable now to the ordinary traveller. The small passenger, banana and mail boats no longer operate. Only private yachts, big container ships and a few water barges ply between the islands these days, so my original plan of a tropical voyage around this jewelled crescent took a knock from the word go, even from the one British line that still does take passengers between some of the islands in the big Geest banana boats.

'No,' the man said in their Bridgetown office. 'I'm sorry. All our cabins are booked at least a year in advance, on the round trip from South Wales.' So it was back to the Ocean View Hotel with a local airline timetable and thoughts of moving on to the island of St Lucia sooner than I'd expected. Mr Lynch was carefully setting up his rum-punch mixes in the bar. He was a reserved, polite, methodical fellow, like many Barbadians, but he ventured a slow smile now at the news from Miss Macleod's radio in the lobby that England, against the West Indies in the Test, had once more collapsed in their second innings.

'Yes, man,' he nodded gently. 'We can surely play that game.'

'That – and the coral beaches,' I said.

'You don't like the beaches?'

'Not crazy about them.' I told him I was out here on my own, looking for something different. This idea didn't make a lot of sense to him. 'We get plenty honeymoon couples out here. But everyone else – they spend *all* their time on the beach.'

That evening the austere old lady and I took our separate tables in the dining room once more – conspicuously unbronzed, the only two white people in Barbados, it seemed, who had not been on the beach that day. Over the flying fish and tartare sauce I pondered what to do. Hire a snorkel or a scuba suit and dive in like everyone else? Tax the honeymooners with a few impertinent questions in a disco? Sign on for the package limbo-dancing and barbecue in a phoney pirate's cove? Walk the plank and run the gamut of rum punches on the 'Jolly Roger' cruise down the coast?

In bed that night, I thought what a very comfortable, amiable holiday island Barbados was: the ideal 'wish-you-were-here' postcard place. But I wasn't on holiday. Perhaps the other islands, with a more troubled past and present, would offer more to talk about. I'd get tickets onwards from a travel agency tomorrow.

'Houses,' the director of the agency said to me in his office next morning. 'If you don't want to lie in the sun, Barbados is full of interesting old buildings: barracks, lighthouses, signal stations, churches, great houses, chattel houses, suburban villas.' And he elaborated. One needs the luck in such haphazard travel, and I had it then. The director of the travel agency was Paul Foster and he turned out to be the President of the Barbados National Trust as well.

He gave me a recent book – *Historic Houses of Barbados*, a fine collection of ink drawings by Henry Fraser, with historical and architectural notes from Ronnie Hughes, and several introductions to the present owners of some of these great houses. 'All you need is a car now – and a few phone calls,' he said. 'I'll make your ticket out for St Lucia *next* week, shall I?'

I arranged to hire a car that afternoon and went on to the police station in Hastings to get a local driving permit. The duty sergeant was filling in a charge sheet in a fine copperplate hand which I could read upside down. 'Petty Larceny,' he'd just written, 'One Brass Bell Alarm Clock'. And I had clear confirmation then, along with the book

I'd been given, of what was special, what was real in Barbados beyond the lotus eating. It was the past; in the sergeant's copperplate hand, in this meticulous, almost Victorian attention to the theft of one alarm clock, the past amidst the Edwardian splendours of the Ocean View, the bandstand in Marine Gardens and now in all these old houses – forty or more of them in the book – and that only half of them on the small island. Barbados, I realised, isolated from the world as much as from the other Caribbean islands over three-and-a-half centuries of uninterrupted peace, had kept a lot of its history in aspic. Lurking everywhere inland behind the palms and coral beaches was a past that I'd not suspected, blinded as I was by the garish coastal-strip tourist elements of the place.

I had expected present unrest or the remnants of violent drama in the West Indies, and no doubt I'd find that later on in my trip. But Barbados, I could see now, offered something quite different. This was no treasure island with parchment maps smeared in blood and no one had ever really walked the plank here. In this well run and profitable democracy there was little if any contemporary unrest. Unemployment, yes; some drug and other problems with the tourists, and the sugar industry – largely subsidised by the government now – is no longer a natural money spinner. But the island, with its very high literacy rate, good shops, health and communication services (all phone calls are free within Barbados) offers little for any doom-laden commentator to chew over. My role as Jeremiah, which I've played successfully and with ample reason elsewhere on my travels in the world, had no future here.

I returned to the Ocean View for my last night in a better mood. Mr Lynch was going through his rum punch rituals once more. I had a Planters to celebrate. A little of this and that and this; a dash of Cointreau, a sprinkle of nutmeg. Mr Lynch's Planters were the best in Bridgetown. I had two of them.

'Bin out on the beach today?' he asked, surprised at my good humour.

'No.' I showed him the book of historic houses. 'That's where I'm going.'

'Ah, I see.' He thumbed through the drawings. 'Well, you won't have far to go,' he went on, stopping at one of the illustrations. 'Marine Lodge here – that's opposite the hotel, far side of the road. And Retreat House right next to it.'

'Just opposite?' I was surprised. In three days coming and going I'd never noticed these splendid seaside villas. None so blind, I thought. Looking for an angle in Barbados, I'd been living in it, and next to it, ever since I'd arrived.

2

Barbados:
Colonial Ghosts
(February 1985)

The wind rattled the tops of the palms as I drove out of the city in the blowy heat. Out of Bridgetown and into the country – to see Barbados properly; the place beyond the package tours and to get a sense of the island's past.

The first fascinating – and ubiquitous – evidence of this in Barbados is the endless little chattel houses which were literally, in the old sugar plantation days, a 'moveable possession'. The local people, though they owned their wooden huts, could only rent the land they stood on in a plantation 'tenantry' and had to be ready to move everything at short notice. Today, though the site is owned and these houses stationary, they still follow the earlier design, the exteriors elaborated now. Indeed some of these chattel houses have a wonderfully quirky, ornate air, minute gingerbread palaces, Mad Ludwig fantasies, Bavaria in Barbados, and driving out of Bridgetown is a splendid education in how to express yourself in wood, tin and paint for a pittance.

The basic form of the chattel house is always the same. It is scrupulously symmetrical – a small, box-like, red tin roofed, clapboard wood structure built on a groundsill of coral stone; the nose of a hall door bang in the middle with two small, unglazed jalousie windows like eyes at either side. But any development can become a riot of extension and ornamentation. The larger houses have several sections, additional cubes tacked on, going backwards, upwards and sideways from the original structure, each with separate gables, windows, trellises, sometimes tiny balconies, all intricately set off in fretworked wood. Their façades mimic the great plantation houses. Some have a pedimented front porch; classical columns, with carved traceries above canopied windows; or even a handsome double flight of steps up to the tiny front door – and all of them painted in every shade of pastel or bright colour, so that going out of Bridgetown that morning was like driving through a little toy-town, paint-box kingdom.

The countryside beyond, as you rise up the gentle slopes, heading east towards the Atlantic coast, is supposed to be very like England. I wasn't entirely convinced of this, since I don't know any parts of Britain entirely covered with sugar cane, still the major crop in Barbados. However, if you can turn a blind eye on all this tropical greenery, there is a comparison in the narrow winding sunken lanes (there are few, if any, main roads on the island), little hidden dells, windblown coppices on hill tops, neat stone walls still clinging round old sugar estates with the odd Great House poking up between the trees beyond. Though again, if you look at all closely at these trees they turn out to be pretty un-British: Cabbage Palm, Mahogany, Banyan, with great clumps of bougainvillaea and red hibiscus beneath.

Perhaps it's the eleven Anglican parish churches that most give the island its British air. They are splendid, hill-top, coral-stoned edifices rising up every few miles, rebuilt after many hurricanes and fires, but still more or less exact replicas of their originals at home. They are constructed in the early Victorian Gothic style: four-square, castellated belfries, steep sloping roofs, tall diamond-paned windows and buttressed walls where the white coral stone has weathered over the years into honey-coloured Cotswold shades, so that travelling across Barbados can become a splendid succession of church-goings, a tropical version of Larkin's poem: 'A serious house on serious earth it is', and here the matter is still taken very seriously indeed. All the churches are active in some shape or form every day of the week and full as a boot on Sundays, as I was to discover.

The other transplanting in Barbados is not English but Scots, Welsh and often Irish – in all the family and place names that litter the island, brought from Britain in the seventeenth and eighteenth centuries: poor whites from the Scottish glens, Welsh valleys or Catholic exiles from Cromwell's Irish campaigns. Their presence on the island is recorded in the telephone directory, above shops and pubs, so that I wasn't surprised that day when I stopped at a little crossroads village shop up-country and saw the old sign over the door: 'Martin Finnegan: Licensed Dealer in Beer, Wine & Spirits, On or Off the Premises'.

Inside the mood was just as it might have been in some Irish grocery-cum-bar, on a crossroads in the middle of Tipperary about thirty years ago: the same in every respect except that Mrs Finnegan, along with her few customers drinking beer, was several shades darker than your typical Tipperary woman and of course, the game under discussion was cricket, not hurley. Otherwise there was just that reserved, quietly friendly, spit-and-sawdust, Irish country-pub air about the place, a smell of twine and carbolic soap, where the sardine and baked-bean tins shared shelf space with beer and rum bottles. There was even – just as there would have been in Ireland – a mission-box on the counter, collecting for the lepers in Africa.

As I sipped my beer in the dusty shade and talked cricket with a young red-haired countryman called Patrick Hayes, I wondered what long history of suffering, exile and covert miscegenation had given him this name? He himself, when I asked him, knew nothing about Ireland. As far as he was concerned all his ancestors were black, though the name and the reddish hair clearly suggested otherwise. They were the marks of some Irishman many years before who, as an indentured labourer under the British sugar plantocracy, occupied a position little better than that of the African slaves. The history of Barbados is indeed very British; these Lords and Masters saw little difference between a man from Galway and one from the Gold Coast. Behind the fine Anglican churches, the great Georgian Houses, are very *un*-English names, I thought, which tell a much less splendid story, one of black and poor-white exploitation on a vast scale. Though had it not been for the labour-intensive, that's to say African, slave requirements of the sugar industry in the late seventeenth century, the story would have been rather different.

The slaves would never have been brought here and Barbados, along with several other British West Indian islands, would have become miniature Australias and New Zealands, populated today largely by the descendants of British colonists, exiles and convicts.

This was the case in Barbados to begin with, until the 1660s, when the sugar trade took off and the imported slaves began to outnumber the local white settlers. An interesting thought, for we tend to see the West Indies as having a Black African majority, as being a slave society from the beginning. While in fact, it was only the collapse of the original white settlers' tobacco and cotton crops here – and a raging taste for sugar in smart London drawing rooms – that brought the three million slaves out to the Caribbean and killed half of them on the infamous Middle Passage over, or during their first few years out here. A sobering reflection, I thought, as I drove away from the little pub towards the Atlantic: the sweet tooth that had done for them all, the Holocaust in a grain of sugar.

Nowadays, remarkably, West Indians and Barbadians in particular, have either forgotten or tactfully avoid mentioning this tragic colonial past with Britain or the other European powers. Remarkable, too, is the way in which, over the years, they have adapted to their island exile in the Caribbean. One has to remind oneself that the West Indians are a people from a continent 3000 miles away and are island-bound here, as in a prison, with strong race memories of a lost freedom in their own lands.

These days, it's the Americans not the British who most influence Barbados – as I discovered that afternoon when I checked in at the sumptuous Crane Beach Hotel, sensationally built on a cliff leaning right out over the Atlantic, huge waves lashing the rocks below on one side, a white coral beach on the other. The Crane Beach, even on this off season, was filled with up-market American tourists and it was the 'Food and Beverages Manager' who offered me a rum punch in the cliff bar that evening. And later, after a lobster dinner, I met a group of trendy New Yorkers who were amazed, disbelieving, when I told them that the Queen was still nominally Head of State in Barbados – not an idea that appealed to their Republican sentiments, but very typical of the strong (and forgiving) Barbadian sense of tradition in such matters. The Americans were quite huffy about the whole thing, for they automatically assume a *Pax Americana* throughout the Caribbean, where Reagan rules the roost, as titular Emperor, not some dame in Buckingham Palace. Of course, as a result of the present great power play in the West Indies, the future of most of these islands will be moulded (or dictated, as it was in Grenada) by Washington. The British appear here only as a memory – another race memory for the locals – in the great houses and churches they left behind, incongruous as the Pyramids now, mysterious evidence of a lost civilisation.

I visited many of these memorials to the British: Sunbury House, a fascinating museum of that civilisation; Clifton Hall, drenched in a floral waterfall of hibiscus, bougainvillaea and alamanda; the white jewel of Villa Nova where Anthony Eden moped in his retirement; the Jacobean St Nicholas Abbey, oldest house on the island and still the centre of a working sugar plantation; Malvern House with its unique hurricane cellars; Goldenridge, a lovely, musty, high-ceilinged, Irish rectory-style house set on a hilltop amidst a windblown mahogany grove; the huge ruins of Farley Hall, a Victorian Governor's country weekend palace set at the end of a sensational avenue of Royal Palms. These were some of the great houses from which the plantocracy ruled the island for three centuries: waited on hand and foot, literally, by dozens of willing slaves, since a household job was much to be preferred to twelve hours a day, six days a week, slogging out in the blazing cane-fields. There were several slave rebellions in Barbados – mere impotent gestures, for the island was always heavily garrisoned and hence a very docile place for all of its colonial history. There was the time, the security and above all the money to build these great houses and maintain the large sugar estates and retinue of slaves that went with them. An indefensible society – and thus heavily defended by regiments, naval squadrons, fierce dogs and Anglican clerics (it was only the non-conformists here who were against slavery) and of course, by the usual bevy of honest but short-sighted colonial administrators and civil servants, few of whom ever saw much beyond their claret-reddened noses. A highly conservative, reactionary society which, way into this century, maintained its haughty privileges along with a rigid, if unspoken colour bar. The travel writer Patrick Leigh-Fermor, visiting Barbados in 1949, described the British here as operating 'one of the most disgustingly hypocritical systems in the world'.

Today British influence, such as it is, is enshrined in a small Embassy above Barclay's Bank on a side street in Bridgetown, while the Americans preserve the Caribbean status quo from very much larger and more handsome offices on the main thoroughfare.

In the space of a generation, black–white snobberies and antagonisms have been replaced by a joint search for reds under the bed. What counts in Barbados is that the locals should avoid a new enslavement under Moscow or Castro and in such pursuit, Britain can offer little clout. Only the past belongs to them here: evident today in the Protestant work ethic, the fervent church-going and cricket-playing, the old Leyland buses and the great houses. But it's the past, not the package-tourist present or the American-dominated future, that makes Barbados interesting – for anyone who wants to do more than lie on the beach.

Driving on from the Crane Beach Hotel the next day I saw the ruins of a large, isolated house, splendidly set out on the cliffs of St Philip against a sensational backdrop of raging, foam-driven Atlantic breakers. The remains of a long, twisting drive led up to this tropical Manderley; a grove of palm trees and outhouses lay beyond it with a track down to a small private cove where the waters tore and roared. The house itself was a magnificent coral-stoned building, two-storied, with a long arcade and terrace on the leeward side, windows and doors all heavily boarded up, a desolate wind-blown place. But I managed to squeeze through a window at the side and walked the large, empty rooms where dusty slits of sunlight shone on unspeakable mounds of garbage, household detritus from years gone by. I trod gingerly up a large double flight of mahogany stairs while the wind creaked in the broken slates above me.

On the first floor landing I turned at the sudden noise in the hall below – the wind again, but rushing through the shadows beneath me now pushing things along with it, a patter of – leaves, old paper, footsteps? A strong wind – wind with a presence in it. But when I got downstairs all the doors and windows were still firmly boarded up, and the wind had stopped, nothing moved.

Two weeks later, in Martinique, I met an elderly French woman who knew Barbados well in the old days. I told her about this house on the cliffs and the strange wind. She looked at me, surprised, two strangers with something vital in common now.

'That was Harrismith House,' she said. 'I knew it well. Knew the family before the war – rather a difficult old father, a very big sugar planter. He built the house just as a holiday home. I stayed there several times. . . .' She paused. She had something to say, but wouldn't. 'And the wind?' I asked, prompting her. 'Yes, a difficult old man,' she went on. 'And the wind . . .' She looked at me then. 'One night I woke up, in the middle of the night, I don't know why, and went out onto that landing, the one you were on – and there was the same wind. And then I saw . . .' Another pause, as if I wouldn't believe her. 'I saw a girl, dressed in Edwardian clothes, about eleven or twelve, coming through the hall from the sea, carrying the drowned body of a boy, the same age and looking exactly like her: they were twins. Both soaking wet, the boy dead, as if the girl had just taken him back from the waves.'

She was the most exact, literal-minded old French lady. I believed her completely, for I had felt, if not seen, just the same thing myself on that blazing afternoon in the musty coral house, where the wind came from nowhere – only from the past of the island, full of pain and secrets. Behind the jolly tourist façade of Barbados today, beyond the happy coral beaches, lurk all sorts of unhappy, uneasy spirits, black and white, slave and planter, the crying-out of colonial ghosts.

3
St Lucia and Martinique
(March 1983)

Why didn't I like St Lucia, the second island I went to on my West Indian trip? Had the off-season heat and humidity begun to get at me? Was it the pretentious and expensive hotel looking down on the harbour, with the crowds of cheap-season package tourists everywhere, yelping over their rum punches, forever on about the 'Yewkay' and Arthur Scargill. Was it the town of Castries? – a strong contender for the dingiest and dirtiest of all Caribbean capitals. Or was it the series of rows I had with the local airline office about my onward flight up through the islands, because they wouldn't give me a ticket unless it was also a return to Barbados, the island I'd started out from?

Whatever the reasons, St Lucia was a place that didn't work for me. Perhaps it was as much my fault. I wasn't in the mood, didn't stay long enough and I didn't have any pre-arranged introductions to the island bigwigs – the President, Governor, Prime Minister or whatever, which, according to one of Alec Waugh's old Caribbean travel books is a vital requirement in all West Indian peregrinations. It was a pity since those old travel books tend to share the opinion of the Encyclopaedia Britannica in describing the island as 'One of the loveliest in all the West Indies'. This seemed true enough, from what little I saw of it. St Lucia is mountainously volcanic; flat at both ends, but with splendid green-clad peaks in between; it has dramatic rainforests and a unique species of parrot in the interior. Beautiful no doubt, though I never got to see much of these natural wonders.

Instead I got stuck in Castries, wandering about the stinking market, arguing with airline clerks, moving my bags from one room to another in the hotel, floor by floor, as the water ran out . . .

Things seemed to conspire against me in St Lucia and the more I imagined this conspiracy, the more annoyed I became. It was the classic progression of traveller's paranoia, made worse in my case by a sense of professional failure: a travel writer failing to cope, unable to discover that magic moment, fascinating image, the bizarre conversation or turn of events on which I could dine out for months when I got home.

'No,' the bad-tempered woman in the airline office said to me once more. 'No onward ticket – unless it takes you back to Barbados.'

'But I don't want to go back to Barbados.'

'We can't issue you with a ticket unless you do.'

'Why?'

'New regulations.'

'Listen, I've no intention of staying in St Lucia, if that's what you're worried about. I'm going on to Martinique.'

'Certainly. But you'll have to go back to Barbados as well.'

'But I've just left Barbados.'

Soon, I realised, it would be a real shouting match, even sharp backhanders to the cheek, and I'd be hauled off to the local clink. 'Listen,' I said carefully. 'I'm a tourist on my own, not a package tourist, and I want to go on up the islands as I choose, fancy free, stopping and starting as I want – do you see? And I want to go to Martinique now. You have four flights a day. So what's so difficult about it all?'

The woman looked at me, alarmed now at such independent news: this tourist, escaped from a package, looking for single tickets without a final destination. I was a dangerous species. She said nothing more. Dumb insolence, I thought. Perhaps that's what most put me off St Lucia: the feeling of being trapped in this surly paradise, a place where there was no room for people who wanted to make their own choices and decisions, only a welcome for those who had delivered themselves over to the package-holiday merchants. Though perhaps that's unfair, too, and the only fair thing for me to do is draw a tactful veil over my visit to St Lucia and move on, as I did then with the help of another travel office, to Martinique.

The difference between Martinique and the other West Indian

islands is astonishing. I saw that at once, walking towards the smart new glass-and-aluminium airport terminal: a vast French tricolour on the terrace; the neat pill-box hats of the police and customs officers inside; marble halls with digital clocks beyond; strong wafts of Gauloise and *café filtré*; men in blue dungarees downing mid-morning rum snifters at the bar. The place was aggressively French, coldly efficient; the people typically correct, distant. 'Mais alors – j'm'en fiche, j'm'en fou . . .' All that. I might have arrived at Nice airport and the motorway to town was almost the same as it would have been there. It was jam-packed with speeding *camions* and brand new Renaults and Peugeots, madly switching lanes in between them, going even faster. There were great *gaz* depots, oil refineries and industrial estates between the road and the sea. The whole tempo here was hard, quick, vibrant, *French* – and the message everywhere was equally clear. This was no easy-going *mañana* island. Here people had work to do; life was *sérieuse*. Here there was money, but you had to earn your *bifteck* – here the food didn't just fall off the trees.

The political reason for all this Gallic attack is clear enough as well. Martinique, along with its sister island of Guadeloupe to the north, is not a forgotten French colony or some vague overseas possession, but a fully-fledged *département* of France. The 350,000 citizens suffer the same obligations, but enjoy exactly the same rights, privileges, social security benefits, free education, health services and so on as someone living in Normandy would. Instead of howling for independence a generation ago, the Martiniquais pressed for and obtained just the opposite: full political integration with France. Unlike the British, who've dropped all their Caribbean islands with resounding thumps during the same period, successive French governments have more or less willingly assumed full responsibility for their old colonies out here. The famed French *Mission Civilisatrice* continues in these parts, though nowadays it is more an export of French commercial know-how and package tourists than any spreading of Racine's plays or the felicities of Flaubert's prose.

Nonetheless, a much older French Republican influence continues to make up the predominant features of life on the island today – in the language, food, architecture, religion – but also in the nature of the local people who, psychologically and racially, have a more educated and confident approach than most other West Indians. The French never had a colour bar here and the results of this are apparent everywhere now – most obviously in all the easy 'ça va mon vieux?' café chatter, in the market or at street corners, between black, white or coffee-coloured people. The races mix here, without tension: white café proprietor or local black *flic*, together with their variously-hued chums, all absolutely equal over an evening apéritif. This, after the guarded distances between the races in the ex-British islands of Barbados and St Lucia, was very refreshing, as was the local Alsace-type beer, quaffed down in the heat with a half baguette, salami-and-olive sandwich.

Fort de France, the capital, is supposed to be like Nice. It has a neat grid of late nineteenth-century streets behind the seafront promenade on the Baie des Flamands, with high, narrow, blue-washed, green-shuttered terrace houses, laundry blowing from tiny balconies overhead, smart boutiques or little *épiceries* and *boucheries* on the ground floor. Certainly the sense of being in the Mediterranean is very strong. The hotel I stayed in, the Malmaison right in the centre, was just like some Left-Bank hotel in the Paris of the twenties: a splendidly archaic, dark-staired, cubby-holed place, with ancient wall bracket telephones, erratic plumbing, noisome gurgling stand-up lavatories way down the landing and the traditional sawdust-hard, tree-trunk-like bolster on my bed. I had a wonderfully carved four-poster in West-Indian mahogany and each morning a dark, slippered shuffling crone woke me with a tray of French bread, strawberry jam and café au lait. Yes, I thought, after my first night in the Malmaison – this was my first taste of life in the Caribbean where, if life was earnest, it was also real: a world blessedly without package tourists.

However, I soon realised that without one of Alec Waugh's classy introductions or paying a fortune for a private car, I'd have to join some sort of package if I was to see anything of the island. I wanted to see places like La Pagerie where the Empress Josephine was born and brought up and the town of St Pierre in the north, utterly destroyed by the eruption of Mont Pelée in 1902. I'd have to take a day tour at least – stuck in a bus with a lot of Frogs . . . But why not? I could see that I'd have to lose the arrogant virginity of the lone tourist at some point on my Caribbean trip. Only the very rich can always beat the packages – I'd have to join them. Besides, I thought, they were likely to do these things better in France and this island was indubitably part of the main.

Aside from the smart boutiques, Fort de France doesn't cater for the tourists and you have to cross the bay, a half-hour ferry trip, to Pointe du Bout to get in among the package brokers. Taking the ferry that morning I exchanged the much more interesting workaday France of the capital for *La France Tropique*, the French version of an Island Paradise. I can't say I was much taken by the creation when I got there – this pleasure drome all done in that futuristically chic French style which yet remains half le Corbusier, half Berlin bunker. Between these tourist barracoons the beautiful people walked the hot paths en route for the beaches, almost naked, shoeless, so that soon in the burning heat, their *savoir vivre* rapidly fading, they were hens on hot bricks, breaking into a run, their string bags bouncing with Eau Vitel Delices and the latest Barbara Cartland in French. Dodging between the palms and nudes myself, a deserter in long pants and a sun hat, I found a travel office: a coach, a 'Tour Historique' of the island, including a beach barbecue, was leaving in half an hour.

Climbing on board, I found myself the only Englishman among thirty or so fairly elderly Parisians. They were married couples mostly, from the old middle- and working-class suburbs – very far removed from the bare-breasted Club Med types, I was glad to see.

One or two had rashly coloured shirts and hats on but most were kitted out as if for a sensible picnic on the banks of the Seine about thirty years ago. Indeed the picnic element in our trip attracted most of their conversational attention as we set off up the coast for St Pierre and Mont Pelée. A barbecue on a tropical beach seemed to them a curious, even a doubtful proposition. Who would be there to cook it? Where was the equipment, the *charbon*? Where was the food and most importantly, what sort of food? 'Mais alors . . .', 'Ecoute!' Such gastronomic imponderables, rather than the dramatic scenery, occupied the hour's drive to St Pierre – which, when we got there, was something of a disappointment. Instead of the charred remains of a Caribbean Pompeii we found a perfectly ordinary little coastal town in front of us, hugging the shoreline, with the towering Mont Pelée looking very dormant a mile away. Apart from a few specially preserved blackened walls down by the beach and the old foundations of the town jail higher up, nothing remains now to suggest the incredible volcanic holocaust that struck this Paris of the West Indies eighty-three years ago, when in the space of minutes, the 40,000 inhabitants of this sensuously cultured French outpost were entirely wiped out. There was only one survivor; a murderer protected by the thick walls in the town jail's condemned cell.

Instead, for news of this biblical wrath, we wandered round the small volcanological museum where there were fused coins and perfume bottles and an old Singer sewing machine which had melted, an object straight out of a Salvador Dali painting.

'Ça – c'est grave,' a Frenchman next to me said to his wife. He was speaking impatiently of his lunch.

And the lunch, half an hour later on a palm fringed beach, was splendid. After liberal 'Planteurs', we all sat round the barbecue pit on little camp stools over salade Niçoise, grilled red mullet, *coups* of chilled Rosé and finally the *pièce de résistance*: a vast tray of *bananes flambées* heated over the coals so that the white rum burst out in flames all over the fruit to excited exclamations: 'Oh, la-la!' 'Magnifique! . . .' Then there was coffee and a stronger rum as a digestif. The lunch, which wouldn't have disgraced the Tour d'Argent, lasted a good two hours and afterwards not one of our party bothered (or would have been able) to walk the beach or swim in the limpid, turquoise coral waters.

The *déjeuner* was what mattered and our next trip; to La Pagerie, the Empress Josephine's old home, was another anticlimax. The chimney of the old sugar mill was still there amidst ruined walls, with part of her entirely rebuilt and refurbished family house some distance away, got up now as a frightfully neat and proper little bijou museum, full of *bibelots* and larger *objets d'art*, none of which, almost certainly, could have been there when Josephine lived in the place. But this didn't matter one bit. Our stolid Parisian group – wined, well fed and still picking their teeth – weren't fussy over exact historical provenances. There was the Empress's bed, a near-naked marble torso of the lady and a photocopy of a passionate letter to her, from Boney away on his Italian campaigns – all of which attracted some cocky, Gallic, post-prandial interest. 'Ah, comme it était méchant, ce petit Buonaparte . . .' one of the women remarked.

On the coach back to base, the tour guide told some banal, faintly smutty jokes and then encouraged us all in a sing-along: 'Auprès de ma blonde, qu'il fait bon, fait bon . . .' with subsequent risqué changes and interpolations. It was all pretty frightful and yet on balance, for twenty pounds and given the beach, museums and the marvellous lunch, the day had been good value, worthwhile. I was forced to think again about this package-tour business.

They certainly did these things better in France and I could see now why the local Martiniquais had so pressed to become a full part of the Republic. Liberty, equality, fraternity – these words had some real substance in Martinique – not to mention the cuisine or the subsequent ease of my departure for Domenica. When I went in to book my ticket onwards there was absolutely no attempt made to send me back to Barbados.

4

Domenica:
Paradise Regained
(March 1985)

Flying into Domenica, we seemed to be doing literally that; the little plane turning steeply in from the sea, making a right-angle straight towards a cliff of jungle-green above Roseau, the capital. The nose dipped as we headed for the mountains – then there was a last minute, stomach-turning bank to the left, great trees below our other wing, before we sank again at a startling rate and sat down with a thump on the tiny Canefield landing strip. The dashing pilots from Martinique, I'd been warned, like to make the most of an only fairly difficult approach to this toy-town airport, set on a narrow strip between the steep hills and the Caribbean. But these aerobatics didn't matter, they simply served to heighten the excitement I'd felt earlier as we'd flown along the coast, looking out on the astonishing shapes and colours of this volcanic, egg-box-like island. The mountains rose and fell in jagged, saw-teeth formations; sheer from the turquoise sea, up into jet-green tropical rainforests, then into cloudy peaks before diving into fathomless, dim ravines beyond. There was even a rainbow then, prism clear, arching out from the peak mists into the sunlight over the coast.

I felt it at once – that lucky serendipity in travel where you sense before you arrive that you've found somewhere special, unique perhaps. That morning, my stomach turned as much from this strange knowledge as from the antics of the French pilot. Domenica *is* something special in the West Indies; all the travel books admit that. It is a large island, but unspoiled, undeveloped – undevelopable one hopes, given that the girth of sheer mountains round the coast allows for very few beaches, while the interior, with equally few roads, is still largely impenetrable: virgin rainforest, one vast natural botanical garden. The usual tourists don't come here, the packaged rum-and-sun crowd. They couldn't anyway, for neither of the two airports are big enough for jets; only smaller planes can land – hence the attraction for someone like me, on the run all over the West Indies from the lotus locusts. Domenica has nothing to offer them. But it has everything else. It is an island that remains very largely itself – secret, rather forbidding, a lost domain in the Caribbean.

Something of this isolation and freedom from tourist convention was evident in the airport terminal building: a sensible, low wooden hut, which had the radio and 'control tower' at one end, customs and immigration in the middle and a tiny departure lounge and bar at the other. A spick and span, blanco-belted police sergeant with a swagger stick made up the airport security. He was very much an old Empire-style figure, in his red-piped trousers, full of stolid dignity; a man who still felt his place in some lost British order of the world, the Royal arms rampant on his peaked cap. Domenica, a British colony since 1805, achieved full independence in 1978 – yet the mood in the terminal remained sunset imperial, set somewhere about the summer of 1947.

On the way into town I asked the taxi driver about the big tanker in the bay. I feared it might be bringing oil for burgeoning cars and industry.

'No,' he said. 'That's a water tanker. We export fresh water, to Antigua and Curaçao.'

'Water from one of your 365 rivers,' I said knowledgeably, repeating an item from the guide book I'd been reading on the plane.

He nodded. 'Yes, water. We have too much of it. You'll see. It rains here.' I knew that from the guide book too – as much as 300 inches a year fell up in the mountains. 'Water and hurricanes,' he went on. 'Though they don't start until August usually. You'll miss that.' And I remembered another paragraph from the guide: Hurricane David, which made Domenica its epicentre for twenty-four hours in 1979, killing only a few people, but completely devastating part of the capital, tearing great hunks out of the mountains, smashing a lot of the tropical rainforest.

When we drove through the little seafront town of Roseau you could still see the damage five years on: some abandoned roofless houses, the Fort Young Hotel in the same state and a great tree in the Botanical Gardens that had fallen right over a bus, squashing it like a fly, kept now as a curious, chilling memorial to the fearful whirlwind. But the rest of the town had been rebuilt or had survived as it was: a neat grid pattern of small, turn of the century streets – Great George Street, Queen Mary Street, Hanover Street – a series of wooden town houses and shops, with cool verandahs, jalousie windows, pillars, porches, and airy balconies overhead.

Three handsome stone churches were grouped over a rise above the seafront: Catholic, Anglican and Presbyterian – in descending order of importance for the islanders are largely Catholic, given their French connection before the British won control here.

Along the seafront itself, beyond the cannons of Fort Young, was a splendid coral-pink, tin-roofed building, tropical Edwardian in the grand manner. It was the Carnegie Library, and next to it were the Marine Gardens with the traditional bandstand and war memorial at the other end. On the far side, running out of town to my Anchorage Hotel, was a long narrow road, filled with little old grocery-cum-rum shops, dark interiors, big sacks in doorways. The road itself was a pedestrian tumult: hefty gents with heftier burdens down from the hills passed by, smart young men sporting bright kipper ties, barefoot ragamuffins and washerwomen at streams that ran in gullies by the road.

People, with their gossip, travels or handiwork, owned the roads here – that was the first obvious, nice thing about Roseau, unlike the other West Indian islands I'd been to, where tourists and the motor industry had taken everything over. Roseau, I could see at once, was a town before the fall of towns. And that afternoon, out on one of the hotel's complimentary boat trips, snorkelling for the first time in my life over the reefs off Scott's Head at the bottom of the island, I was pretty certain I'd come to a genuine Caribbean paradise at last, a dream island at the end of the wide Sargasso sea.

Coloured fish spun and dived as I glided down among them, a miraculous guest in their world: angel fish, pike fish, transparent minnows whose tiny dark insides were clearly visible. An encrusted cannon from the old fort above lay further down the reef, next to an old water jar: I was in a sun-filtered, ice-clear museum and aquarium filled with blue and pink and black confetti, darting above the shards of buccaneers. I'd thought to spend only a few days in Domenica. But I changed my mind as I came out of the water, gasping, literally goggle-eyed and encountered another rainbow, three of them in fact, rising in successive domes out of the emerald, mist-topped hills.

On the other windward side of the island, was the last reserve in the West Indies of the Carib Indians, the once fierce cannibal tribe from the South American mainland, who had completely dominated the Caribbean until the arrival of the Europeans in the seventeenth century. Somewhere in the jungle interior was a Boiling Lake, a Valley of Desolation; elsewhere a miraculous gorge, an emerald pool and everywhere the rainforests. They were bursting with every kind of exotic tree and plant, and bird; a volcanic greenhouse supporting sixty different tree types in a ten-acre plot, the 'oldest and richest collection of vegetation on earth, containing the ancestors of virtually every modern plant and tree' – according to the Domenican Nature Conservancy. At last in these islands I found a place for action, travel Lost-World style, crocks of gold at the end of every rainbow. Domenica certainly wasn't for lazing on the beach.

Here, too, might be the site for the early chapters of a novel I was planning, in which the child of an Edwardian colonial family grows up in some distant Eden. I was imagining an old plantation house lost in the hills, a citrus estate, called 'Lime Hill' perhaps. And perhaps there was just such a place here, in ruins now, waiting to be resurrected in words.

For in coming to Domenica, I was conscious of two other writers, Jean Rhys and Phyllis Shand-Allfrey. They had been friends here; white Creole children who had shared a similar upbringing on the island sixty and seventy years before. There were travels in the mind to be made here, through their splendid books and my unwritten one, apart from all the literal trips.

'Phone Albert Astafan,' the hotel receptionist advised. 'He runs the best tours.' So I did.

'Forty US dollars a day,' he told me. 'If you or I can find another person to come along. It's the off-season.'

In the event, he found another person to share the expenses. Mauri was an independent-minded young woman from Los Angeles, a movie production manager, and we set off next morning in a four-wheel drive, over a rackety iron suspension bridge out of town, eastwards up into the mountains.

'We'll do Trafalgar Falls, the Emerald Pool, maybe the beach at Castle Bruce today,' Albert said. He was a quiet, but congenial, bearded man in shorts and sandals, owner of the tour company – so we were honoured – and scion of an old Lebanese family, who had come to these parts, among many other Middle-Eastern traders, several generations before.

Mauri – windy-haired, camera-strewn, in floppy Bermuda shorts and T-shirt – was making a haphazard, adventure tour round the Caribbean between movies. We were a varied trio, a curious package of nationalities and interests, as we moved up into the hairpin bends, over increasingly narrow, pot-holed, land-slipped roads, between ever denser, taller banks of trees and forest on either side. I began to see the point about ten different sorts of tree to the acre now – and the profusion of different fruit and beans we could have picked from the truck as we drove along: coconuts, coffee, cocoa, breadfruit, banana, mango, papaya, grapefruit, oranges, limes, all growing up in little terraced smallholdings by the roadside. Eden indeed. But were there any snakes?

'No poisonous ones,' Albert said. 'Just pythons – the Caribs sell the skins.'

'And what else?'

'Possums at night, along with land crabs and Crapaud – big frogs, mountain chicken we call it, a great delicacy but it's out of season. And the birds,' he went on. 'The rare *siffleur montagne* particularly. You'll probably hear it.'

And so we did, an hour later, some thousands of feet up in the centre of the island, walking a tortuous, moss-slippy forest path down to the Emerald Pool, where the temperature dropped suddenly and it was mould damp as we moved beneath vast, vine-clad trees. The invisible bird opened up somewhere above us, five or six sweetly repeated, flute-like notes on a scale, a human creation it seemed, like the start of a symphony.

'I had one of these birds at the end of our garden in the hills a few years ago,' Albert told us. 'I whistled back to it every evening, trying to teach it a new tune. It wouldn't catch on. Then I was away for a few weeks. And the first thing I heard when I came back was – my tune.'

The pool, when we got there down a steep path, wasn't emerald – just a muddy brown from the recent rains, with a sheer fall of the same-coloured water from a gash in the cliff fifty feet above us. The rock bowl beneath was shrouded by huge trees, the mammoth buttressed *chataigner* tree and the *gommier*, a totally smooth, pillar-like hardwood rising a hundred feet or more above us. Beneath these primeval giants, in the filtered sunlight, were the climbing plants, epiphytes of all sorts: lianas, vines – growing up from a carpet of silver and gold ferns, this last magic shrub gold-dusted on the underside, so that its leaf left a meticulously detailed imprint on your hand when you grasped it. Another truly Sensitive Plant, 'Shamelady', a delicate tendril in the moss, withdrew and seemed to die when you touched it. A tiny mushroom, cupped in my hands, glowed luminously in the dark. Razor grass – precisely that – guarded the approaches. The pool was a botany lesson at the beginning of time – secret, empty, a no-one-else-in-the-world-place, the whole air a scented green even if the water wasn't.

Something scuttled into the ferns nearby. Albert – pretty bravely I thought – put his hand into the greenery and pulled out a large snapping land crab, a startling orangey-pink colour, holding it judiciously by the back of the shell.

'No frogs, I'm afraid. They come out at night.'

'Are they really big?'

'As chickens – some of them.'

Away in the distance just then, over the hills towards the Atlantic, I suddenly heard a mournful horn, a single drawn-out funereal note, slowly, faintly repeated on the still air.

'What's that?'

'A conch shell. The Caribs use them out in their boats, warning the villagers to expect them back from fishing.'

'Paradise regained,' I said lightly.

'Oh, you've seen nothing yet.' Albert was very matter-of-fact, as he put the strange crab back among the golden ferns.

5
Domenica:
Snakes in Eden
(March 1985)

As you go through the West Indies, moving out of the developed tourist areas and into the more interesting islands, the local telephone books get smaller and smaller. In Domenica the book wasn't much more than a pamphlet, so I'd no difficulty in finding the name or in contacting the writer Phyllis Shand-Allfrey, Jean Rhys's old friend.

'Yes, indeed,' she said. 'Come and see us when you've done the Carib Reserve, Trafalgar Falls, the Boiling Lake and so on.' Albert Astafan, our guide, had quite a programme lined up for Mauri and me – that day and the following one – in an expensively-hired four-wheel drive. 'Saturday then,' Phyllis suggested. 'If you're still in one piece. You have to *walk* to the Boiling Lake you know, up hill, and down dale, and through the Valley of Desolation. At least six hours each way. And with these rains . . .'

'Pilgrim's Progress,' I said. 'But I'll be there.'

Pilgrim's Progress indeed, I thought, as we set off that morning, winding up the bumpy roads into the hills once more, where as soon as we were well up in the mountains, crawling round the blind hairpin bends, we were further blinded by the rain: first great silent marbles of it, gradually increasing, until a downpour engulfed us, and then a real tropical storm crashing out of the mists higher up, hitting the windscreen with such force that the wipers were useless. We'd left the capital, Roseau, in bright sunshine barely half-an-hour before.

'No point in going on to the Freshwater Lake,' Albert decided. 'We'd see nothing of it.' So we turned back, taking another road north-east, making for the Carib Reserve.

'This is nothing,' said Albert, as the rain became a complete thrashing grey curtain and we skidded and churned out of pot-holes that had become small lakes. 'Only twenty-five years ago we'd have had to walk through all this to the Carib Reserve – or taken a two-day boat. There was no road across the island then.'

'Hardly one now,' I observed. Though in fact I was loving it all, a little adventure at last, away from all the too-smooth tourist runs on the other islands. Here was a real Treasure Island; all the others had long since been looted.

'There really aren't many pure Caribs left,' Albert told us. 'Fifty maybe. Though the tribe generally, marrying with the locals, is increasing if anything. A thousand or so now I'd say.' On the other side of the island at this point, the sun out again, we turned off the dirt track road and onto a much grander, newly tarmacked driveway which led up into the hills again.

'A real reserve,' I said. 'Like the entrance to a suburban housing estate.' And there were houses very soon, on either side – but far from suburban: little shingle-walled, palm-thatched or tin-roofed cabins on a groundsill of stones looking over the Atlantic. 'I suppose the tourists have changed everything here,' I ventured, for most of the cabins had a display of baskets and other wickerwork hanging up outside.

'No, not so many tourists make it across. The Caribs are doing well in other ways – selling fish and bananas from their smallholdings. They've become pretty skilled farmers. Not much lying about in the sun for them these days. They're practically all part of the island community now – a cash economy.'

We stopped at one of the little cabin shops and I bought a lovely double-skinned (and thus waterproof) wicker picnic-basket, the different coloured reeds interwoven in an intricate diamond design: a snip at four pounds. The boy who sold it to me didn't look very Carib at all, but later on, higher up in the hills, I saw a little of the real thing: a marvellously beautiful girl, long jet-black hair, a pearly-copper skin, wide cheek bones, high forehead, slanting eyes, a Gauguin south-sea-island face. And then a tall, thin man who certainly wasn't negro: straight-haired, the same light bronze skin, from another world certainly. He was walking towards the Carib banana-packing co-operative, where trucks were arriving on their weekly trip to pick up their crop. Money was being doled out under the gaze of an armed policeman and there was quite a crowd round the travelling market cars and pick-ups, filled with trinkets and goodies from Roseau. Most of the crowd, by looks at least, wasn't Carib at all.

'I told you,' said Albert. 'The pure ones are nearly all gone.' While we waited, Mauri bought a pair of plastic sandals, made in Taiwan.

'I rather thought,' I said flippantly, 'that I'd see them deep in the woods, in some remote forest glade, smoking an exotic weed or chopping someone up with a cutlass.'

'You might have done, twenty-five years ago or more, before the road came here. But they couldn't live forever as museum pieces, could they?'

'No, I suppose not.'

On the way back out of the reserve, slowing down, we saw the beautiful Gauguin girl again. She walked alone, away from the market, but carrying nothing, looking straight ahead, taking not the least notice of us. A startling apparition, light-footed, with an airy sensuousness, she didn't seem to fit the heavy, tree-filled, rain-drenched island landscape at all. She was as much a stranger, I felt, as I was here. Her tribe must be disintegrating, inter-marrying, but in her sharp Amerindian features – that classic arrogant regard – you clearly saw all the old race memories, the days – a few centuries before – when there was nothing in the Caribbean which didn't belong to these people and no rivals on any of the other islands who wouldn't, finally, end up as lunch or dinner for them.

I asked Albert on the way back if there were any old plantation houses left on the island – a site for the novel I had in mind – or any remains of the country estate called 'Geneva' where the writer Jean Rhys had been brought up.

He was quietly mystified. 'There were never any grand country houses in Domenica,' he said. 'Just large tin-roofed bungalows at best. And most of those went with hurricane David in '79. Nothing like that lasts here.' He looked up at the sky. And indeed the rain clouds were sweeping down on us again even as we spoke and we were soon engulfed once more in another wind-lashed storm – the whole sunny, steam-filled landscape of ten minutes before turned dark as evening now.

Though when we swam at Titrou Gorge that afternoon the sun was brilliantly out once more, in this extraordinary damp-and-dry, rain-and-shine island. Not that the sun mattered very much as the three of us sank into the chilly waters at the mouth of the long, cave-like gorge; a great volcanic split in the rocks. The fern-shrouded roof narrowed to less than a yard high above us and a deep stream ran out of the mountain through a twisting cavern, coming from a waterfall which we could hear faintly beyond the shadowy corners ahead of us.

'The thing,' advised Albert, 'is not to lose your breath.'

'Or your head,' I added.

'Same thing. Any panic – just turn and let the current take you back. Don't try and fight it.' I said I wouldn't.

It was an interesting swim. It was extraordinary. As soon as we entered the narrow gorge the light turned into a lot of mottled green shades: moss green, yellow, olive, tweed dark and black green. The sun fell in wispy shafts from far above us, changing all the colours with light, dappling the current which was smooth now, oil-green as we moved through it. It pushed you gently, deep underneath, in ways you didn't want to go, backwards or against great black boulders, like buttresses, that jutted out of the walls.

The light was the strange thing, full of these subtle, constantly varying motes and reflections; soft, cathedral-like. We were moving lengthways along the bottom of a vast green bottle, treading unknown depths. It was Jules Verne's *Journey to the Centre of the Earth*, as we swam round narrowing corners deep into the mountain, the current gradually increasing as the crash of the waterfall approached.

Albert and Mauri were well ahead of me. And I had a long moment's panic then, doubting my strength ahead, yet surely too far to go back. But I made it – I had to – round the last corner and into a diamond-green splashing grotto where the water spurted like some vast plumbing fault out of the rocks into the middle of the pool, with a narrow ledge right behind the cascade. The two of them pulled me up onto it, through the falling water, which almost pushed me back, a raging, suffocating, pulsating shower. Finally, safely on the ledge, I managed to shout out in some glee, 'Don't suppose many tourists make it up here.' Albert agreed.

'And not many tourists make it to the Boiling Lake either,' our new guide told us early next morning, at the village of Landau up in the hills again behind Roseau, the rain threatening once more. 'No,' he shook his head, a youth in jeans and plastic sandals with just a big panga. 'Most tourists don't even try – and those who do, well, they usually come back halfway.'

This news gave us some not-to-be-numbered-among-them courage as we moved off upwards through the thick rainforest, climbing a narrow twisting path, made fairly easy to begin with by log steps. But very soon these steps became ladder-like, an almost vertical ascent and, within twenty minutes, I was gasping.

'Don't worry,' our guide called back to me. 'It's downhill very soon.' And so it was, the only problem being that the descent was almost sheer as well and just as exhausting. Up and down we went like this for several hours – though we must in fact have been gradually rising all the time, since finally we emerged on top of a ridge, with views right back to the village far beneath us.

A ridge? It was much more a knife edge, this path along the mountain top now, little more than a yard wide, where the crest dropped almost sheer away from us on either side into deep valleys far beneath. Ahead were much higher peaks, covered in swirling mists, bruised rain clouds sweeping in over the top of them. And then, of course, the rain hit us in great swirling gusts. I'd brought along a telescopic umbrella together with our lunch packs. The guide laughed when I opened it up and indeed it was quite useless. We – or rather I – struggled on. The whole thing became a matter of fearful will power, legs aching unbearably, drenched, wind-buffeted. The already tortuous, high-wire path became wet and slippy with the rain, my feet sank into greasy mud, squelched into holes, calf-deep. This couldn't go on, I thought. But it did – and we did.

The rain blew over eventually and we stopped ourselves for fifteen minutes and afterwards I got a second wind. The going was a little easier in any case; we were moving down the slopes of great boulder-strewn hills, towards a sulphurous valley below: the Valley of Desolation. Here all the lush vegetation disappeared completely, replaced by jagged white stone, flaky or pumice-like; hot streams oozing slowly through these outcrops; sulphur geysers sighing, hissing, slowly erupting every ten yards or so. There was a noisome, choking smell everywhere, nothing moved or lived here and the muggy, smelly silence was broken only by frightful wet gawks and belly laughs; the awful flatulence of the geysers.

Rising up the other side of this nightmare valley we reached the top of a plateau, a smooth square of rock, with mists and steam vapour swirling all about us.

'It may not clear,' warned our guide. But it did, quite suddenly, a few minutes later – and I stepped back quickly, kneeling down for safety. We'd been standing near the edge of a vast grey cauldron of rock. It was almost sheer-sided right round, with a lake at the bottom of it, a quarter-of-a-mile wide, and all of it bubbling steadily, great porridge-like eruptions, rising, spattering, fuming with clouds of steam. The Boiling Lake. It was an Old Testament vision, a Bible illustration by Gustave Doré, symbol of Jehovah's wrath, the very mouth of hell where the damned would fall and boil for eternity. I stepped even further back from the edge.

'The shore temperature is approximately 197 degrees Fahrenheit,' our guide said neatly. 'In the middle no one has been able to measure it.'

'Has anyone ever fallen in?' Mauri asked.

'Not with me,' the guide said. 'But a few years ago an American nearly did.'

'Nearly? Surely it would be one thing or the other?'

'No. He only got his toes boiled. There's a path down to the lake. He slipped. They pulled him out just in time.'

A few minutes later the wind changed and the steamy clouds covered up this yawning horror again; and we left, for another six-hour trek back, through the rain, over these startling, Lost-World plateaus and highlands, where the sun finally came out once more, brilliant gold streaks through the clouds, turning the wet rainforests into a glistening green carpet, with rainbows arching out from the hills, successive rainbows, one after the other, just thrown into the sky. It was a completely spendthrift landscape, an unbelievably sumptuous, painted thing, in which God had run amok with the colours and contours.

'Well, what did you think of it all?' Phyllis Shand-Allfrey asked next day in the tiny old mill-house where she and her husband live in the foothills just above Roseau.

'It's hardly believable – most of this island. Beginning-of-time sort of place.'

'Yes. It's not really for people at all, is it? Never was. You see, with these great mountains and rainforests everywhere, there was never any real colonial development or settlement here. No possibility of sugar plantations for a start. Just limes on a few slopes, and now bananas. Besides, with the climate, nothing lasts anyway. Mildewed or overgrown in a year if you leave anything. I suppose one could never really win here – beat the elements, the hurricanes.'

'Something a little malign?' I asked.

'Yes. So much beauty. But there's a threat of something behind it all, isn't there?'

'Chaos, disruption, disaster,' I pondered. 'The Boiling Lake, the Valley of Desolation . . .' She nodded. 'Tell me about Jean Rhys,' I said after a pause.

'Well, it's rather like her work, isn't it? – this island here. There's a sort of poison in the beauty of it, don't you think? "A worm i' the bud".'

'Snakes in Eden,' I thought, as the rain came down once more, pattering, then hammering on the tin roof – while we talked about Jean Rhys, about the hell-and-heaven of this island at the end of the wide Sargasso Sea.

6

Antigua and Barbuda:
A Hundred Dollars US
(March 1985)

When the plane landed that evening in Antigua I was tired and I'd no idea where to stay. I knew where I didn't want to stay: in some modern tourist-package hotel and Antigua, I could see from the brochure, had plenty of these. Then a small advertisement at the back of the guide caught my eye: 'The Admiral's Inn, English Harbour. Bar, Restaurant, Rooms. A special place to make a little history of your own.' Was this some frightful, plastic, false-beamed American idea of an old English seaport inn? I simply couldn't tell. Antigua was the only place on my Caribbean trip where I had absolutely no contacts and almost no previous knowledge about the island. I'd come to Antigua because it had the only airport in the Leewards where I could get a connecting flight on to Jamaica in four days' time. I was starting blind here, when all you have is that sixth sense – the sense you develop if you travel haphazardly a lot – which you hope will lead you to the right hotel in the brochure.

So, 'The Admiral's Inn', I said to the cab driver in a lordly fashion, like an old *habitué* of the place, knowing all its select glories, though in fact doing no more than praying for them now in my careless tones.

I had assumed that the inn must be somewhere down the road from the airport, near the main tourist resorts and island's capital of St John. So I was a little alarmed when we soon left the holiday coast, sped through the town and out into the pitch-dark countryside beyond. Fifteen miles and twenty-five dollars later, I was entirely alarmed, certain that my intuitions had gone haywire. The road was getting worse, moving up into the hills, far from any inns or harbours. I was obviously being taken to some forgotten guest house in the middle of nowhere – or worse. Then, on top of a rise, I suddenly saw a necklace of lights round dark water beneath me, porthole moons from boats riding at anchor: English Harbour which, having crossed the entire island, we drove into ten minutes later. When I brought my bags through the old wooden doors of the inn, along a brick passageway and straight into a genuinely oak-beamed bar where the reception was, I knew it was going to be all right: that sixth sense triumphant once again.

Above the bar hung a magnificent Admiralty blueprint of a late eighteenth-century British Man of War, the forty-eight-gun HMS *Boreas* – the ship that Nelson, as a young captain, had sailed into this harbour, just in front of the inn, in 1785. And the inn itself, I read from a much more detailed brochure now, was almost the real thing: not a hostelry in those days, but the dockyard engineer's head-quarters. He and his men had worked upstairs and the ground floor, where I was now, had been used as a store for pitch, turpentine and lead.

Indeed, you could see some of the original pitch marks at the foot of the stairs and the bar countertop, an old workshop bench, still had the names of British warships – in here for repairs 200 years ago – carved on it by the sailors of the time. This dockyard store and offices, almost a ruin ten years before, had since been converted into an inn, using the original old wood and brick. There was nothing false-beamed or plastic about it. Nelson himself must certainly have walked in this very doorway here, along the same brick passage, checking with the carpenters and engineers on repairs to his ship.

I went out into the gardens with a rum punch. A huge moon gazed over the flamboyant trees. There were old steps down to a small jetty in front of me and the dark harbour, with shadowy boats, was immediately beyond. To my right, I saw some twenty or so squat Corinthian pillars, spotlit, in two parallel lines, the stone heavily eroded, like the remains of a Greek temple. Coming closer, I saw the shallow water between the pillars, fish swimming in the light. It was the old dockyard boathouse with the roof gone, the original dry dock for the harbour to one side of it. Turning back, I saw the light in my dormer bedroom window, up in the old attics of the building; a small room perched in the eaves, a crow's nest over the harbour. What would daylight show of this strange, museum-like inn and harbour? I was suddenly excited, smelling the past here, great whiffs of empire-thrusting history, Jack Tar ghosts and phantom British ships of the line which all together, for better or worse, had made this island what it was.

But when I opened the slatted wooden shutters of my window next morning, letting in the brilliant light, Nelson had disappeared and I saw another quite different maritime world spread out everywhere in the almost landlocked harbour in front of me: a collection of the loveliest, largest ocean-going yachts I've ever seen. I got out my binoculars and panned over the marvellous vision; it was a most extravagant Dufy painting come to life. There were yachts of every cut and size, make and colour; each boat set in the finished canvas now, fixed in the dawn, motionless on the blue, ice-smooth water, their tall white masts long exclamation marks against the thick green wooded hills and mangrove trees beyond. Several of the larger boats – including one vast-hulled yacht from Panama – seemed of the old, exclusive pre-war sort. They were wide-beamed like great shallow spoons on the water; white, pumice-stoned pine decks, ropes coiled neatly as Catherine Wheels, with great wood and brass-spoked tiller wheels set in mahogany-railed cockpits behind – the sort of graceful leviathans that Sir Thomas Lipton sported across the Atlantic on his tea fortune sixty years ago.

I realised almost at once that, exchanging Nelson's colonial ghosts, I had come among another, later neo-colonial power in the West Indies – the very rich. A civilian force whose forays here were packaged not in jumbos but in million-dollar yachts. I had spent my time avoiding tourists of any sort on this Caribbean trip. But now, isolated on the far side of the island with three days to fill before my flight, I should have to face them at last: not the surf-and-sex crowd but the stinking rich.

The very rich have always been the dominant loungers in the West Indies, of course. But now, with the arrival of the common man, the moguls have taken to vast motor cruisers and sumptuous yachts as the only means of appropriate isolation left to them in the Caribbean. And English Harbour, Antigua, as I discovered, is their mecca, their principal watering hole in these eastern islands. They hold a mighty regatta here every year and at other times, drop anchor for a few days, replenishing their crates of Chivas Regal and rolling over to the Cable and Wireless office, conveniently placed right next to the inn, to make heated contact with their brokers in Wall or Threadneedle streets. I found half a dozen of them there after breakfast, when I went to telephone home. Far from being out in the sticks, I was almost on the floor of several stock exchanges here. As well as a stuttering telex machine, there were three or four only partly insulated telephone boxes and the air above them was thick with urgent financial questions and commands, vital arrangements and rearrangements dependent on the equally shifting vagaries of the gold market, General Motors and the dollar/yen exchange.

Before lunch – after I'd spent the morning wandering round the nicely reconstructed dockyard with its charming museum and little craft shops – these same sated financial wizards, joined by friends from other yachts, were propping up the bar at the inn, swilling Red Stripe lagers, while others attempted darts at the far end. They were nearly all American and there were no women: stag-party sailors, hefty middle-aged Americans, deeply bronzed, often bearded, rather in the latter Hemingway-mode, though probably with false hair on their chests, in neon-coloured T-shirts, designer trunks and flip-flap sandals: they were rather gross. Several of them, sitting at tables, were in rapt or staccato conference with neat little men in business suits, brief cases open in front of them. They were accountants and brokers, specially flown out that morning from Miami or New York to consult with their masters. Lunch, when these rough, gruff types and their minions deigned to take it, was either hamburgers drenched in ketchup at the bar, or lobster and champagne out on the terrace restaurant. Mentally counting my own steeply diminishing dollars, I was not impressed.

There is always something ugly about sheer money, when there is nothing behind it but just more of the same thing. On the other hand, a slim billfold, in such circumstances as these, can be almost as depressing. So I went out and had some lobster myself for lunch – though I decided not to bother with the champagne.

That evening – having walked to the top of Shirley Heights, the ruins of a vast British army fort on the other side of the harbour – I found the money-no-object men back in place round the bar once more. It was cocktail hour, not lagers but tall, humdinger drinks, exotically fruity, coloured and strong – the sub-Hemingways much more smartly dressed now, in shiny white evening jackets, one or two scarlet cummerbunds, a few of them even with women in tow at last. They were wispy, unseaworthy girls, straight out of a *New Yorker* fashion ad, wearing the flimsiest of haute couture cocktail frocks – I suspected they'd just been flown out from Miami for the night as well. One of these Americans, waiting on his friends, was attempting, unsuccessfully, to play darts down at my end of the bar.

'Goddarn it.' He turned to me, assuming I was another Yankee. 'This crazy Limey game.' I put him right on it and we got chatting. Subsequently and delicately, I broached the topic of the very rich in these parts. 'Oh, this is nothing,' he told me. 'You should go to the other island here, Barbuda. That's where the real high flyers go. Big island. But no one and nothing on it really – except the hotel at Coco Point, and that's almost out of my range, starts at around 500 bucks a night. But maybe you British would find it interesting. One of you people, Lord Something or Other, had it as his own private estate for a long while: had this idea about breeding the perfect slave in the old days, some genetic experiment: brought all the biggest and best looking guys and dolls over from his other sugar estates in the Caribbean – and set them to it. Don't know how it worked out. Why not take your boat over in that direction and go see? Only forty miles due north of St John's, can't miss it.' When the man heard I didn't have a boat, he made his excuses and left.

Barbuda: I'd not heard of it. But that night I got all the tourist brochures out again. And there, on a back cover, I saw the ultimate in full-colour, coral-beach, Paradise-Island advertisements: 'Barbuda Day Trip. No Passport. No Taxes. No Bother. Much Fun. 100 dollars US'. I booked myself a seat to this strange paradise first thing next morning. Genetic experiments, the perfect slave? – all at the hands of an English Milord. What next? It called for some investigation, whatever the price.

We flew straight out over the sea at dawn the following day in the small aeroplane; two honeymoon couples, myself and the pilot. The water changed beneath us in the twenty-minute flight from dark to turquoise blue, the lovely iridescent shimmer of sunken coral reefs everywhere as the sun rose before we landed. The strip was just a strip, nothing else, set in a scrubby clearing between stunted trees. The island was certainly quite deserted. A guide met us in a minibus and we drove off towards the single village of Codrington, going on afterwards to the lagoon. 'Yes, about a thousand people live on the island,' our guide said. 'But only in the village.'

'Codrington,' I said. 'Lord Codrington.' The woman had given us a splendid Treasure Island sort of map to Barbuda as well as a guide and I read aloud from it now. '"In 1685 the Codrington family, who controlled large sugar estates in Antigua, were given Barbuda by the British Crown in return for 'one fat pig a year if asked'. They retained the island for over a century and a half".'

'Yes,' the guide said.

'I understand this family tried to breed the perfect slave here on the island?' I went on.

'There's a rumour to that effect,' she said neatly, saying no more.

We passed through the village, with hardly anyone around. But the few people I saw looked entirely ordinary – no reflection of super slaves so far. We took a flat-bottomed boat up to the far end of the lagoon to look at the Frigate birds. There was a unique sanctuary of them here, the young, in their thousands, nesting in the mangrove bushes, where you could get right up to them, either because they were so unused to people or couldn't fly, or both. The smell was appalling. Afterwards we drove right down the island on its single dirt road, past a ruined Martello Tower, towards Coco Point Hotel and its beach for our barbecue lunch. The landscape remained scrubby.

'There are wild horses here. And pigs,' the guide said. 'There used to be deer as well. Lord Codrington brought them out from England.' I'd sooner have heard from her about the slave experiments and so would one of the honeymoon couples that I got chatting to, who had heard just the same rumour. But our guide, with her Paradise-Island responsibilities, wouldn't ever enlarge on the topic.

We crossed over a much grander, grass-clad, private airstrip and the next thing we were through the gateway, going up the tarmacked drive to Coco Point Hotel. There wasn't a lot to see – the hotel was closed for the six summer months – nothing except lush tropical gardens, grass sprinklers, smart tennis courts, a long low building giving straight out onto a three-mile-long coral beach. We wandered through dust-sheeted furniture in the lobby, great Marlin and other record fish-trophies on the wall, into a big silent kitchen filled with elaborate utensils. 'It's owned by an American,' we were told.

'Really just kept for his personal friends who come every year. That's why they charge so much, just to keep outsiders away.'

We had cold rum punches and barbecued lobster and other goodies for lunch under palm-thatched umbrellas on the beach and later, we snorkelled out over the fantastic reefs, beyond which, there are over eighty wrecks, large boats, which we could have discovered with scuba suits. But we didn't bother. We messed about in the shallows all afternoon or strolled up and down the tide line, over the pink, powder-fine, untouched sand. We couldn't have easily reached either end of the beach, for the two promontories that enclosed it were almost invisible miles away. Not even Man Friday could be expected here, in this shimmering palm-fringed paradise. The rum punch, lobster, eighty Treasure-Island wrecks, a hundred different coloured fish – it all belonged to us, and only us, that afternoon as we played the ultimate rich, having each bought Eden for a hundred dollars US. It was all there: the beach, the crystal water, the murmuring palms and the coral reefs. I've never experienced a cliché so completely in my life.

Then I thought of the last few days and how it all hung together in quite a different way when one considered the dark side of these paradise islands: Nelson on the rampage first; the very rich who colonised them now in the name of the Dow Jones Index – and in between, hidden as unspeakable history, the perfect slaves, bred here on this perfect island. The cost of our day trip, I saw then, was a lot more than a hundred dollars US.

7

Jamaica:
Pleasure and Pain
(April 1985)

I started to unpack my bags for the umpteenth time in the West Indies in the splendid twelfth-floor bedroom of the even more splendid nineteen-storey Jamaica Pegasus Hotel in Kingston and then, tempted by the view, I left my old socks and dirty clothes, slid the vast picture window open and walked out onto the balcony. Immediately beneath me, surrounded by a high wire-fence, lay some of the hotel's luxurious facilities: neatly-tended tropical gardens, big TV satellite dish, jogging track and a magnificent swimming pool, kidney shaped with a cascading fountain as an island at one end; steamer chairs, cool drinks and bronzed visitors set up all around it.

Beyond this beautiful ghetto lay the city of Kingston; the dusty, dreary concrete of this uptown area – New Kingston of the banks, smart hotels and embassies – and, behind this, running down to the bay two miles away, the city proper, Trench and Whitfield Towns and the shantytowns. From this height and with my binoculars, I could get some slight vision at least of the poverty and inequality that lurked beyond the grand hotel. And I had that sharp sense again, felt so often years before when I worked for the UN or the World Bank, and traipsed round the poorest parts of Africa, India, South East Asia: why am I here in such cossetted luxury, while the others, most of the local people, are out there with little or nothing?

I went back into the bedroom and started to sort through my dirty socks again. I'd found no real answer to my unease in those earlier days, and there was none now. I couldn't deny that after a month slogging round in the humid mid-summer heat of the Caribbean, I was pleased with the endless comforts of the Pegasus: the discreet air-conditioning, satellite TV, direct dialling home, a room-service directory fit for Cesar Ritz himself, not to mention all the cool tropic temptations outside: the blue pool, the terrace bar, rum punches among the beautiful people . . .

Of course, I could have arranged to stay somewhere else, among the ordinary people, in some fly-blown establishment down by the harbour. But I hadn't. I'd taken the easy, the comfortable way out – insulating, isolating myself from uncomfortable reality. I can make no excuses for myself.

When I got to Jamaica I knew I was coming to a country which was more than just an island. It has getting on for three million people and is over 4,000 square miles in size; the third largest piece of land in the Caribbean. It is also an island of acute social, economic and recent political disruption – a victim of all those perennial Third-World exacerbations: depressed industry, agricultural neglect, an ever-widening gap between the minority rich, majority poor, an endlessly rising tide of people and unmet expectations, a drug problem, all sorts of night and daylight robbery and just plain murder. I was suddenly back in the real world, no longer a tourist soaking up the sun, though the sun was there all right, but it shone on poverty, dissension and shantytowns – not on happy beach boys and umbrellas.

When I looked at a copy of the Kingston paper that morning the big headline confirmed this shadow side of Jamaica. 'Killings up by 9.4% at end of May', it said, like a stockmarket quotation. 'The number of people killed by criminals and enraged citizens . . .' it went on.

'Enraged citizens,' I thought, an apt euphemism covering a multitude of sins. I'd been told to watch myself in Jamaica by friends on the other islands, particularly in Kingston. I was not to walk anywhere after dark in the city, not to walk in Trench or Whitfield Towns at all, to keep the car doors locked going through Spanish Town, my head down and so on. It was all the usual rather scary advice with the odd real horror story thrown in, but one can never be certain of the truth of the matter until it's too late and you've proved it conclusively with a mugger.

Of course, such rumours, and the fear they induce in the

newcomer, tend to *invite* the mugger, attract the violence as you walk along the street – eyes going hither and thither, looking nervously over your shoulder. If you don't look and behave as if you expect to be attacked, the chances almost certainly are that you won't be. So that afternoon, I set off out of the hotel's wire compound with a confident step and spent more than an hour exploring New Kingston without anything untoward happening to me at all, no sight of any 'enraged citizenry'.

Later, back at the hotel, I phoned one of my contacts in Kingston and arranged to meet him and his wife at a local theatre that evening, half a mile away, for a new production of *Fiddler on the Roof*. I walked there too, in the dark, with some qualms, but without any mischief whatsoever in the shadows beyond the broken streetlights. Though my friend, who had spent some time in the city, was rather aghast. 'You simply shouldn't risk it,' he told me, driving me back to the hotel afterwards with all the car doors locked.

Next morning I walked to an excellent bookshop and art gallery a mile from the hotel, walked on to Devon House another mile away (a lovely late Victorian merchant's home restored by the Jamaican National Trust), then back a third mile to a car hire firm near the hotel and finally, a mile in the dark to a restaurant in the area. By the time I drove out of Kingston next morning, I was exhausted with walking, and offering myself up to the 'enraged citizenry' with absolutely no bidders. I'd survived Kingston with no trouble at all.

But what I'd really come to Jamaica for was to get a proper look at the country. I wanted to do a haphazard tour here and there, over the Blue Mountains, along the north shore to Port Antonio, a look at Ian Fleming's house and Noel Coward's villa, 'Firefly', a visit to the Maroons, an almost lost tribe of runaway eighteenth-century slaves still hidden deep in the strange Cockpit country in the north-west of the island. Was this sort of itinerary tantamount to avoiding the real issues again? Perhaps. But then, my reflections or pronouncements are not likely to influence Jamaica's problems one way or the other. What I thought I could do – what any visitor can best do – was to travel the island decently: not just lie on a beach, not be frightened but look at the landscapes rather than listening to the rumours. Some of these horror stories are true, of course. But then the number 11 bus may get any one of us as well.

The main, the proper road from Kingston to the north coast avoids most of the steeper, 5000-foot passes through the Blue Mountains, cutting almost straight through to Ocho Rios or Annotto Bay. The second minor road north – which is the one I took of course – twists frantically up to some of the highest points of this spectacular range, and now, an hour out of Kingston, I was in trouble. The other local traffic had quite disappeared and I could see why: the recent rains had washed most of the hard surface of the road away, leaving just the sharp stone-foundations beneath. And great chunks of this had gone in places too, fallen in landslides into steep ravines. It seemed an impossible journey, just as my friend in Kingston had warned me. But I couldn't turn the car back, for the narrow road – hemmed in by the jungle on one side, sheer cliffs on the other – was never wide enough to do so. It was stay put, or go forward. Madness either way, I thought and just punishment for my exploring temerity.

But the car was new and Japanese – and as I made my way slowly up through the hairpin bends I came on tiny villages hidden in the folds of the great green, rain-washed hills. Local children, mostly little girls in neat green smocks, had just got out of school and were walking along the side of the road. I waved at them. They were surprised – at my white face or the car up here or both. A second group of them came in sight, picking up stones from the road, and before I got to them, these cheeky little girls were throwing the stones at the car – bouncing off the roof, one coming straight in the window. And now *I* was surprised, ramming the car forward over the potholes. I ran this gauntlet several times before I reached the top of the mountains, the last pass at Silver Hill, before I swept down the far side on better roads, getting to the north coast an hour later and turning east then for Port Antonio.

'Ah, yes,' Mr Mullings said that evening at DeMontevins Guest House. 'But there was no malice in them – those little girls. Just mischief. It's a nice quality in Jamaican women. Though I agree entirely – that's not the way to show it at all.'

Mr Mullings, local JP in Port Antonio and proprietor of the guest house was a splendid patriarchal figure, abundant in every way – in years, girth, height, kindness, a soft-eyed man topping out with a froth of white hair at well over six feet.

'And I suppose it is,' he went on appraisingly, as I moved towards the dining room, 'that they don't see many people like you in cars up on that wild road. You were obviously a sore temptation to them. I'm sorry you didn't let us know you were coming,' he added. 'We could have arranged some nice Jamaican dishes.' And I knew from my guide book and my friend in Kingston how true this was; some of the very best local cooking in Jamaica is done by Mrs Mullings at DeMontevins Lodge, the famous Mrs Mullings who was Errol Flynn's cook . . .

Port Antonio, at the eastern end of Jamaica and 100 miles from today's tourist strips around Montego Bay, was in fact the crucible of the Jamaican tourist business. In the 1890s American cargo ships, carrying salt fish from New England and taking away bananas, brought enquiring, intrepid Yankee visitors as well, the poet Ella Wheeler among them.

'The most exquisite harbour on earth,' she called Port Antonio. 'Five distinct colours in the bay, tropical verdure everywhere, and summer, and joy, and life was good,' – just as it was for Errol Flynn here in the 1940s and 50s when he bought Navy Island out in the bay, making merry hell among the locals with his Hollywood cronies. In those days, the port itself was still an El Dorado for bananas, the fruit piled up on long, narrow bamboo rafts, coming out of the lush interior, shooting the rapids of the Rio Grande.

Today the roaring boys are long gone, most of the bananas are shipped out elsewhere and the tourist trade is limited to a few American cruise liners, the blue-rinse women and their henpecked husbands in for the day to do the raft trip. Consequently, the town – as I discovered next morning – has an ancient, decrepit but genuine air, without any appalling modern tourist developments, high-rises or apartment hotels. The late-Victorian DeMontevins Lodge, set on a hill peninsula overlooking the two harbours, was a perfect reminder of older and better times in Port Antonio. It was a bright pink-bricked, terrace house with beautiful maroon and white, elaborately-cast iron pillars and balconies all along the front, evergreens in the small garden bounded by a neatly railed wall and pillared entrance gate, the whole place kept up, inside and out, just as it would have been seventy or eighty years ago.

Now here was just the sort of place to come to and stay in Jamaica, I thought, an hour later, starting off on the raft trip on the Rio Grande ten miles up-river. The slim, twenty-foot bamboo craft moved gently on the still current, as I sat on a kind of throne at the back, the raft man in front with a huge pole. Then we encountered the shoals of rapids, the raft bending and ducking about through the fast channels, grating over the stones, waves splashing on my feet, moving quickly now through great shadowy ravines, the green rainforests towering above us: then the wide stream again, the calm, the silence, before broaching the choppy turquoise water in the estuary.

Yes, I was playing the tourist once more here, in love with old Empire-style guest houses and a great river, a sybarite in the sun, far from the problems of contemporary Jamaica. But then, 'Shall there be no more cakes and ale?' – Suckling pig or lobster? There is pleasure as well as pain after all. Jamaica offers both in abundance.

8
Jamaica:
Bittersweet
(April 1985)

I walked down some winding steps to the tiny cove hidden beneath the tropical garden, where the sliver of coral beach was equally invisible from the rest of the shoreline, hemmed in on either side by great protruding rocks, the water running out, diamond clear all the way over the greeny-blue shallows, to the white reef. It was the last word in private Caribbean bathing places, even if the shingle-roofed bungalow above was rather a spartan affair. It consisted of one long drawing-cum-dining room, with holiday chairs and tables, looking out over the sea through unglazed jalousie windows; a bedroom next to this with simple, locally made hardwood furniture; a carefully lit and posed, very fiftyish studio photograph of a man with a long cigarette holder on the dressing table; several other small bedrooms and a kitchen behind. I ran my hand over the ink stains on the bedroom dressing-table, thinking of marvellous girls and master crooks, Pussy Galore and Goldfinger, of vodka martinis stirred and not shaken, touching this dressing table where James Bond was born and where annually, every winter for twelve years, he sprang up reincarnate, to save the West, bed those girls, sip Dom Perignon and gorge on soft-shelled crab.

'Yes, this is where the Commander wrote his books,' Violet his old cook and housekeeper said. 'Every morning, after he swam, with coffee and scrambled eggs for breakfast.' I looked at the old photograph again – the heavy-lidded, rather supercilious, broken-nosed features of Ian Fleming who, in 1946, had this bungalow built, called it Goldeneye and escaped here every year from the London cold to create those sizzling thrillers, the ultimate in high-life, derring-do romance.

Though Ian Fleming's own life here, in Oracabessa, on Jamaica's north shore, was fairly austere: a strict regimen of two months work and simple local food cooked by Violet, which suited the Commander's tastes but not those of his friend Noël Coward who lived up the road in Port Maria. 'Whenever I ate with Ian at Goldeneye,' Coward said, 'I used to cross myself before I took a mouthful.'

'Yes,' Violet told me, 'the Commander, he was a man of very regular habits: he like Calah soup, goat fish, salt fish and ackee, oxtail and liver. Especially that goat fish.'

Not much like James Bond, I thought, as Violet sold me three raffle tickets for a Methodist harvest supper she was involved with. You can rent Goldeneye now for twelve hundred dollars a week all in during the winter, or for nearly half that in the summer: play your own Bond vodka-martini fantasies or remember an equally suave but less lucky man – almost a prisoner stalking these same rooms – Anthony Eden, who as Prime Minister, came straight to Goldeneye as a hideout after the Suez fiasco late in 1956.

You can't rent Firefly though, Noël Coward's beautiful white bijou villa, sensationally perched on a hilltop above Port Maria ten miles away, where the Master lies under a vast marble slab, covered in a sort of gilded cage at the end of the tropical lawn. Coward gave the house and its contents to the Jamaican National Trust and it's been opened now as a little museum where you can inspect his sleeping pills, cigarette holders and other night things on his bedside table together with old scores of 'Bittersweet' on the grand piano downstairs. Coward, much more in the Bond mode, entertained fairly regally at Firefly, with such as the Queen Mother and the island Governor as guests. And further along this prosperous north shore, Peter Finch and his Jamaican wife bought a classically elegant Georgian plantation house, Cardiff Hall, set way above the ocean in the jungly hills looking over Runaway Bay. Mrs Finch showed me round that afternoon: the perfectly proportioned, honey-stoned house with its long terrace looking out on a lovely overgrown garden filled with tropical fruit trees, a decaying swimming pool at the end of it, with the sea – a long shimmering reef-broken vista – in the blue haze beyond.

The rich and famous visitors saw the paradise in Jamaica's north shore many years ago, in the days after the last war when Jamaica was still a settled colonial outpost, without all the problems and disruptions which, as a small developing nation, it suffers today. So that in the last decade, and especially as a result of the political troubles of the late 1970s, many of these foreign residents, as well as many skilled Jamaicans, have left the island.

Oliver Moxon, an Englishman and Rural District Councillor who I met the next morning at his excellent restaurant at Boscobel, felt that the racy, intelligent 'push' had largely gone out of Jamaican life today, partly because the old vigorous ethnic mix in the island is weakening; those earlier habits of inter-marriage or breeding between the local black population with Asians, Chinese and whites which gave the place its energetic fizz and must certainly have contributed to the varied and startling beauty of many of the inhabitants.

A lack of foresight was another problem, according to the manager of a large hotel further along the coast. The hotel employees union wanted a 100% increase in wages. The manager repeated the dialogue he'd had with them. '"Okay", I said to them. "But I'll have to sack a third of the staff to pay the extra." "So go ahead," the union told me. Though quite apart from the unnecessary unemployment they were creating, they were going to lose a lot of union dues as well.'

The problems in Jamaica today often revolve round the problem of simply being a Jamaican, without interference from Castro or Washington, and without the old colonial admixtures; that at least stabilising mix of paternalistic help and hindrance which the British brought to the island. After hundreds of years of slavery and taking a back seat, many Jamaicans today are understandably anxious to take over the wheel – driving madly towards any short-term advantage and let the devil take the hindmost. And the tourists, upon whom a large part of the economy depends, don't help in any effort at sensible self-identification. It's these tourists indeed, provocatively lazing on the beach and burning their money, who supply a far too ready image of the James Bond life. A world where charm or cash, sex or drink or even force can always win the day: modes of expression which naturally appeal to many unemployed Jamaicans.

On the other hand the tourists, conspicuously lazy and unadventurous, confine themselves almost entirely to the beaches of the north shore. You only have to go inland a bit, up into the mountains, to find an entirely different Jamaican life. It is a world of small banana patches and little tin-roofed churches of every creed and eccentric persuasion, all hidden in the steep valleys where the narrow roads are awash every Sunday with portly matrons in cotton prints, hefty shoes and airy hats, together with their much thinner old men, making for the local Moravian, Baptist, Pentecostal, Seventh-Day Adventist or Methodist church. Up here one finds a puritan aura of nineteenth-century fundamentalist belief and hard work; a strongly matriarchal world where powerful grandmamas and spinsters rule the roost, looking after their grandchildren while the young women, wives and menfolk all go beachcombing along the El Dorados on the coast.

But one can exaggerate these social divisions in Jamaica, for Jamaicans – as evidenced by their myriad different faiths – have always nurtured strongly individualistic traditions, and survived them. The most notable and isolated of these survivors are the Maroons, an almost lost tribe of early eighteenth-century runaway slaves who still live high up in the Cockpit Country. This is an extraordinary limestone plateau, potholed like a vast egg-box, largely impenetrable, some forty miles inland from the north-west coast. After a comfortable night in the splendid old Coral Reef Hotel in Montego Bay, I set off at dawn next morning on what looked like something of an adventure, since I'd been warned that access into this area was even now pretty difficult – which of course was why the Maroons fled here in the first place. For fifty years after 1690 – when they first rebelled and escaped from the sugar plantations – these skilled guerilla warriors defied whole regiments of British Redcoats until a peace treaty had to be signed with them in 1739, giving their colonel local sovereignty and the tribe full freedom as well as 1500 acres of land and the right to maintain their own laws and taxes, so that in effect a state within the colony was created.

Of course the British, biding their time, tried to rid themselves of this independent principality later, after a second victorious Maroon War in 1795, when the governor transported 600 Maroons to Nova Scotia of all cold places, thus breaking the armistice agreement he'd just made with them. However, sufficient remained in the wild Cockpits for them to build their numbers up again and they remain there to this day, still paying no taxes and thus without roads or services, but still, as they see it at least, living in a state within a state.

After more than four hours doubling back over endless hairpins with a final appalling track up the mountainside, I got to the Maroon capital, the tiny village of Accompong on the southern edge of the Cockpits. It was just a few tin-roofed cottages on the plateau grouped round a big war memorial commemorating the Great Colonel Cudjoe, victor in the first Maroon war. The place was deserted. Where was I to start? I had to find the present day colonel in this strange mini-state and I felt rather like Barbar searching for, and finally broaching, the mysterious lair of Father Christmas. At last, down a back track, I came on two raggedy youths.

'I'd like to meet the Colonel,' I said.

'Yes! – we will take you to him.' They were very confident, leading me down the lane to a shabby bungalow at the end where a wheezy ancient with bloodshot, weepy eyes in an old cloth cap was smoking a damp butt on the terrace.

'Here he is!' the youths said brightly. But he wasn't the real Father Christmas, the real Colonel. The old man stood up in his tattered clothes, introducing himself in a shaky voice. 'The Honourable Mr O. Rowe, Maroon State Secretary,' he announced, very forthcoming and pleased to have an enquiring British visitor. We were obviously pretty rare in these parts. He took me into a little cluttered, musty front room with old linoleum on the floor and I sat at a kitchen table while he rustled about for the 'State Papers', as he called them – finally presenting me with an extraordinary eight-page document, written in fine copperplate, each page carefully enclosed in plastic. It was the original treaty signed between the Maroons and the British after the first Maroon war in 1739, giving them their freedom in perpetuity along with their 1500 acres and much else besides. And at once the State Secretary took up the burden of what for him was obviously a long and well rehearsed argument.

'You see,' he cried, suddenly breaking into a stentorian, backbench, parliamentary voice. 'I ask you, in all justice – it is all there. And they have betrayed us. The British have done that thing.' He went on for a long time elaborating on these injustices, going through all the neat clauses in the old document and in reading it myself, I thought the State Secretary had a very good case.

Later he took me across the village to a much bigger, nicely painted house where I met the Maroon Colonel himself: Colonel Harris N. Cawley, a tall, well built, reserved young man in a Maroon stamped T-shirt, who took me inside to meet his wife in a book-lined parlour with ordnance survey maps on the walls. I presented him with a bottle of rum and we all sat talking very formally for an hour, like a cabinet meeting, over present and past Maroon betrayals.

'We are simply asking for our rights, as laid down and agreed by the British Crown,' the Colonel said. 'It is all our land, as you see in the treaty – our country: "1500 acres north west of Trelawny Town to the Cockpits".' He fingered the relevant clause. 'We had one of your parliament men over here some years ago, a Mr T. Driberg. He agreed with us and brought the matter up at Westminster.' The Colonel showed me a letter from Tom Driberg, MP, confirming this. 'And we have written to your present Queen,' he went on, 'at the High Commission in Kingston, many months ago. But we have not yet heard from her.'

'Perhaps you should write to her direct,' I said.

'You think so? But we do not have her address.'

'Her Majesty Queen Elizabeth II,' I told him. 'Buckingham Palace, London, SW, England. That will find her.' I wrote it all down for him, like an ambassador, and the Head of State in this wild forgotten place was grateful to me in a gracious way, inclining his head gently several times as he showed me and the State Secretary out. Once outside, the nice, wheezy, raggedy old man asked me for a cigarette and I gave him the rest of the pack.

What else could I have done to help? It was such an old argument; the rights and wrongs of it have long since been overlaid with later history – the end of empire, a new independent Jamaica. Yet the Maroons still eke out life in their imagined free state, a kingdom of the heart at least, remembering their glorious warrior past, while they wait in their threatened Ruritania for a letter from a distant queen that will set their world to rights.

FLASHBACK

I
France:
Meeting with the Master
(May 1987)

Last autumn, I took a cross-channel ferry to Dieppe. The sea mist swirled around the windows, the fog-horn barked as we crawled over the waves to France and I recalled my first trip there, which had been rather different.

In 1950, as a schoolboy in Dublin, my grandfather, using a contact in the Irish cargo shipping line, had fixed me up with a week-long, midsummer excursion to Dieppe and back. All very nice – except that the ship turned out to be a horse boat, with several hundred of the wretched, scraggy beasts incarcerated below decks in the sweltering heat. Innocently at first, I'd thought these horses were going to France as working animals of some sort. It was soon explained to me: the French, among their other exotic characteristics, had a taste for this kind of meat.

Halfway over, in the smooth blue drift of the English Channel, a rotten smell began to bloom from the covered hold. The horses had started to die. The hatches were opened, a derrick swung over and a first beast was yanked up by the neck. I was astonished not so much by the horse's death as by its grotesque deformities now: it had a tiny head, with a drastically narrowed neck where the hawser bit into it, tight under the throat, the body bloating out extravagantly, like some monstrous seahorse, legs akimbo, before the garotte was slipped and the suppurating carcass dropped like a stink bomb into the briny.

An inauspicious start to France. Yet, young as I was, I soon forgot
about it all – until the whole grisly scene came back to me years later,
living in Paris, when I first saw Buñuel's surrealist film *Un Chien
Andalou*. There, suddenly, were just the same sort of rotting
carcasses; the two donkeys draped over the grand pianos. And,
equally suddenly, I was back on that horse boat, my nostrils filled with
the putrid odour of dead and dying animals.

As a consequence of such strange juxtapositions, I've always seen
France with a divided vision; through its cinema with one eye, reality
with the other. And I think this bifurcation started at the end of that
ghastly horse-boat journey thirty-five years ago, when we finally
berthed in Dieppe.

I'd walked up into the town with one of the younger crew members.
We'd guzzled a litre bottle of fizzy yellow Norman cider at a lively
harbour bar – the Universe Bar, I remember – then sauntered up and
down the main street like practised *boulevardiers*, before coming upon
the exciting sexy photographs outside the picture house. In the vividly
coloured and dramatised display someone called Gerard Phillipe – a
smiling d'Artagnan in a chest-baring frilly shirt, pantaloons and
flourishing a rapier – was carving up a succession of lesser swordsmen
or having his way with a number of scantily clad, bosom-bursting girls
in hayricks. The film, *Fanfan-la-Tulipe*, seemed to offer all the illicit
thrills expected of France – certainly none of it would ever have got
past the censor in Dublin – and we made inside with indecent haste,
enthralled thereafter by all the tremendous swashbucklings and the,
to me, giddily explicit tumblings in the haystacks.

And there was the moment, I see now, in that little Dieppe picture
palace, where the drug took without my knowing it: instilling a
passion for films, and then for the making of them, which would draw
me back to France a few years later to work in the industry there.

Though now, as the Newhaven ferry came alongside the boat quay
in the sheeting rain and I fought through the drizzle for a seat on the
train, all that fun seemed beyond recall. I looked across the customs
sheds and cranes, along the quay front and there was the Universe Bar
again. Now a drab grey harbour dive, with water coursing down the
peeling stucco. Keep faith, I thought.

The prayer was answered. Just after Rouen the sun came out and
we ran into a dreamy, green-and-gold autumn landscape, skimming
along by the light-dappled river, barges plying up and down, coloured

washing strung between the rigging: willows sighing, poplars swinging, little boathouses, hidden creeks, bosky islands, waterside café-restaurants, fat men in braces fishing. Here was the essential France. But equally, for me, here was Jean Vigo's pastoral swansong, his last film, *L'Atalante*, about barge life on the Seine, and of course Renoir's bittersweet *Partie de Campagne* as well. I basked in the double vision then. Both seemed equally real.

That evening I took a room in the old Hotel St André-des-Arts, set on a long winding alley behind the Boulevard St Germain – a favourite of mine and unchanged ever since I first went to Paris. It was here, opening the window of a tiny, top-floor maid's room next morning, that Paris began to live for me once more. Absorbing the skyline panorama, it was as if I'd never left the city. One of the most extraordinary things about this Left Bank area is how much of it has remained unchanged, not just since I first lived here in the mid-'fifties, but from so many earlier visions and versions I'd had of it. There – almost within touching distance at that height in those narrow streets – were the crazy-paving roofs, louvred shutters, drunken chimneys, serpentine gutters. It was a higgledy-piggledy chiaroscuro, made as if to confirm the cliché of roof-top Paris, yet entirely real; a seemingly elaborate set taken straight from René Clair's *Sous les Toits de Paris*, but created over hundreds of years. Paris is where we always promote the cliché, never the city itself, which remains simply there, for its own usually quite unromantic purposes.

Then, as if to prove the point, I heard three young men playing some sweet, slow jazz arrangement from the Deep South from the pavement below me. The tempo changed, quickened, and I smiled, hardly believing it. They'd started on the theme music from Marcel Camus's famous *Black Orpheus*. 'This is where I came in,' I thought, for it was in Paris, in 1957, that I'd worked as an assistant to Camus on his very next film, *Death in Saigon* – a time when, with *Black Orpheus* just released, this theme had been all the rage in the city. The past was running strongly now, coming together with the present, perfectly juxtaposed, as if I were editing the whole production myself.

When I first lived in Paris, through the freezing winter of '56 – anxious to get into French movies, but having to give English conversation lessons instead – I had another maid's room in a hotel in Passy. But it was at the tiny Ranelagh repertory cinema nearby that I spent most of my time. It was in this narrow, *belle époque* railway carriage of a cinema, that most of my real education took place. There were often half-a-dozen different films a week to see – all the classics – and warm radiators to go with them, so that I sat practically round the clock, immune from the snow outside, cocooned in celluloid dreams promoted by Buñuel, Vigo, Clair, Carné, Clouzot, Clément, Cocteau and above all by Jean Renoir.

It was his film *La Grande Illusion* that moved me more than anything else I saw then. In particular, the scene where Erich von Stroheim – the brutish-looking, neck-braced but highly sensitive prison camp commandant – has to shoot his friend, the French officer Boeldieu, and afterwards goes to the window of his own room and cuts his prized possession, the single geranium growing there, the only flower in the whole barren castle. This would have been a blatant piece of sentiment in the hands of any lesser actor, but with von Stroheim's uncanny personification of the up-tight Prussian officer, the gesture seemed entirely appropriate. I marvelled at the finesse of the great bullet-headed man, determined that one day I, too, would get behind a camera with such actors, arrange such spellbinding emotion.

When I returned to the city that morning last autumn, it was a day between seasons, with that stillness in the weather when a long time of heat is dying and winter is no more than a hint on the calendar. The streets were bright with a fine sharpness, a little crackle in the air of an Indian summer. Yet somehow I wasn't part of it all. There was more past than present in the air of the city for me.

I walked up the Left Bank quays, crossed over the Pont d'Iéna and on along the Quai Louis Bleriot until I reached the gateway of the old Boulogne Studios. It was here that I'd finally made it into the French film world, assisting Marcel Camus on his Saigon movie – albeit as little more than a messenger boy. The job was menial, the pay ludicrous, but it was seventh heaven. How had it all come about?

The year following that bitter winter, one of my English conversation 'students', who lived in a heavily furnished flat in Passy, turned out to be an even heavier, middle-aged banker and entrepreneur about to start dealings in America. An abrupt, excitably genial fellow, swarthy-fat with a walrus moustache and shiny dancing pumps he was of Turkish extraction, he said, though he looked more like the very essence to me. After half a dozen 'conversations' in which I'd explained American idioms from that day's Paris edition of the *Herald Tribune*, we became good friends, finishing our hour's chit-chat with fiery thimblefuls of Turkish rakia. I told him that I wanted to work in films and it transpired that he, too, had an interest in the business, backing or investing in the product. And more than that, he went on casually, he knew several people in the French industry. Why, Erich von Stroheim – had I heard of him? – he was an old friend. Would I like to meet him? He wasn't very well – right now – that was the proper Yankee expression, wasn't it? But we could drive out there anyway and see what advice he might have.

We did indeed drive out together, the following autumn weekend, in a huge Cadillac with a chauffeur, to the little village of Maurepas, twenty-five miles south west of Paris. Von Stroheim lived in a small, rather Charles Adamish château, behind high walls and elms at the edge of the village. The old master, by then in his last months, was upstairs, bedridden, and we were entertained by his friend the American *chanteuse* Cynda Glen, in a setting almost straight out of one of von Stroheim's more extravagant epics: a vast, tatty-dark *salon* crammed with incongruous furnishings: Prussian sabres on the walls, pistols and spurs, blackened Louis Quinze mirrors, a great dusty ship's lantern hanging from the gilded ceiling, frayed Aubusson carpets, together with contemporary knick-knacks, electric candelabra, Hollywood photographs and silver cigarette boxes inscribed by Douglas Fairbanks. Then, as the *pièce de resistance* in this already bizarre setting, there were the ducks – a little flock, tame and vociferous, wandering in and out, pecking at the grand-piano legs and relieving themselves happily while we sipped Kir Royale.

My Turkish friend, asking me to wait while he saw how things were, went upstairs with Cynda. I went outside, walking the grounds, down a back drive towards a little gate lodge I could see in the distance. It was a dank, decaying, misty autumn afternoon and the cotton wool smoked round me as I passed von Stroheim's old exercise yard – rotting parallel bars and hand swings looming up in front of me.

The gate lodge was deserted, locked in front, but a door round the back was ajar. I peered, then pushed inside. It was a musty film-cutting room. There was a moviola on a bench and cans of old film piled up beneath it. On the wall were various notices, mementoes from other cutting rooms and sound stages, in Paris, Hollywood, Berlin: 'Silence – Le Rouge Est Mis!', 'No Smoking', 'C'est Interdit de . . .', 'Verboten . . .'. On the opposite wall were pale, torn photographs with scrawled signatures: D. W. Griffith, Mary Pickford, Chaplin. A room beyond was filled with other tatty bits and pieces from von Stroheim's career, thrown haphazardly to the winds: trunks bursting with old props and scripts and call sheets. In corners lay larger objects: a smashed aircraft propellor, a set of polo sticks – and there, too, a collection of neck braces, from *La Grande Illusion* no doubt.

Elsewhere lay a scattered wardrobe of lavishly gilded uniforms, spiky Prussian helmets, swords and riding boots – the buckles tarnished, the leather green with damp – the romantic, violent, stoic detritus of von Stroheim's life, half fact, half fiction; a life only as long as the nitrate film stock scattered about, which kept these props company now in a damp sea change.

I took a car out to the same village on my return trip last autumn, recognising the gates, the high walls, the big trees. But I let it go at that. I had no appointment at the Château Maurepas now. I remembered instead the Kir Royale and the incontinent ducks and the moment, later that afternoon, when I finally got to meet von Stroheim.

He lay flat out upstairs beneath a blackened baroque crucifix, a shrunken figure, a shadow Prussian officer, in which the child had become all too obviously father to the man, the white sheet tucked right up under his chin like a great bib. Yet his eyes were alight, filled with glittery life, unblinking, fascinated by something, gazing straight upward – as if at some last, perfectly imagined, ultimately extravagant, uncut epic of his being projected onto the ceiling.

Then, as I was introduced, the shrivelled bullet head turned a fraction towards me – a momentary glance, a finger raised for an instant above the sheet. A blessing in disguise? – accompanying the little note he'd signed, recommending me to that thronging celluloid world he was about to leave forever.

And that was enough to remember, I thought, as I drove back into Paris – nothing sentimental, nothing of the decaying props and nitrate film long since dissolved, but a finger raised and a wan smile: gestures beyond corruption.

2

Nice:
The Silence is Golden
(May 1987)

Thirty years ago I took the Blue Train to Nice. It wasn't blue – that was the colour of the sky and the sea, the azure, sybaritic tones of the world you were headed for. The train was a long streamlined silver bullet, all first class, divided in spacious private compartments, which edged out of Paris at a civilised ten in the morning, a champagne lunch as you neared Lyons at a hundred miles an hour, and got you into the Hotel Negresco with plenty of time to unpack your linen tropicals and spruce up before dinner. It was the sort of journey and destination one might well dream of, which I *had* dreamt of, and which had then come to pass. Yet how, at twenty, with no money to speak of, had I managed to embark on this, *La Vie Grande Luxe*?

Well, I was working in the film business, and in those last, balmy, free-spending days of the industry, before television put a damper on things, everyone involved – even the lowest of the low, as I was – travelled on the Blue Train and stayed at the Negresco. The film industry then, even among the canny, penny-pinching French, was still a spendthrift world. The big spending was seen as an inevitable feature in the tinsely dream and glitter of the movies, part of the whole lavish conceit the producers had to promote and in which their employees were only too willing to share.

I'd arrived on this extravagant stage, as a third assistant director, several years before, working for the Rank Organisation, running round their Pinewood studios as a call boy. Then, tiring of the dull country-house mausoleum of British movies, I'd asked for a transfer to their Paris office, to work on various Rank-financed French films there. With some luck, and a nudge from Erich von Stroheim, this was arranged and I was attached to a Paris company just about to start shooting a James Hadley Chase thriller: *Retour de Mainivelle*, or *Kickback* – on location along the Cote d'Azur and afterwards at the old Victorine studios in Nice. All of which explains why I was sipping Veuve Clicquot at a hundred miles an hour that midsummer afternoon, thirty years ago.

Thirty years later, aiming to revisit the scenes of these happy charades, I was stacked up like a galley slave in the foetid, overheated air, among a lot of grunting, garlicky passengers, on the top couchette of – yes, the Blue Train, as this – criminally to my mind – now way-down-market conveyance is still called. It was now a dreary yoke of shabby night-time carriages, without refreshment, prone to juddering halts and starts; a travesty of the old Blue Train, which spat me out – an aching, sweaty wreck – at dawn next morning.

Sic transit, I thought, eyeing the vast and vastly expensive Mercedes taxis lined up outside Nice station and struggling instead on foot to a small hotel in the old town. Before, on my first arrival here, I'd been met by a big studio limo, taken straight to the location where they were already filming – at Edouard de Rothschild's sensational villa and exotic, glass-walled gardens, perched right on the tip of St Jean Cap Ferrat. Here, expecting to start in on my most menial tasks as third assistant, I was instead treated with suspicious deference, offered a canvas chair by the production manager and a front view of Daniel Gélin, as the crooked chauffeur in the story, pulling up repeatedly in an elegant old Rolls at the front porch of the even more elegant villa.

It was some days before I managed to play any active part at all in the production – clearing crowds away, calling the actors and so on – and even then reaction to my labours remained one of surprise, disbelief, mistrust. Eventually, I discovered why. The French lighting cameraman – a wry, withdrawn, amused soul, fluent in English when he wasn't pondering the sun through a smoked glass – told me that the producers assumed I was a spy, sent out directly by that puritan J. Arthur Rank himself no doubt, assigned to the unit in the guise of assistant, but in fact down here to see that Milord's money wasn't being squandered on fripperies and extravagances.

Of course, a film unit in those days, especially on location, drew its life's breath from just such excess and *Retour de Mainivelle* was an expensive production before the camera even rolled. It had a three-month schedule, costly locations and studio sets, with Michèle Morgan – still France's number one female box-office draw in those days – as co-star with Gélin, together with a number of other major French and German performers. And all devoted to this trivial *série noir* thriller, a serpentine but entirely banal tale of murder, blackmail and subsequent double-dealing among the perpetrators, both sexual and financial. Truffaut, or especially Chabrol, might have made something of it all. But this, in 1957, was just before the onset of the French New Wave, when the industry there, fatigued after its long brilliance, was settling for less, with Hollywood tough guy imitations, costume romps, theatrical adaptations and general run-of-the-mill, bourgeois-titillating pap.

Our director, Denys de la Patellière – a tubby, pipe-clenching, quick-footed little man in a suede jacket who looked just like my prep school French teacher – did the best he could with the rigmarole of a script, transforming many of the trite scenes and much of the flat, tough-guy dialogue with deft invention, encouraging the actors to play against the lines, promoting ironies, games between the players, which were never in the script to begin with.

As for me, these basic flaws in the story didn't matter a whit. Here I was, working in the illustrious French cinema, on location at Eden Roc or Rothschild's villa all day, in a back room of the fabled Negresco at night, with several months of the same to come, in the company (since it was part of my job to call and generally minister to the actors on set) of the very approachable Daniel Gélin and the less approachable, and therefore more idolised, Michèle Morgan. She was the ultimate in ever-cool suavity: the palest honey blonde hair, arctic blue, sour-sweet eyes, bamboo thin in wind-drifting white *voile* – an ice maiden, in those voluptuous southern airs.

They were halcyon days, wine and roses, all that: but above all, sharing in that sheer physical fun which is movie-making. And I was part of this playing God with life which is at the heart of the attraction of feature filming: the setting up – with vast concentration, care, expense – of a succession of quite unrelated images, which yet one day will cohere in the editing room, displaying their secret design. But first, trapping these vivid, free-floating pictures: the splendid old Rolls driven over a cliff and spinning into the turquoise sea near Antibes (this piece of extravagance would have given Milord Rank a real fit); Gélin, in just his underpants, gingerly climbing into bed with the similarly clad maid – the sheet pulled up slowly over their heads, leaving provocative shapes against the camera; the grizzly, time-delaying ploy of the murdered body kept in the deep freeze, then withdrawn, stone hard, to thaw.

These were the seemingly irrelevant parts – the common currency of the garish *série noir* thriller – but here transformed into something possibly of vital import, the birth of quite a different story which, in the haphazard blessings of the celluloid recording angel, might transcend the banal genre. Here was the magic that, standing behind the camera, took us all away from every other concern. Intent, on location or on the sound stage, gazing into a circle of dazzling light, we were all celebrants in a mysterious rite, where time, stuttering through a little mechanical gate, was snatched from oblivion and trapped for ever.

On most days, at the end of the shooting, the unit was offered apéritifs by the producer, director or one of the stars. Glasses were set out on trestle tables, pastis and vermouth bottles stuffed head first into buckets of ice. It was during one of these little herb-and-aniseed get togethers, when we were filming back at the Victorine studios on a hill to the west of Nice, that Gélin, knowing I was Irish, told me of another Irishman, Rex Ingram, who'd made these studios famous back in the mid twenties. I hadn't heard of the man, then.

'But you've heard of *The Four Horsemen of the Apocalypse* – of Ramon Navarro and Rudolph Valentino,' said Gélin. 'Well, Ingram made them, all of them, huge successes in Hollywood in the silent days. Then he had some sort of row with MGM, came out here and set up business in these studios with an epic called *Mare Nostrum*. He was a great silent director, a "primitive" – great friend of D. W. Griffith and von Stroheim. But a much more mysterious figure – the prints of most of his movies never survived. And nor did he as a director. Disappeared when sound arrived. Never made another movie.'

Gélin finished his pastis, and left the sound stage. Following him out onto the back lot, we came across another company at work in the Victorine. They were setting up for some night shooting, on a ghastly, ultra-modern, suburban street set, with an even uglier, quite futuristic blue-striped plasterboard house dominating one end of it, a bijou res., with cold round windows, like eyes, staring down at you. A beanpole of a man was pondering this monstrosity, seeming to relish its horrors, beneath the ten-kilowatt arc lights: Jacques Tati was putting the finishing touches to his film *Mon Oncle*.

'Look at him,' Gélin nodded. 'Just like Rex Ingram: a great silent director, another "primitive". No dialogue, you see. Can't be doing with words.'

A little later they started to shoot. 'Dégagez le champ!' 'Silence partout!' The clapper board snapped and Tati cagily embarked on some manically comic business with secateurs. He was trying to even up some broken *espalier* branches set against the wall of the house and finished by massacring the entire plant.

Silence. Just the slight hiss of burning carbon in the arc lamps, a vaguer whirr from the peering camera – and beyond an ever more agitated, wildly pouncing, stabbing figure in a pork-pie hat, shrunken mac, trembling pipe, doing battle with the ever diminishing shrub. That magic again, taking shape in the silence – a benison, an epiphany, beyond words. The silence was golden.

Thirty years later, I walked the streets of Nice, dodging the continuous smears and piles of dogshit everywhere on the pavements, the endless shuffle of rich geriatrics, towing their incontinent poodles and spaniels, the raucous shoving bands of tourists. From a height by the castle I looked right down the Promenade des Anglais, smothered in stalled cars, all jammed up with nowhere to go – then along the curve of the Baie des Anges with its packed tight litter of sun-bathers and *sportifs*, occupying every scrap of the pebble beach – then up to the hills behind the city. Not a piece of open space left: it was all gross apartment blocks, shoddy new villas, suburban houses of just the same sort of design that Tati had created here on the back lot thirty years before. A cold, isolating, traffic-snarled panorama, where everything that Tati had forecast – in *Mon Oncle* and his later film *Traffic* – had come to pass.

In Nice these days, as elsewhere in France, there's little left of that other life which Tati, in *Mon Oncle*, proposed as the only antidote to all modern poisons. He celebrated the quirky intimacies of the old *quartier*, built around café-bar and open market, with all its slippered denizens: pensioners and gigolos, fishwives and saucy sweet sixteeners, washing flapping over lurching houses, a canary singing only in the carefully reflected sunlight from a window pane.

Most of that sort of local colour, which I remembered in the old town of Nice, has quite disappeared. The whole place now, old town and new, is a mix of second-home, battery-hen apartment blocks and of fearful hamburger and other fast food joints. Though the sun was hot when I returned there, I felt cold. It was not nicer to be in Nice.

I had a drink in the Negresco, now a national monument, but all fearfully tarted up, its beautiful *belle époque* tones and furnishings ravished by an overwhelming, entirely inappropriate Louis Quatorze décor. I traipsed round the galleries. But the one I really wanted to see, the Beaux Arts Jules Charet, which so epitomises the old Nice with its skittish Dufy and sensuous Bonnard paintings, was closed for redecoration. I went instead to the austere Anglican church in the centre of town – their harvest festival service – and with a vociferous congregation of British exiles bellowed out, 'We plough the fields and scatter', which made me homesick.

After the service I visited the grave of an earlier exile here, the hymn writer, the Reverend Henry Francis Lyte and studied the words cut on his tomb: 'Abide with me; fast falls the eventide . . .' Indeed, I thought. All in all, something of a sad Sunday.

But then, next morning, I phoned the manager of the Victorine studios and took a cab there straight away, leaving the shadow-sad old town, winding up the hills, soon sailing into that true blue element of sun and sky, balmy bright and soft, the last promise which the Cote d'Azur still keeps. I stopped outside the old arched gateway of the studio and set off along the palm-shaded drive as the iron bars closed behind me. I was free then, free as the many fantasies which now surrounded me. There were old sets stacked against a wall; the cutaway sides of plywood houses; a mock-up of an ancient café-bar; the hum of moviolas from an editing room; a line of wigs on faceless heads set up against a window like a coconut shy; a big camera crane stalled in front of the open doors of a sound stage. And inside, that piquant, nail-varnishy film studio smell, a mix of pine resin, fresh plaster, and make-up; lights being set, camera rails laid out for some long tracking shot, a man gesticulating with a viewfinder, a woman delicately tending another, with combs and powder puffs.

I waited for M. Galerne, the new manager, in the studio bar-restaurant, looking at the old production photos round the walls: of

Marcel Carné and his *Les Visiteurs du Soir* and *Les Enfants du Paradis*, both made here; of René Clément and his *Forbidden Games*; of Tati, Max Ophuls, Cocteau, Luis Buñuel, Jean Renoir. Almost everyone of any note in French cinema over the last fifty years had filmed at the Victorine.

And I, too, I thought, had lived and worked in this arcadia – the vicarious, precarious world of film making. But it was too uncertain for me; I never managed to continue my career in the business and turned to words instead. I felt that it was a pity then, thirty years later. For I could clearly sense the old thrill of playing God with a camera. Behind the iron gates the real world, with its changes and failures, was locked out. Here you built alternative worlds, putting on the incorruption of make believe and I had isolated myself, cast out of this plaster-board paradise with its powder puffs and arc lights. This return trip to Nice was beginning to seem little more than an exercise in romantic masochism.

However, when the genial M. Galerne appeared, offering me an iced pastis in the heat, I felt encouraged to tell him about my past in the studios, with Tati, Gélin, Michèle Morgan and finally to admit how it had all gone.

'Ah,' he cried, 'but it hasn't!' He borrowed a copy of that day's *Nice-Matin* from the barman. 'I noticed it this morning,' he went on, pointing now to the TV programmes. 'There it is – that movie you worked on here: *Retour de Mainivelle* – it's showing on Channel 2, this evening!'

Afterwards he took me to watch the shooting of a television commercial on the big sound stage. And despite the banality of the whole thing, storyline and product, and because they were filming mute – the dialogue and jingles to be added later – the old, that oldest, silent magic of movies was immediately renewed for me. 'Le rouge est mis!' 'Silence partout!' – a clapper board snapping, action, the camera gliding along the rails, ever forward, nosing into the dazzling circle of light.

The silence was golden once more and I was spellbound: time regained in the stammer of a negative through a little mechanical gate. I remembered then what James Stewart had once said that summed up the whole business: 'That's the great thing about movies – you're giving people little, tiny pieces of *time* that they never ever forget'.

3
Italy:
The Dark Wood
(May 1987)

The evening I left Nice, French television was showing the old movie I'd worked on there, thirty years before. But I wasn't able to watch it, for I was at the station making for the couchette I'd booked on the Rome Express, pushing and shoving among beery bands of rucksacked youngsters and operatic Italian families already giving tongue, gesticulating, lamenting, dangerously overweight in fur coats, swinging demi-johns of vino and barrage-balloon salamis.

Mama Mia, I thought – another rough night, a real sardine-tin job ahead of me. So I was surprised, giving my ticket to the carriage conductor, when I was politely ushered into an empty couchette-compartment and more surprised still when, for the next fifteen minutes, nobody else joined me, the crowd filling up all the other compartments, chock-a-block, instead.

Then the real shock came. Looking out of the window, I could see a smartly dressed, officious looking man, accompanied by a uniformed *flic* and the conductor hurrying down the platform. They got into the carriage and stopped by my door.

'Ah, vous êtes ici, Monsieur! Très bien – et milles pardons. Je suis en retard, de vous dire au revoir.' The plain-clothes man, and he was obviously that, was full of apologies, shaking my hand. 'But you will be comfortable.' He looked round the empty compartment. 'We have arranged for you to have it alone.' He went on chatting, speaking broken English now. 'Très bien,' he finished, for the train was about to leave. 'We wish you well at the conference in Belgrade – the first Interpol conference in a communist country! I'm sorry I won't be there myself.'

He took my hand warmly again and I took other hands and there was a lot of friendly pumping and smiling and saluting before they all left, except for the conductor, who stayed behind, solicitously organising my couchette. Then he pointed to an interior bolt-lock at the bottom of the compartment door. 'When you sleep,' he told me, 'make sure you close that. Thieves,' he smiled. 'Ils sont partout dans ce train, après la frontière.'

'Bien sur,' I responded knowledgeably, and he left, full of respects, as the train pulled out of the station.

I was pretty dazed – an Interpol conference in Belgrade (where my rail ticket was in fact made out to) and I was some sort of delegate to it, a British policeman, detective or some such? I might have invented it all as the opening of one of my thrillers. Then it occurred to me just how strange it was, because thirty years before, finishing on that film in Nice, I'd returned to London to work as an assistant on another film called – *Interpol*. And after the studio work at Boreham Wood, we'd flown out to Rome to film some exteriors. Trevor Howard had played the canny Interpol man, Anita Ekberg and Victor Mature were the other busty, heavy leads: a cops-and-robbers nonsense writ internationally large.

Now, as I headed for Rome again, there were just the same thieves and hit-men and I was the Interpol man myself. I'd missed seeing the film I'd worked on in Nice, that evening on TV, and instead appeared to be embarking on, indeed starring in, a whole new production – but working blind, without a script.

I had planned merely to revisit Italy, where I was married twenty-five years before; look again at Rome, Florence and remember and compare. But already an entirely fictional element had intruded on my journey. I was cast as a different man, with quite a different past – an English detective or policeman. I probably lived in a neat, pebble-dash villa in Uxbridge or Gerrard's Cross, with a wife called Molly and three equally strange children. It was all unnerving. Who was I? 'The past is another country,' L. P. Hartley famously said. 'They do things differently there.' But not *that* differently surely?

Looking for a landline, I took out the book I'd been reading – Sir Harold Acton's elegant and sensible *Further Memoirs of an Aesthete*. Turning a page the Italian couplet caught my eye: some lines by Dante: 'Nel Mezzo del cammin di nostra vita . . .' 'In the middle of the journey of our life, I found myself in a dark wood.' Well, that didn't help much, but it certainly summed up the situation.

Who had I been then, on this same train, on my first trip abroad, when I'd gone out from Ireland on a holiday exchange, staying with distant acquaintances of my family in Genoa to begin with, then with others in Yugoslavia? Genoa itself was fast approaching, an hour down the line and beyond that, turning southwards, the big naval port of La Spezia, the hilly white-wine land of *Cinqueterre* and the jade-blue waters of Lerici, where I'd been married.

Now, in the autumn dark, I could see nothing of all these places. There were only the old images, my own private library of film clips to run through my head . . . The plump, intensely houseproud Italian Mama in her exquisitely tasteless, marble-floored apartment where I'd stayed in Genoa. She was a tightly silk-sheathed, glossy-haired, still vivacious woman who constantly patrolled the shiny floors with chamois leathers attached to her feet, forever gliding over the icy marble, until the day she fell, lying out spreadeagled by the heavily draped piano: a fervent, frustrated woman who, as I was helping her up, had suddenly started to embrace me, furiously, clumsily, hopping about on one leg.

The incident remains indelible. The baking summer afternoon, in the smooth marble-glinting flat, high above the roaring city; the taste of warm caked face-powder on my lips, a strong rumour of *pomodoro* and garlic on hers. At eighteen, that had been my first real taste of a woman. Was that where something had begun, or changed? The excitement and distaste I felt at the episode had balanced each other out, leaving me empty of feeling at the time. Of course, looking back on it, I saw how essentially comic the incident had been.

Distracted by the bibulous laughter all down the carriage, I ate the cheesy snack supper I'd brought with me, with a half bottle of nasty, fizzy Italian red wine, then bolted the door, heaved myself up into the couchette and eventually fell asleep. The dream that followed was dramatic. I was on a wave-lapped beach, lying out on a crackling funeral pyre, the flames licking up all round me, several unidentified men in frock coats with stovepipe hats in their hands standing above me. But I wasn't dead. I was being burnt alive, unable to escape. One of the men said, 'Dante!' with heavy irony and laughed.

When I woke, I readily identified the source of this horror. It was not Dante, but Shelley, whose body had been burnt on just such a beach, a little south of Lerici, where I'd lived and married twenty-five years before. In those days, before the coastal autostrada, it was a lovely, largely unspoilt resort, washed in soft ochres, brilliantly lit in gold and blue. We lived high up, near the castle, on a hill and headland which fisted out, then subsided into the Poet's Gulf where Shelley drowned, but which cradled me, and where, in E. M. Forster's apt words, 'The pernicious charm of Italy worked on me and, instead of acquiring information, I began to be happy.'

Now, sweating after the nightmare, I unlocked the door and made for the lavatory down the shadowy corridor. When I got back, leaving the bolt open for the moment, I released the window blind and, standing up, looked out at the dark seascape. The brilliant bowsprit lights from a necklace of small fishing boats glittered out in a bay. Rapallo station whizzed by. These were images, places I knew well from my life here in the past. But a daylight life, where now there was just the curtain of night.

Then, to my horror, there was the sound of my compartment door – gently, almost imperceptibly, opening. I turned. Two thin, thuggish, stubble-encrusted young faces appeared at the opening, malign halloween masks in the faint light. We stared at each other for a long moment, undecided. They clearly hadn't expected me to be awake and on my feet. In any event, they slammed the door and made off fast down the corridor.

God, I thought, mistaken identities, nightmares, a queasy stomach and now the forecast thieves. This journey was seeming less and less necessary. And nor was that all. Putting on the light, still shaking, I saw a taped plastic bag, filled with white powder, lying by the compartment door. Heroin? It looked just like it; the thieves had dropped it, or tried to hide it, or plant it on me. Would I hand it over to the conductor? No. What the hell was an Interpol man doing with a bag of heroin? – or worse, a man who, as it would emerge, had nothing at all to do with Interpol, an impostor. I started to push the crime firmly under the seat, when I stopped, remembering something. But of course it was the little plastic bag of soap powder, fallen from my case, which my wife had packed for me.

Rome, in a late heatwave, swirled with fumey sunshine and murderous cars all that day – aggressive, discordant, harsh. I felt ignorant and lost, the more so since the hotel where I'd reserved a room denied all knowledge of me. Though the clerk said they did have a booking for a Mr Holmes that day, also from London. But he had already checked in.

'Sherlock Holmes, no doubt,' I said to the man acidly, feeling myself pursued once more – in this case pre-empted – by policemen and detectives. Leaving my bags, I walked round looking for another hotel. They were all full, even in mid-October, tourists and cars everywhere, clogging the streets, when the former weren't jumping for their lives.

It was midday before I got to the old Hotel Inghilterra off the Via Condotti, where we'd first stayed after we were married. It had been horribly tarted up, in the trendy de luxe style: brash mirrors, painted marble, bright lights, the foyer filled with punk fashion models and skin-headed Cockney photographers. And the rooms, if they'd had any, started at around a hundred pounds a night. Twenty-five years ago, at less than a tenth of this price, it had been the nicest hotel in Rome; a nineteenth-century albergo with handsome antiques in every room. Outside the area was worse, all the distinguished shops and little restaurants ripped out, replaced by garish pop music filled boutiques. The Piazza d'Espagna, a cauldron filled with touts and boozey, half-naked hippies, was impenetrable. This whole once gracious Condotti quarter was now a horror. *Italia Mia!* But it wasn't mine any more, a ghost at noon, as I escaped down a side street.

And then, twenty yards ahead of me on the Via della Croce, I thought I'd seen a ghost. A big, burly, bear of a man in a rumpled white linen jacket emerged from the famous wine shop, Pacellis, and walked away purposefully with that well remembered, roly-poly gait, a whiteish, crinkly flush of hair rising sharply up over the ears. The vision hit me like a blow over the heart, for there seemed no doubt that it was Laurence Gilliam, head of the old BBC radio features department, with whom I'd worked in London years before; a wonderful broadcaster and good friend.

But there was a doubt, and more, for Laurence had died in London in 1964 and been buried out here, in his favourite city, in the old Protestant cemetery. Yet how eerily appropriate that his double – or his ghost feeding on the wine breath – should have emerged from

Pacellis, since Laurence had been a great wine lover: 'Paths of duty lead but to the Graves', as he said at programme meetings every September, before sending himself out to do a quick feature on the Bordeaux *vendage*. And indeed the last time I'd seen him, shortly before he died, had been in a rather similar wine bar down the road from Broadcasting House, where we'd fixed up all our programme business, throughout half a morning, over a bottle of Frascati.

It was Laurence who first enthused me about Italy – I've never known a man whose enthusiasms were so virulent and catching: the happinesses there, the colour, sunlight, love – all the things I subsequently discovered in the country. Now, losing his shade in the crowded street, I returned to the cool wood and marble of Pacellis, the musty-tart oak smell, where water played over the white wine barrels, and remembered Laurence with more chilled Frascati. In Pacellis, at least, nothing had changed. But I had, a survivor from those better days, holding the chilled wine glass, a chalice offering communion only with the dead.

Old men forget – which is perhaps why, around fifty with one's faculties still intact, one starts, in panic almost, to remember too much, gorging on the past, knowing that soon, in the vacancies of real age, even this satisfaction will elude one. And so, appalled by present Rome, I fed on the past, all set to bankrupt my assets there.

It wasn't until I got to Florence a few days afterwards and was sitting with Sir Harold Acton one late, sun-slanting afternoon in his beautiful Renaissance palace of La Pietra outside the city, that I began to put some credit into the account of my life. At the end of a long, dead straight cypress avenue an Italian Jeeves had admitted me, through picture and fountain-filled halls and corridors, to a large shaded drawing room, crammed with graceful antiques and old masters, where we sat by the window, chatting over drinks – looking out at the hillside gardens, sloping away in myriad terraces, vast ilex hedges, lovely arbours, colonnades, marble statuary. And above it all an arc of sky – a canopy from a Quattrocento *Adoration* – that pure, faint blue, sunset-tinged Tuscan light.

I told him I'd been reading his *Further Memoirs of an Aesthete* and how sad the lines of Dante were that he'd quoted: 'In the middle of the journey of our life, I found myself in a dark wood.' And then I suddenly thought, what lugubrious nonsense for me to feel anything of the sort, sitting in this dream palazzo, surrounded by these triumphs of art and nature, being regally entertained by so considerate and witty a host. Everywhere around me was the antidote for all the wounds and defeats of the past: the consolations of a classic order – in paint, wood, marble, horticulture, hospitality – an air where ghosts could not walk. In that limpid, dove-gliding evening light I could not now be mistaken for other than who I was, impregnable against nightmare, those faceless hungry characters on the train, the ghosts of old friends, all images of disruption. So that when I left La Pietra, even in the gloom of the long cypress avenue, I was no longer in a dark wood.

4

Zagreb:
Two Women
(June 1987)

When I first went to Zagreb in the mid fifties, I stayed with the Curčins, friends of my family, in a large, bright, modern apartment on a hill beyond the Cathedral. Dr Curčin was a great friend and admirer of the famous Yugoslav sculptor, Ivan Meštrovíc, then living in America, and the flat was crammed with his work, a petrified forest of heroic statuary, mostly in the Great Mother Earth department.

It was here, lying out on a steamer chair on the sunny balcony recovering from a bout of 'flu, that I first met Marija, who happened to visit one morning. Marija was an art student, with long, Rapunzel-like rings of braided hair, wound round and round her head, forming a honey gold crown at the top, a sharply retroussé nose, very high pointed cheekbones, a flawless pale skin and a look both virginal and provocative, making haughty distances with her big blue eyes one moment, filling them with scandal and mischief the next.

When I was back on my feet she showed me round the city, particularly the old mediaeval and baroque town on the hill, where we took the little funicular railway up, buying newspaper cones of hot chestnuts next to the ticket kiosk at the top, before wandering off round the pastel-washed streets with their baroque, barley sugar stick churches, candle-lit street shrines and sudden leafy vistas over the latter Hapsburg city far beneath.

One day we learnt that President Tito was due to visit Zagreb, and

Marija and I went downtown for the great event. He arrived more like a movie star than a president, at the head of a long motorcade, resplendent in a white suit in a white American limousine, streaming through the wildly cheering, waving crowds in Republic Square.

It was a real delirium and tumult. And that was my first vivid taste of Yugoslavia's most obvious quality then: a sense of tremendous optimism among the people, a sure faith in their ability to create a new and united country out of their previously so divided and impoverished land; to forge a middle way between Marx and Capitalism. Those were days of hope in Yugoslavia, when young people from all over Europe came out to spend working-holidays helping on vast construction projects, like the Belgrade to Zagreb motorway. For many people then Yugoslavia was a promised land, offering a clear way out from the impasse of conflicting East–West ideologies: a country where communism quite obviously had a human face. And there's no doubt that, what with Marija's sensuous company and all that other buoyant political enthusiasm of the time, I became a Titoist myself.

In those days, with its sharply controlled currency and economy, life in Yugoslavia was ridiculously cheap. For the equivalent of a shilling, Marija and I had the best seats in the cinema, and twice that sum would take us out dancing for the evening, at a University club or student café, with wine and accordian music. Often joined by some of her friends, I became part of the city, an almost invisible foreigner, picking up the language as the autumn developed, leaves falling lemon yellow in the light – embarking on a love affair and a political conversion at the same time, the one seeming naturally to go with, and depend upon the other.

Yet neither Marija nor her parents were Communist. Quite the opposite: they were Catholic and Croatian – and strongly nationalist in the latter cause, for the family had come from the old Hapsburg bourgeoisie, when Croatia had been a comfy province of the empire and Zagreb had always looked north to Vienna for its intellectual and material sustenance – and even further north. Marija's parents, for instance, when I went in the afternoons to their dark, heavily furnished flat looking over Strossmayer Square, always served up an English tea with Earl Grey's Best Darjeeling.

Thus it was – Marx and Cupid rampant, so that I wasn't at first conscious of it at all – that I began to deviate from Marija, praising this great new socialist society, while she in return first mocked it gently, and then, when I persisted in my encomiums, condemned it roundly.

'Everything in Yugoslavia is run by the Serbs,' she told me bitterly one day, walking in Tuscanatz woods among the crunchy leaves. 'And the Serbs have no ambition but to dominate us up here, feed themselves on our wealth and hard work.'

It wasn't clear to me then that, like many Croatians, she regarded most Serbs, with their Turkish colourings and Orthodox faith, as rough and dangerous peasants; vile bedfellows, forced upon them most recently by Tito and his godless social order. All unaware, I countered like a commissar.

'But Marija – surely you and the Serbs and all the other republics here are in this together: for the sake of national unity, the greater good, sink or swim.' This was my sort of response and hers was one of bitter laughter.

'If the Serbs really believed that themselves we wouldn't mind so much. But they don't. They simply want to use this enforced national unity as another opportunity to crush us!'

It finally became clear to me that Marija's inbuilt antagonism against communism and the wicked Serbs was rather stronger than her affection for me. The affair waned on her side and I reacted in the worst way by trying to save it with more specious Marxist argument – by pointing out to her, among other things, that appropriate emotion between people could only bloom in an appropriate society. For me, in my arrogant naïveté, those days of hope depended entirely on the personal and political going hand in hand. And so I persisted in propagating this dubious equation.

Ah, that I might have temporised, dissembled! But I hadn't the wit to do so. It all came to a head one day between us when, passing through the candle-lit shrine to the Virgin in the old city gate, I mocked the superstitious, outmoded values perpetuated there, in a world where so obviously there was a new and properly caring God. Such things, particularly in Yugoslavia's special Marxist canon, would inevitably disappear, just as nationalist antagonisms and the State itself would wither away in the coming Balkan millenium. After this spiel Marija was not available for any further political or emotional re-education. Crassly, I had ruined the affair.

Now, more than thirty years later, the train pulled into Zagreb station – the same elegant, ochre-washed Hapsburg building at the end of Strossmayer Square, the long leafy park with its elegant bandstand and fountains running right through the centre of 'Little

Vienna', as Zagreb used to be known and as it still appeared, I found, as I walked with my bag up to the old Palace Hotel.

The same blue trams still clanked in the autumn sunlight beneath the huge plane trees – trams I'd taken with Marija most afternoons somewhere happy or other. And later that morning the same funicular railway drew me up to the baroque town on the hill, with the hot chestnut stand next to the kiosk still miraculously there, and beyond that the same ornate, pastel-washed houses, the barley sugar stick churches, and the candle-lit shrine to the Virgin in the gateway of the old city wall. Nothing had altered.

But further along there was something new – a restored baroque mansion, with an arched gateway to an inner courtyard, filled with vast statues, mostly nude women. I recognised the overblown, exultant style at once: this was the Meštrovíc Gallery, a permanent exhibition established after my time in the city, and going inside I recognised a great, buxom, vast-thighed, splay-legged nude straight away. I remembered it well. It had stood near the doorway of Dr Curčin's apartment, and had rather embarrassed me each time I entered the place. But Marija, when I opened the door to her, had made light of this shameless marble colossus, draping her raincoat over it one day, before crowning it with one of Dr Curčin's Homburg hats.

'There – you'll feel easier now,' she'd said, kissing me quickly, before I chased her round the now most unsuitably veiled monument.

And at that moment, thirty years later, staring at this same cold, sightless block of marble, mute as I was in the silent gallery, the past suddenly had voices for me again, Marija's scandalised jokey tones invading the silence. Light shone back down the years and her much more vivacious shapes and movement floated back to me through the lifeless stone. Encouraged by this strong memory, I looked Marija up in the phone book back at the hotel. Of course, beautiful and dutiful woman that she was, there was no sign of her – she had disappeared into marriage and another name.

But that evening I met Enka. I'd gone out to eat alone in the Gradski Podrom, the famous 'caves' restaurant in the Republic Square, and was given a table right next to a celebrating group of students, a dozen of them, singing with the orchestra, guzzling cevapčiči and lowering a lot of Riesling. Halfway through my meal, the girl almost opposite me at the end of their table, turned and suggested I join them.

They were a bunch of Slovenian architectural students, down from Ljubljana. But Enka lived in Zagreb and studied economics. She was different in every way from the blonde, statuesque Marija: a petite, self-confident, fidgety-quick girl with glasses, jet black, fashionably cropped hair, dark almond-shaped eyes – something shrewish and Jewish about her, in the old tradition of Mittel Europa blue stocking, I thought: inquisitive and intellectual where Marija had been all emotion and intuition. Enka's English, for example, was well-nigh perfect. We talked of my past in Zagreb and her present.

In the thirty years since Marija's time, with subsequent experience of the Soviet Union and other east block countries, my enthusiasm for Marx had entirely disappeared, replaced by the lineaments, at least, of Colonel Blimp. So amongst other grim criticisms of communism, I pointed out to Enka how Yugoslavia, in this cause, had gone steadily downhill. Inflation was now running at 100%, unemployment at nearly 20% and there was a foreign debt of nineteen billion dollars.

'The great experiment of Yugoslav socialism,' I told her sententiously, 'in national unity and economic "self-management" has failed.'

Enka had started to smile as I spoke; now she laughed scornfully. 'Your figures may be right. But the experiment hasn't failed,' she said. 'It's still going on, just with different factors in the equation now. Our problems today are simply a result of the *success* of our earlier experiments – the boom years in the 70s. But there was greed of all sorts then. And now we're having to pay for it. And we – or they – don't like that.'

'They?' I queried.

'The old – and the new – bourgeois: the ones who did so well in the 70s. But I'm not one of them. I'm a party member. I *expect* to pay!'

I must have shown my surprise, for as if to forestall any idea I might have that Communist party members were a sober and unadventurous lot, she said, 'Have some more wine' – and later, 'Let me show you something of the *real* Zagreb tomorrow, the new Zagreb!'

We met next day in a workers' café-bar, a smoky, narrow room, smelling of salami and plum brandy, filled with heavy set, swarthy men. Enka arrived late, in designer jeans, smart navy anorak, happily breathless, smoothing her silky dark hair back after the wind outside, textbooks swelling a Gucci plastic carrier bag.

'I thought I'd bring you here,' she said, 'because this bar is always full of Serbs – *and* Croats – and you said last night how we Croats didn't get on with them.'

'One bar – one swallow – doesn't make a summer,' I replied. 'And besides, as you must know, it's not the Croats but Slovenes who've been having the great rows with the Serbs lately.'

She sipped her coke, looking at me carefully, big eyes quizzical and amused behind her spectacles. 'What knowledge! What concern!' she mocked me. 'What *you* don't know is that's really a paper row, a lot of politicians and economists spitting words at each other. The truth is everyone knows we're *all* in this together – have to survive as a *united* nation or not at all.'

I remembered this truth well. I'd said just the same thing to Marija thirty years before. But now I took an opposite view, playing devil's advocate.

'It's sink or swim certainly, but you don't seem to see the hatchets out, in the hands of the better-off republics like your own, trying to cut the arms off the others reaching for the lifeboat.'

'That's simply human nature,' she answered.

'Does Marx have a sure antidote against that?'

Enka was splendidly sardonic. 'We're pragmatic here – and socialist, much more than Marxist.' Then she was mock-mournful. 'And you, Gospodin Hone, you really are a most heavy and pessimistic old person!'

I suspected I was well on the way to jeopardising my friendship with Enka, just as I had with Marija thirty years before.

'I tell you,' said Enka, relenting, 'I'm bored with politics.' She reached out suddenly, touching my hand on the counter.

We went out into the windy afternoon sunshine, walked over the Sava river, and Enka showed me new Zagreb, with its splendid trade-fair pavilions, concert hall, university, and glistening white high-rise apartment blocks. Her parents had a flat halfway up one of these airy towers. It was empty when we got there, but filled with every mod con: colour TV, video, along with handsomely patterned, red-and-white weave Dalmatian carpets, cool Habitat-style furniture, cabinets crammed with books – economics, science, philosophy and copies of Anthony Burgess's novels in Serbo-Croatian, for both her parents were academics. I had to admit it then: this bright, refreshing city and apartment certainly had some of the shapes of a new Jerusalem.

I looked out the high window, to the grey stuccoed Hapsburg city in the distance, and beyond that the old mediaeval town on the hill, with its baroque churches and candle-lit street shrines: Marija's town, and mine, long ago.

Enka had gone into the kitchen. Now she put her head round the door. 'So?' she asked. 'It's not all as bad as you thought, is it?'

'No, indeed.'

'And now,' she went on, 'for you old bourgeois Englishman – I am making a cup of tea. That's what you must have in the afternoons, isn't it?' she teased, coming towards me, taking her anorak off, smoothing her silk-dark hair again, bright eyed, inviting.

The tea, when she made it later – a present from someone back from London – was Earl Grey's Best Darjeeling. Well, some things never change, I thought.

5

Belgrade:
Greene-and-Ambler Land
(June 1987)

Belgrade, to some of an older generation, may still suggest the start of the Balkans: rough adventure and revolution; plum pudding bombs and white eagles over Serbia; gateway to Asia and all the romance of the orient; the Orient Express and 'Stamboul Train. The very name readily evokes early Graham Greene or Eric Ambler, seedy spies and revolutionaries, nursing all sorts of mayhem, lurking in third-class carriages. And musn't it have been somewhere out here that the Lady Vanished and Hercule Poirot, waxing his moustaches, pondered that grisly *wagon-lits* murder? Here, certainly, was the ragbag of fictions I took with me when I first travelled to Belgrade more than thirty years ago. Now, all these years later, older and wiser, I was returning.

Belgrade, or Beograd, meaning the 'white' not the 'beautiful' city, is neither white nor beautiful now. Far from it. The Americans, while the Germans were still in occupation during the last war, flattened most of the old Serbo-Turkish city. And later, the Yugoslavs themselves did for what remained of the quaint wooden houses and old stucco mansions, rebuilding much of the centre in the monstrous Stalinist style before really taking their coats off in the boom years of the 70s with a rash of ghastly high-rises, glass matchboxes, flyovers and dreary 'boulevards', topping all this by creating a whole new city just across the Sava river where it meets the Danube.

When I first went there back in the mid-'fifties, few of these horrors existed and fresh from some happy months in Zagreb, where I'd become something of a convert to Yugoslavia's special brand of Communism, I was prepared to think the best of Belgrade. I hadn't forgotten the Greene-and-Ambler version of the city, the lurking spies and shadows. But all this seemed pure fantasy to me then, a product of the degenerate West. Belgrade, after all, with Tito, was the centre, the powerhouse of this great new Socialist experiment: it was a world without shadows, where the real revolution had at last taken place. Subsequent events in the city that autumn rather changed my mind and, incidentally, started me out on my own spy-thriller career.

The first problem was Mrs Stolnač, in whose apartment I stayed, and her young teenage son, Peter. Mrs Stolnač, a small, intense, short-fused woman, had been a brave and successful partisan fighter with Tito throughout the War. And I soon realised what the Germans had been up against with such people when, swapping guns for words, she shortly came to deal with me as she had the *Wehrmacht* – in a series of vehemently executed verbal sallies, ambushes, feigned retreats and vicious counter-attacks. A guerilla war broke out between us, with her son as a fifth columnist – at first, as I thought, on my side but soon showing his true colours and returning across the lines.

The *casus belli* lay in the fact that, through other Belgrade friends, I'd met a number of very dissident, not to say bizarre students – painters, poets, musicians who were beyond the pale in every way. They weren't just against Tito or Communism – these were the least of their antagonisms. They were against everyone and everything. They were Serbian anarchists in the great Balkan tradition of the student Princip and his plum-pudding bombs at Sarajevo in 1914 – these half-dozen Byronic souls and some equally headstrong, dark-haired, arrogantly beautiful girls. Despite my earlier political conversion in Zagreb, I soon took to them, attracted by their vagrant spirit, talent, wit and idealism.

And it was this which came to infuriate Mrs Stolnač, dedicated hard-line communist that she was. She laid into me, every inch the commissar, condemning my friends as anti-social, anti-State, enemies of the people in every way. She stormed at me. I was abusing her hospitality, consorting with criminals.

At first, since I'd told her nothing of these new friends of mine, I wondered how she'd found out about them. Then one day I spotted Peter, the wily son, following me secretly as I crossed town to one of my 'anti-social' meetings. Pretending ignorance of his pursuit, I stopped at a shop window, watching his reflection in the glass as he paused as well. Then I hurried on, crossed the street among the crowds on the Terazije, before doubling back, going in the front door of the old art deco Moskva Hotel and slipping out the back entrance, losing Peter entirely in the process. And that, without my knowing it, was my first exercise in the art of espionage, mimicking the role of hunted man. All unaware, in slipping my tail that afternoon, I'd lurched into Greene-and-Ambler land, taken a first step into that shadowy world of spies and counter-spies which, though apparently dead in the brave new world of Belgrade, still survived – indeed, as I was to discover, prospered mightily as a result of all the secret manœuvrings in Tito's communist, but non-aligned, state.

A distant acquaintance of my family's – a Mr Radovič as I shall call him here, the chief, indeed the only, representative of a large Western multinational company – had an office in this same Moskva Hotel. And shortly after the incident with Peter, I used my introduction to him.

A number of Western enterprises had offices in the Moskva then – a sort of safe house at the time, when Tito's relations with Stalin, with whom he'd broken only a few years before, were still very shaky and a retaliatory Soviet takeover was not beyond the bounds of possibility. Mr Radovič's bedroom office, reflecting the clout of his company, was particularly spacious and lavish, in the crude art deco manner imposed by the generally tawdry and extravagant decor of the hotel. It was a flashy suite, with Tiffany-style lamps and Balkan-Gothic stained glass windows. It all rather suggested an upmarket Turkish brothel.

Yet Mr Radovič himself – middle-aged, withdrawn, professorial – seemed entirely at odds with these louche, chorus-girl surroundings. Offering me a tasteless, watery lunch downstairs in the hubbub of the dining room, he ate meagrely, diffidently, soberly, peering at nothing in particular through heavy-lensed spectacles.

Still, he was friendly in a punctilious way, spoke perfect English, seemed wise and understanding in a Western manner. So I told him of my difficulties with Mrs Stolnač, and with Peter over the anarchist students. He commiserated with me tactfully, but offered no other comments or advice. We finished with a quite inedible Serbian pudding – dumplings in an ersatz chocolate sauce – and that, I thought, was the last of Gospodin Radovič. I resumed my by now very surreptitious meetings with the students.

These devil-may-cares, given the acute housing shortage in Belgrade and their general social antipathies, had created an extraordinary camp for themselves, out of tin huts and sack tents, on a marshy spit of land hidden by reeds and willow trees, next to the Sava river across from the ramparts of the old town. And here, free of all authority, they pursued their 'anti-social' activities. In the daytime, revolutionary *paysagistes* created rather conventional views of the willows and the pearl-grey, misty water beyond. At night, in that warm autumn, things were livelier, the encampment magically lit by dozens of candles, where some of the new arrivals still painted. Indeed Dusan, a most mature student, an emaciated, tow-haired, most morbidly refined Serb, sunken and wild-eyed, who looked like Aubrey Beardsley, would *only* paint at night, by candle-light, and only on one theme: corpses in coffins, surrounded by keening, witch-like women, macabre studies of Orthodox funerals. The others, for the most part simply chatted, played the mandolin, smoked and drank a little, and canoodled in the velvet shadows. The whole thing, in truth, was only mildly dissident, though it all seemed very daring to me at the time.

Mrs Stolnač meanwhile had retreated, for though Peter still followed me, I'd become adept at giving him the slip and had told his mother I was occupying myself daily at the British Council Library, which was partly true. And it was here one afternoon that I spied Mr Radovič, much more at home in these academic circumstances, fingering among various books on the far side of the room. I approached, greeting him and he jumped.

'Ah, I was just looking to see if the new Herman Wouk had arrived – *The Caine Mutiny*. They say it's very good.' The shelf he'd been inspecting contained nothing but biographies.

Then to my surprise, for he had seemed very occupied, he suggested we stroll back together to the Moskva. 'How are all those wicked student friends of yours?' he enquired lightly, as we walked across the Terazije. I told him they were fine, that I found their company a balm after the strictures of Stalinist life with Mrs Stolnač. 'Of course they're all artists,' he remarked. 'Or, do they talk politics as well?'

'No. Not really.'

'No, of course not. Just – bohemians.' Mr Radovič tasted the word nervously.

'Yes, just that.'

He seemed vaguely disappointed. We were approaching the entrance of the Moskva then, when, seeing something or someone at the doorway of the hotel, Mr Radovič suddenly stopped, taking my hand. 'Do come and have lunch again,' he murmured before, quite absent-mindedly as it seemed, he noticed the book he'd been carrying in his other hand. 'Dear me, how careless – I took this book away without having it checked out.' He passed it to me, rather urgently. 'I wonder if you'd be so kind as to take it back to the library for me?'

And then he was on his way and I had the book, a slim volume, I remember and far from Herman Wouk's *Caine Mutiny* – it was an old Hogarth Press copy of Virginia Woolf's *A Room of One's Own*. I couldn't return it that day. The Council library was about to close and would then be shut all over the weekend. So I took it with me down to the charmed encampment among the reeds and willows on the Sava. And there, horror of horrors, I lost it, somewhere in the candle-lit dark that evening.

I went back straight away next morning to the Moskva to tell Mr Radovič, and asked for him at Reception. The clerk, to my astonishment, denied all knowledge of such a man, as did the manager when I pressed him. 'No,' he said, there was no Mr Radovič or such a company here. 'You must be mistaken. Try the Balkan Hotel across the street.'

My friend Mr Radovič had become a non-person overnight. When I returned to the camp to look for the book that same morning (still keeping a wary eye out for Peter), I realised that someone *else* was following me: a rain-coated figure, in a fur lumber hat with ear flaps. I played all my tricks in dropping a tail, but without success. The man was obviously an expert in pursuit. God, I thought, the Secret Police. Then, quaking in my boots, I heard the man closing with me quickly, before joining me casually, walking in step, talking brightly as if he knew me.

'I'm a friend of Mr Radovič,' he said, with an American accent. 'He gave you a book yesterday. You were going to return it to the Council Library. But I don't think you did – he needs it rather urgently now, asked me to collect if from you.'

'I'm terribly sorry – I've just been looking for Mr Radovič at the Moskva, to tell him – I'm afraid I lost it.' The fur-hatted man was, for a moment or two, very much put out by this news.

'Where? Where did you lose it?'

'Well, down by the river, with some student friends. I was just off to look for it now. But where is Mr Radovič anyway? At the hotel just now they said they'd never heard of him.'

'He's, um, he's had to go away –' The man paused. 'But never mind. It's not important. But if you do find the book, bring it back to me at the Balkan Hotel. I'll be there tomorrow, in the cafe, between twelve and one.'

His directions were like something straight out of *The Third Man*, and I realised something fishy was up. My worst suspicions were confirmed when I returned to Mrs Stolnač's apartment, still without the book, and found her with a grim-eyed man, this time certainly one of Tito's Secret Police.

Mrs Stolnač brusquely interpreted his questions to me: 'You have been meeting with a Mr Radovič at the Moskva Hotel.'

'Yes,' I shrugged casually.

'You were seen receiving a book from him two days ago. What have you done with it? This gentleman requires it.'

'Oh, I'm afraid I lost it, very careless of me, left it down somewhere.'

She translated this back. The man posed another loaded question. 'He asks if you lost it down by the Sava last night, among your friends? – all those anti-social elements,' she added her own rude comment.

The fat was well and truly in the fire. It seemed as if I'd become unwittingly involved with half the Western intelligence agencies in the city, together with a platoon of Tito's Secret Police.

The whole thing ended awkwardly. But it could have been much worse. The police, both in looking for the code or letter-drop book – as I suppose it was – and intent as well on liquidating the bohemians, raided the magic camp on the Sava. But they were too late. In the best cloak-and-dagger tradition, I'd managed to warn one of the students in town and when the militia arrived, the camp had been struck, all the mandolins and weeping willow canvasses gone.

News of this ignominious failure must have come back to Mrs Stolnač, for that evening, when I returned, she really levitated in anger, digging out every last one of her old English-phrase-book condemnations. 'You rogue, you scoundrel!' Then, stumbling on the worst term of approbation she could think of, suddenly burst out: 'You think you're Jesus Christ! You will leave tomorrow – you will go, go!' I was more than ready to comply. There was only one problem. In those days one needed a stamped exit visa to leave Yugoslavia. And the next day, a Sunday, the Orthodox holiday, everything would be closed. In any case the authorities were unlikely to give me an exit visa in the present circumstances. I was trapped.

There was only one thing for it. I took my bags next morning and went straight round to the British Embassy, hammering on the door, before eventually explaining everything to the weekend duty officer – about Mr Radovič, the mysterious American, the pass-the-parcel games with Virginia Woolf. It must have all made some kind of serious sense to him or to someone, for after a lengthy confab on the phone in the next room, he returned and wrote me out a diplomatic *laissez passer*, so that much in the old Greene-and-Ambler tradition I made a dramatic exit on the Orient Express that same day, accompanied, in the corridor all the way to the frontier, by a red-braided militia man.

Thirty years later, from the ramparts of Kalemegdan Fortress, with its sensational view over the two great rivers, I looked down to where the romantic encampment had been in that secret willow arbour on the Sava. The space was occupied now by the great bulk of the new Sheraton Hotel, in a city racked by inflation, nationalist dissension, foreign debt and unemployment. It was no longer a powerhouse of any great socialist experiment or vital fulcrum between East and West; a place where spies must have meagre pickings these days.

I mourned the end of youthful high adventure here, of assignations in the Balkan Hotel, code books and letter drops in the Council library, diplomatic *laissez passers* on the Orient Express home – a time when, with Mr Radovič, I had perhaps looked into the Mask of Dimitrios and rubbed shoulders with all sorts of seedy and romantic destiny, with the fur-hatted man and the bright girls, with mandolins and candle-light, down by the river.

Then, walking along Knez Mihailova Street, I suddenly stopped. It was the window of the new British Council Library – a display of British feminist books. And there, looking up at me temptingly, was a copy of Virginia Woolf's *A Room of One's Own*. Peering carefully to either side in the glass reflection, I moved off, very sharply.

6

Cairo:
The Banquet at Saqqara
(June 1987)

Very early that first morning back in Cairo, while the *muezzins* were still casting their first prayer over the shadowy city, I crossed into the empty silence of Gezira island and watched the river mists dissolve. The whole downy, blue-and-white carapace gradually lifted as the sun rose and the essential motifs delicately emerged: first the vague charoal strokes of the giant palm trunks along the island corniche, then the wild bougainvillaea and the big ilex and catalpa trees in the botanical gardens. They seemed to blossom suddenly, glossy green and milk-mauve in the dew-drenched light – then other bolder daubs shone through the vapour like a Chinese print. The white hulk of the long-stalled *Omar Khayam* river steamer seemed to glide forward into the picture, before finally the Nile itself gave up its wispy shroud: noiseless, millpond smooth, flecked with bronze-green lights, a last treasure unearthed by the rising sun.

All this was an island, an Egypt, a world I knew. What I saw in that misty light had changed not at all in the thirty years since I'd first come to Cairo, nor very little for many years before that. But a few hours later, back in the heart of the city, I could hardly believe – or bear – the changes. It was almost impossible to move: cars jammed, double, triple parked, the rest stalled from end to end of the streets, while the people on the pavements were so thick as to be wedged together, glued, having to move en masse, in step, like troops, or not at all. The sense of sheer physical crush was like living in a beehive gone beserk. Here was a city – of hardly three million in my day – which had become a raucous, panicky lifeboat with up to fifteen million people contending for a place in it. It's a global cliché, of course: dozens of great cities are now like this, with the human dimension entirely thrown overboard, the happier intimate buildings all gone, where the humans themselves are left to sink or swim in the dense foul airs, in tin shacks or concrete bunkers, without hope or remission.

Yet in Cairo, in Egypt generally, there is one unique and redeeming feature in all this mutation and mayhem: the past, though apparently gone without trace, often remains available, not far from the surface. It's the historic and climatic luck of the country: Egypt, where everything changes, is buried – by the mists, the sands, the bulldozers, yet at the same time preserved – by the desert and the sun. Perhaps even time itself might be retrieved from this great filing cabinet of history, I thought, since when I returned to the utterly transformed city, in that familiar dream-filled dawn on Gezira island, I somehow sensed my earlier self in Egypt still lying there, untouched by grave robbers, in the gilded tomb of youth, a soul hanging fire waiting its own rebirth.

Yes, first in Egypt, always those misty or pellucid dawns. I've never known a country where each day, every day, started and ended so well. Only all the other hours were difficult when I first taught there at the English School in Heliopolis, the heat storming up the lead-blue dome of sky, voices dying in the clasping, choking air of the classroom, as we all finally gave up the ghost in *Hamlet*. There was no thought then but for the one o'clock bell, the end of the day's work, which brought me to sleep for the afternoon in my curtained bedroom.

Yet this soul's fire made each day two days then. And at twenty I had the pep to fill the gift of this double life easily. By six o'clock, with a second wind, shaved, showered and wearing a fresh shirt, I'd start over again, going out to meet Geoffrey or Leila, out into the cooling canyons of the city, or along the aromatic side streets smelling of cinnamon, paraffin, brick dust, urine. We'd go for coffee at Groppis, drinks at the Continental, or a seat on the roof terrace of the old Semiramis Hotel by the Nile and watch the sun slide down the pyramids, spreading a veneer of rose and purple over the town, cutting out the huge triangles of stone in soft blue from the apocalyptic orange beyond.

'A man goes into Egypt and is changed forever,' so they say. Certainly the year I spent there changed me completely, gave me directions which, though I wasn't to take them until ten years later, formed the impetus behind my later career as a writer. Egypt gave me the need to remember and record; gave me the emotions – sad, happy, farcical – that made such records imperative for me.

So that now, with my friends of the time all dead or vanished and the city itself changed almost beyond recognition, perhaps I may trace a last record from some of those originals, relying for line on that indelible spirit of place, hovering mist-like over the river, which I sensed that first morning when I returned to Gezira.

We were a mixed bunch in 1957, a job lot of good friends: McGuire, Leila, Geoffrey, Lola, Tadros the Greek auctioneer, flabby, gold-toothed Cherif from the Ministry of Antiquities, and lecherous old Rex, with his equally libidinous terrier 'Spot'. The two of them had somehow managed to stay on in Egypt after the British had been chucked out of the country. Rex was at the centre of every devious web; he lurked in his sensational Mameluke harem, restored beneath the citadel, ever ready to pounce, swooping down the hill with Spot up beside him in his great cream-and-coffee coloured Rolls, the two of them all set to scour the fleshpots of the city.

Cairo has always had its bizarre denizens, a rich pot-pourri of exotic misfits, refugees from one sort of wound or another, or just fascinated hangers-on like me. We lived like cave people in that broiling heat, emerging only at night, looking for variety and pleasure. And so it was all the more surprising when, one evening at the Continental, with Leila's birthday a week hence, we decided to mark it with an outing in the full blaze of noon. It had been Cherif's idea – he had access to Saqqara, the legendary royal burial ground ten miles south of Cairo because of his job with the Ministry of Antiquities.

We'd have a proper feast, he said, from hampers supplied by the Estoril, on trestle tables under parasols. Cherif was very English in his preferred traditions and had private means. He had been to Oxford at some point in his vague career and argued that 'This was how one did things.' And besides, Cherif was rather besotted with Leila, just as I and Tadros were. Everyone was a little in love with the willowy, grave-faced Leila. She was obliged to work as an airline clerk, because, though her father had been a Pasha and a Minister under Farouk, they were now dispossessed by Nasser's new socialist regime.

And if not Leila, then some of us hoped for success with the less complicated Lola, her puppy-fat Lebanese friend who, waiting for unlikely success as an actress, did a little amateurish belly dancing at Le Perroquet, one of the slightly more select nightclubs in the city. Rex had different sexual inclinations. But with his equally developed gourmandising, our projected pleasure tickled his epicurean fancies. And besides, as he knew, his huge Rolls would be a very necessary part of this *déjeuner sur le sable*. Geoffrey, a wry South African who taught in the posh boys' school of Victoria College at Maadi, was a collector of droll Egyptian events, and foresaw a choice example here, while McGuire, another Irish teacher with me in Heliopolis, a thirsty pedagogue who'd developed a passionate taste for the local Stella beer, viewed the outing as a heaven sent means of prospering this lust in the hot noonday sun beneath the step pyramid.

Thirty years later, remembering the banquet but never having been back to Saqqara, I took a packaged tourist coach out there, leaving the frightful city, going south down the Nile road. And quite soon we were in another landscape and one I remembered well. It was a world of Biblical men and donkeys in little mud-brick villages by greeny canals, set amidst cool, moss-damp palm groves, with fields of berseem and water buffalo trudging round in circles, turning *sakias*, irrigating the billiard-table land. Here was the ancient landscape which we'd sped through so many years before: necklaces of celebratory jasmine round our throats, all crammed into the old Rolls, raising the dust. And going back along that same road thirty years later, the past seemed to stir itself, rising to the surface, waiting for me.

Cherif had staged the banquet elaborately and perfectly. Waiters from the Estoril had preceded us with the food and the trestle table had been set up against a shady wall of the Necropolis, a secluded stone arbour. This site gave out immediately onto a great pot-holed expanse of sand, for Professor Emery was still at work there, digging up Pharaohs, and beyond this to Djoser's step pyramid, a quarter of a mile away. The pyramid was a reddish-beige, brick edifice cut out from the brilliant blue sky beyond, a remarkable structure in any case, but sensational as something built almost five thousand years before, still in place, the oldest monumental building in the world.

As Cherif had promised, there were parasols, glistening white cloths and napery, spicy Syrian rissoles, aubergine salads, cold kebabs, stuffed Nile perch, vast succulent Port Said prawns, delta pigeon, peppery chicken, fresh dates, with a lot of Gianaclis's white wine for us and Stella beer for McGuire, taken from ice buckets by the two turbaned Nubian waiters in long white *galibeahs*, slashed with green cummerbunds. And no doubt we all looked a picture as we sat down in our white linen tropicals and flimsy dresses; mad dogs – including Rex's terrier up beside him – in the midday sun, raising our glasses to Leila in a birthday toast. Leila, who was twenty-five that morning and radiant in her sad way.

The underlying mood of that banquet was one of romance; of frustrated romance among ourselves and the other eerie magic we felt in wining and dining at the edge of this fabulous graveyard, which for three thousand years had received the immortal remains of the kings, queens and courtiers of Memphis. Perhaps some of their gilded tombs still lay there, just beneath our smart party shoes.

Leila liked me, I knew – but how much? Lola was keen on both Cherif and Tadros, the caricature Greek *commerçant*, neither of whom had much time for her in their pursuit of Leila, who in turn seemed to be focusing on the uninterested Geoffrey. Rex, in this *ronde d'amour*, acted as amused overseer, tilting into the delta pigeon, rather fancying McGuire, I thought, who had eyes only for Stella, the one romance entirely fulfilled that day, as he gorged on the golden liquid.

Then it was time for Leila's birthday presents – nice but unremarkable, except for Cherif's, which was staggering: an exquisitely fashioned gold Pharaonic bracelet.

'From the Royal tomb of Sekhem-Khet,' he told her casually. 'The Pharaoh who succeeded Djoser at Memphis – part of his funerary treasure we found here a few years ago: or rather his daughter's, a Princess. Members of the Pharaoh's family were buried with them in the very early dynasties.'

Some of us were pretty put out by this trump card in our romantic game. 'Oh, I couldn't!' Leila cried and Tadros added the sour, *sotto voce* comment that it was surely illegal, the bracelet was State property, that Cherif was no more than a tomb robber. But Cherif heard him and there was a sharp altercation.

'You know nothing about it, Tadros! There were literally hundreds of such little objects –'

'No matter, it's the principle, Cherif. If everyone were to do that, what then? And you especially, taking advantage of your position at the Ministry –'

'Now, now, boys.' It was Rex interjecting. 'Leila is an Egyptian Princess too – at least for the day. An entirely appropriate gift. Leave Cherif be. There are perks to every job!'

But the matter cast rather a gloom over the subsequent proceedings, until Leila suggested we all go and explore the tombs and temples. It was now the rather unsteady McGuire who quite took our minds off the little unpleasantness.

He'd wandered off the track out onto the burning sands, on the way to the fabulous mastaba of Ti – royal architect and pyramid manager of the fifth dynasty – when he suddenly disappeared, a spectacular disappearing trick down a sand-filled pot-hole from one of the many old digs about the place. We found McGuire up to his neck, several feet below the surface, vertically entombed, apparently quite happy to be embalmed in the warm sand, eyes closed, a look of somnolent ease on his already blissful features.

As we bent down to pull him out, Leila helping and tugging, the wonderful gold bracelet slipped from her wrist and disappeared into the pot hole. She was stricken, desolate – and so was Cherif. I was secretly rather pleased. Besides, it seemed appropriate – the lovely Pharaonic emblem was returned to its original site and replaced the squiffy McGuire, now disinterred in his sandy shroud, a stiff, woebegone, relic from the short Celtic pedagogic dynasty in Egypt.

We revived him with some brandy and the party took off again. And later, when we were in the candle-lit shadows of Ti's tomb, gazing at the wonderfully fresh wall paintings of domestic life on the Nile, Leila took my hand briefly in the darkness, pressing it, promising something. It was a first intimation that my suit might be returned; a love affair that started in the darkness of Ti's magnificent tomb, but soon spread out into the light of the city, along the aromatic side-streets, day through night, waking to those hazy or pellucid lemon-yellow dawns.

'A man goes into Egypt and is changed forever.' Ten years later I tried to commemorate that change in my first novel, *The Private Sector*, bringing my squabbling, loving friends together once more, variously disguised, embalming them with words.

And now, twenty years after that, I was back at Saqqara, looking at those same domestic strip cartoons in Ti's funerary drawing room; that paradisal life of the Old Kingdom, which we'd repeated briefly one afternoon on a trestle table above the tombs of these people, but which Ti and the Pharaohs – so meticulously prepared for, and certain of their immortality – had been living ever since. We later, lesser mortals in this landscape were not so sensibly furnished for eternity. Nor, finally, could my past here be unearthed. But it was there, safely buried somewhere out in the sands, like Leila's bracelet – evidence, at least, that I, too, had once lived in Arcadia.

7

Alexandria:
No Abiding City
(June 1987)

Back in a top-floor room of the old Cecil Hotel in Alexandria one
lilac-skied afternoon last autumn, I had a sensational view over the
empty eastern harbour, right out to Fort Kait Bay, where Pharos,
the great Ptolemaic lighthouse and seventh wonder of the ancient
world, once stood. The brilliant white, castellated Arab fortress
there now was an almost equally glittering crown above the indigo
sea, a drift of salty ordure in the damp breeze. At least Alexandria
was full of all her old colours, smells and weather that autumn day:
the scented windy streets under a moist blue sky, the endless sea
glitter of this forgotten watering place, though nothing remains of its
former glory. All that – the world of Alexander, Antony, Cleopatra,
Napoleon, C. P. Cavafy, E. M. Forster and Lawrence Durrell – now
seems pure fiction.

It was impossible to imagine, as I turned to look at the dirty,
dowdy-dull, ugly modern city, how much fabulous history had
bloomed here. It had been Alexander the Great's royal capital,
flower of cities all, with its magnificent palaces, temples and library
of half a million manuscripts – an Hellenic paradise, inhabited
by an equally heroic and speculative race, so dazzlingly bright, a
history records, that people covered their eyes on entering the walls
and even at night a tailor could see to thread his needle. Then it was
Caesar's and Antony's city, where Cleopatra introduced herself, first

inside a rolled carpet, next in a gilded barge: Alexandria in those enchanted centuries, when one fact after another outdoes the wildest fable.

And in much more recent times, here was the poet Cavafy's haunted, erotic city – this shy Greek who lived alone above a brothel in the Rue Lepsius, frequented the cheap cafés with their handsome young men and immortalised these poor clerks and tram conductors as latter-day gods; twentieth-century successors to Alexander and Antony. They were the same sort of flare-lit cafés and rotting slum quarters in which Justine was later rescued, among the rouged and fuzzy-haired child prostitutes, in Durrell's great literary memorial to the city.

When I first came to Alexandria, as a teacher from Cairo for the summer holidays, I and my friend and colleague Geoffrey had stayed at the Hotel Beau Rivage near Stanley Beach, some miles out along the corniche. In the afternoons I paddled over the crystal shallows, while Geoffrey, a familiar holiday maker and socialite here, flirted on the sands with some of the elderly *grandes dames* of the city, so that his shrill laugh echoed to me over the water as he clowned about their deckchairs.

'Tee-hee! Ha-ha!' Like children being tickled. 'Ah, comme vous êtes méchant, Monsieur Geoffrey!' The dialogue came across the waves like snatches from a Molière comedy. For these ladies, Geoffrey, with his old world English affectations, his wry eccentricities and attentions, must have been a happy reminder of their youth; of a time when the Government and Embassies in Cairo had taken their intrigues to Alexandria for the summer and shot duck on Lake Mariout in the early autumn.

Mrs Moffat, a small, sparrow-like, Home-Counties widow would chatter to me as we saw the ladies home to their crumbling villas behind the seafront: 'You simply can't imagine how beautiful it all was here before the war. Now, quite impossible. They can't even make a proper cup of tea . . .'

As we approached the villas' gates, down avenues heavy with flame trees and the smell of jasmine, wizened arthritic porters rose up from the dust like old newspapers in a light wind, saluting stiffly as the ladies crossed the threshold, giving Geoffrey and me the wary, hopeless glance of crippled protectors. I'd say goodbye to Mrs Moffat in front of her gently decaying mansion, the broken arm of a lawn sprinkler clanking somewhere in the velvet twilight, a Daimler lurking in the garage without wheels.

Mrs Moffat's husband had been in cotton and had made a fortune in Alexandria before the war, when the city reached a last etiolated flowering as Cottonopolis. But it was a world already suffocating in its own sweet decadence and the war and Colonel Nasser finally did away with it altogether, leaving these few European ghosts in their decrepit palaces, remnants of the city's last fabled civilisation.

Thirty years later, going down to dinner in the Cecil, I wondered vaguely what had happened to Flora Moffat and whether she was still alive. She would be nearly ninety now, so I thought it unlikely. Or was it? The Cecil's famous gilded mirrors were still in place; the same mirrors in which the narrator first glimpsed the 'dark thrilling face' of the fated Justine some fifty years before, so perhaps Flora Moffat, with her so much brighter, more sensible regard, had survived the rack and wreck of history and was still here.

Next morning I took a long walk, east, down the corniche, the beaches empty and polluted-looking, a dusty rattle of permanent construction and destruction from the soiled and ragged city to my right. Turning off the seafront into the old Cotton-Baron residential quarter, I came to the same tree-lined avenue where Flora had lived, but with few trees left, all gone for firewood now, the pavements torn up, sprouting rusty pipes and wires and oozing sewage. New apartment blocks, already crumbling, had replaced most of the splendid villas, but Flora's rococo-Levantine fantasy, with its spiky turrets, terracotta tiles and gargoyles, was still standing.

The once tranquil tree-filled lawn was now a shadeless chaotic vegetable garden, with tin shacks on it and some fat-tailed sheep foraging on what had once been Flora's rosebeds. A young *boab* sat on the villa steps, chewing sugar cane, a sullen incongruous figure against the elegant portico. 'Mrs Moffat?' I asked. He shook his head. He knew nothing. Behind him, through the open hall doors, barefoot children in smudgy pyjamas played hopscotch in the great paved and pillared hall. The mosaic tiles had been torn up and every sort of rubbish swirled around, dancing in the sea wind with the children. It was here, in this once heavily gilded and furnished hall that Mrs Moffat's Greek Jeeves had received visitors before ushering us upstairs for gin slings in the long ersatz Louis Quinze salon on the first floor. Here that we'd once attended a – for me, panic-stricken – *thé dansant* with these elderly ladies and an Italian orchestra from the Cecil fumbling through Lehar and Strauss. It seemed impossible that neat little Mrs Moffat could survive anywhere in this ghostly slum.

But as I was about to leave, a youngish, smartly dressed Egyptian with a brief case and several flower bouquets emerged from the hall. I asked him about Flora, explaining my past association with her. His English was perfect.

'Why, yes,' he told me. 'She does still live here, only in a tiny flat now. I've just been seeing her. I'm Helmi, her grandson-in-law! I was on my way back into town – but I'll take you to her. She's rather vague and deaf, but she'll be pleased to see you.'

Mrs Moffat lay on an old steamer chair, feet up, almost completely swathed in a patchwork quilt, in what must have been a sort of conservatory on the ground floor. It was filled with exotic potted plants and flowers, tendrils of bougainvillaea creeping in from the ruined garden outside and she, a tiny bird in this hothouse aviary, was surrounded by silver-framed pre-war snaps of her family and other Home Counties or colonial mementos: ashtrays made from riding stirrups, an elephant's foot umbrella stand, horse brasses, English pewter mugs.

Helmi introduced me, we took spindly gilt chairs nearby, and she thought and thought, obviously unable to place me. I mentioned Geoffrey, since dead, but a much closer friend of hers. Then she remembered. 'Ah yes, Geoffrey! – that rascal of an Irishman who wouldn't dance.'

'Er, that I think was me – the *thé dansant* you gave here, when we were both up from Cairo for the summer.'

'From Cairo, during the war – yes, of course!' She found her feet then. 'You must have come up with Alan and his army friends, often in and out here before they went on up to the front at Alamein. I remember! There were parties here then – galore!'

'I don't think –' I tried to say.

'Of course, you must have been with Monty, Eighth Army. Alan's buried there now you know, the war cemetery at Alamein. You knew my son Alan, of course – a wonderful boy.'

'Well, actually no . . .' But she didn't hear me and it seemed

pointless to disabuse her. We chattered on at nostalgic cross purposes, both of us remembering different decades of happiness in
the city, while I tried tactfully to make my memories coincide with
hers.

Afterwards Helmi drove me back to town. Helmi was a lawyer and a
Copt, who'd married Mrs Moffat's granddaughter. He was an
amiable, widely informed professional. I wondered why, like so many
other Egyptians of his sort, he and his family hadn't emigrated to
Canada.

'With Flora still here, how could we? And besides,' – he glanced out
at the shabby city – 'It's not as bad as it looks. We still have the
marvellous weather – and the sea.' He gestured towards the violet
waters of the bay. 'It's true, you can't really bathe in Alex any more.
But there are some fine beaches to the west – swimming, sailing,
fishing. And we're better off than they are in Cairo: all those fumes
and fifteen million people.'

Back at the Cecil we had coffee among the forest of mirrors. 'But
with the old European city all gone,' I asked him, 'and most of the
other Christians, isn't this all rather a ghost town for you?'

'I never knew the old city. And besides, it's been a ghost town on
and off for 2,000 years. Mohammed Ali rebuilt it in the 1820s and
when the Suez Canal came, Alex practically went out of business again
– until the cotton boom revived it.'

'What will come to revive it now?' I asked.

He shrugged. 'It'll never be revived again in your way – or
grandmama's. Islam has no interest in all the things you and she were
talking about, be it gin slings or Alexander the Great. By the end of
this century Alex will be an entirely Islamic city.' He looked round at
the gilded mirrors. 'In five, ten years even this last surviving evidence
of the old Alex will have disappeared.

'And you?'

'Oh, unless Flora lives to be a hundred, I'll be in Canada then. But
come,' he smiled, 'if you're free, I've got some little family business to
attend to. It may interest you: some memorial duties!'

We drove east down the old canopic way, through the heart
of the city, until we came to a vast, high-walled space where
the gateways had all been bricked up, except for one in a far
corner.

'The remains of the old European cemetery,' Helmi told me,

232

reaching for the flowers behind him. 'Grandmama likes to keep her husband's grave fresh.'

Squeezing through a gap in the great iron gates, I was confronted with a vast, overgrown, Amazonian-like tropical jungle. The European cemetery was a mass of exotic trees with falling branches and tendrils, twining round, suffocating an even more riotous assembly of drunken, tossed-about tombstones, vaults, marble sarcophagi, gothic crosses, weeping cherubs, cold statuary: an almost impenetrable necropolis.

'Here's the mortal remains of all your old Alex,' said Helmi. 'No one's been buried here for years. They'd like to build apartment blocks all over it. They probably will.' He found Arthur Moffat's simple tomb, setting down the jasmine and oleander bouquet, clasping his hands a moment, as we stood in the heavy, perfume-damp silence.

'And now,' Helmi looked up, 'the same attentions for Alan, my uncle-in-law, at Alamein, if you'd like to come.'

Alamein proved to be a small village above the white-hot sand dunes, distinguished only by the military museum and the war cemeteries; thousands of identical headstones running away into the forever landscape of the western desert, where this great turning-point battle had been fought. Helmi knew where Alan's plot was, replacing a small withered leaf and fern bouquet with a fresh one, as I shaded my eyes against the tremendous light.

Later I looked through the museum with all its violent shards, where (instead of Alamein) much was made of the Egyptian victory across the Suez Canal in the '73 war and the names of the British generals were misspelt as 'Auknolek', 'Wivil' and – appropriately enough – 'Muntgunery'.

We were the only visitors in this immense dazzling sandscape of death, in which a whole haphazard foreign civilisation had come to die. Those military legions – successors to Caesar's, Antony's and Napoleon's – had last seen the light on that indigo bay in Alexandria before coming out here to their own savage extinction.

Alamein was hot and sad and barbarous – just as the city seemed when I got back to the Cecil that night and looked out over it for the last time from my balcony. I heard nothing then of that exquisite heavenly choir, passing over the bay, which Antony had heard as the Gods deserted him – and the city. Shakespeare's lines in the mouth of this same soldier came more to mind – 'I am dying, Egypt, dying' – as the modern Alexandria slept, oblivious of its great fortune, on the mattress of its fabulous tombs.

8

Ireland:
The House on the Hill
(July 1987)

The four-square, lime-washed Georgian house where I grew up stands beyond two white gates on a rock-clamorous, tree-covered ridge overlooking a sloping lawn. There are beehives, a chestnut-edged parkland with water meadows and the river beyond. On the other side of the valley, one can just see a ruined sixteenth-century Norman castle and a much earlier Celtic round tower before the land rises again in empty, gorsey green hills and distant blue mountains.

When I first came to live here in 1941 and looked out on this wide panorama, no other houses were to be seen anywhere. Now, more than forty-five years later, sitting at the window of my first-floor bedroom, the view is identical, save for the roof of one new house, far away to the right, across the river.

Ireland changes. But the change is exceedingly slow. Or is it? Dublin, where nearly a third of the Republic's population now live, has altered in many areas quite beyond recognition. The developers, over the last twenty years, have cut vast swathes through the gracious Georgian city, replacing some of the finest urban architecture in the world with quite monstrous bunker-trendy or shoddy-modern office blocks. In Dublin, instead of the old graces, a high-tech, money-grabbing, inflationary Gulch City has burgeoned, while the poorer north side – racked by unemployment, crime and drugs – grabs its

235

money in more violent ways, preying on the new BMW rich over the river.

All this is new and unhappy in Dublin. But eighty miles south in Kilkenny – where I return every winter and summer to the old house on the hill – the face of things remains largely the same. From my bedroom there, surrounded by the same furniture, pictures, the same books I read as a child, I live in and look out on a world where almost everything of my past has been preserved.

It is reassuring. Fewer and fewer people of my age can return in this way to their roots, to exactly the same brick and mortar, the same people, the same landscape that nurtured them. The world from my window only alters with the weather and the season – as it had that morning last winter when I got back, looking out on the remains of a snowstorm and saw an enchantment of pearly folds and meringue twists under a brilliant blue sky and sun – a crisp icing along the garden terraces, creamy glaciers running down the lawn to the valley where the trees were canopied in powdery foam. It was a day so unexpected in the normally drear Irish winter – buoyant, tingling, glittering – that there seemed no end of things in the air, bright possibilities, a future.

But Irish landscapes are so often deceptive. Beyond the beauty or cultivation seen in shady parklands, rich farms or cattle pasture, lies so much sad history, old and new horrors: endless ribbon developments of bijou bungalows along once empty country roads; sudden stark ruins, Norman keeps and burnt-out Georgian mansions; wild, ragworty fields, a moist, ivy-creeping growth outside the smartest new boundary wall. Beyond the most placid or secure vision, there is always a feel of impending decay, surprise, disruption, even violence. There's a strong aura in Ireland – in the landscape and the people – of much that will always be ungoverned, untutored, where any imposed order has the air of a mere holding operation, a temporary clearing or civilisation won from a ragged and voracious nature.

And there *is* change here, even in this most rural backwater. Ireland, once more, is a country of departure, where the young especially clamour for any kind of exile: boats to Liverpool or visas for America. Once again, poverty, division, violence and loss have become hallmarks in these homelands. And a principal reason, as so often in the past, is that so many people can no longer find work in or on their own land.

My own memories of growing up here, in County Kilkenny, are the very opposite of all this. The overriding factor then was local self-sufficiency. We and most of our neighbours lived, found work, and sustenance, all within the small orbit of county, townland or parish. As a child, life for me was bounded by the junior school in Kilkenny College five miles north, by the parish church a few miles south and by various other old houses within the county, where I went to children's parties – bran tub and hide-and-seek routs, or grander fancy dress affairs.

I had only the faintest conception of a larger world beyond. The first time I became aware of it was when, at the age of seven, someone, listening to the wireless, shrieked out of a window, 'The allies have taken Rome!' Rome? Yes, didn't I know there was a war on? I immediately forgot about it that afternoon, probably running to meet Mr Hennessy, the local grocer, with his cob and trap, rattling down the high lane with the weekly delivery of candles, tea, sugar, matches – almost the only things which we couldn't produce ourselves.

Electricity was supplied by an erratic and menacing wind-charger on top of a nearby hill. More often, we were illuminated by the lovely creamy or yellow flickering light from Aladdin oil-lamps or candles. Water was drawn from a well hidden deep in the woods, pumped up by a heart-thumping old Croxley diesel engine; the only such mechanism in the place. Our transport everywhere was by cart, with the pony Minny, or in the big, corduroy-upholstered governess-trap with the larger pony, Pat.

As for entertainment, this was almost entirely self-starting, familial and non-mechanical. Arthur Ransome was the most modern author read aloud to us children on most evenings, from a much greater store of Victorian and Edwardian children's classics. And if not E. Nesbit or *The Unlucky Family*, then there were traditional board or card games, Rummy and Old Maid and once in a while, elaborate charades, paper games or a magic lantern show – for me the supreme rapture.

Though all this was in the 1940s, my upbringing was little different from what it would have been fifty years before. Our only reliance on the world outside was via the wind-up telephone. If Mrs Reilly in the village Post Office was out feeding her chickens, no calls could be made or received. Apart from this, with every facility and nourishment to hand, we could have survived a siege in the house almost indefinitely. The world – with its larger obligations, impositions and uncertainties – was elsewhere. High on the hill behind the two white gates, we were a world and law unto ourselves. And that, too was reassuring.

Forty years later the house is no longer, in any of those old ways, self-sufficient. Beyond the white gates very little is the same and the world, the furthest war or disaster, is in the drawing room with us, in full appalling colour, via the TV set. It is inevitable and some will say a good thing too: this instant global awareness and commonplace dependence on all sorts of distant mechanisms. I wonder. I think we have become too concerned with events quite beyond our reach or ability to influence and might better bring our free floating opinions and efforts down to earth, on matters within our scope and competence. But in rural Ireland, with its renewed brain drain of the bright and eager, the human wherewithal for this local involvement is less and less available.

The centralised and, in recent years, often bizarrely mismanaged economy, together with all sorts of local shenanigans – and often just sheer cowboy dishonesty – is such in Ireland now that few rural communities continue to support themselves. Those that did so most ably, now, for a variety of crass and devious reasons, do so no longer. Our nearest village had a railway station, a thriving creamery, a large mill, a famous glass-blowing works and a successful magnesite quarry until a few years ago. None of these remain. The local connections have disappeared.

When I return to the house I have the eerie feeling of compassing a giant span of time, of having travelled, in less than forty years, from an intimately interconnected, almost Victorian world to the threshold of a ruinous twenty-first century, where everyone is divided, numbered, at the mercy of what is anonymous, distant, uncontrollable and usually malign.

This is a common predicament today, of course. What must be less common is to be able to make immediate comparisons between this distant past and present – to return to a house where that older world survives largely intact, where the evidence of that previous order surrounds one, at every glance. Quite suddenly, in one of the rooms or attics, I can find myself back in my own past or in one even more distant. An old house of this sort, which has the space and where things have been stored by generations of the same family, is a time capsule and any serious rummaging is a ticket of leave to a great variety of past instant and incident.

This winter, for example, beneath my bedroom cupboard, I found a fifty-year-old copy of the local newspaper. It told the tale of a visiting uncle who, flying over from London in an air taxi and landing in a nearby field, had later crashed with the plane on take-off. There were no injuries, just his wife's fur coat burnt. But the drama of that day remains in the old coach house, where the twisted propeller hangs on the wall. The house, or its nooks and crannies, is littered with such memorial effects. In the basement is the old dairy, still with its oak churn and rusting Alfa-Laval separating machine, where each evening I turned the whirring, pinging mechanism for Mrs Kennedy, rapt at the miracle of cream from one spout, thin milk from the other.

Here, in emblem at least, remain all those old interconnections and interdependencies. Most of the people concerned with them have left, died or live abroad, as I have done for the past thirty years. But my foster parents, in their eighties now, are still there, not just as custodians but as actively involved inhabitants, of the house itself and the immediate locality.

The question of how long all this may last hovers in the air – it always does, always will. For what is being preserved here is not a museum but life, together with what's most fragile in it: people's roots and memories, the artefacts and visions of their past, things we are more and more bereft of today. But in the end the question is more not *what* will be preserved, but who will do so? Ireland, as all the old Home Rulers so rightly insisted, can only be served *in* Ireland. The present climate for either exiles or locals, offers no encouragement whatsoever for such continuities. Are such houses – like so very many others in Ireland over the years – doomed to extinction?

The poet W. B. Yeats thought so sixty years ago: 'The centre cannot hold – mere anarchy is loosed upon the world' he wrote, as he contemplated the destruction of hundreds of such places during the Anglo-Irish and civil wars here in the twenties.

And thinking only of that always voracious Irish landscape and nature, those destructive mossy-moist growths nibbling away beyond the strongest boundary wall, one feels the odds must be against such survivals. It depends, of course, on many material factors, but equally on how much people value their old toys in the attic.

I do, but only partly for sentimental reasons. My looking back and going back in this series has really had quite another impetus. It's been an attempt to try and remember properly and thus situate myself more appropriately now. The past is so much more than mere sentiment: it can become reincarnate, encrusted with marvels – 'Those are pearls that were his eyes – nothing of him that doth fade – but doth suffer a sea change – into something rich and strange.' Memory lane needn't be a sad cul-de-sac, but a road to an undiscovered country, suggesting exits, not ends.

Our own history – that ever weightier, largely unopened ragbag we lug about with us – offers lodestars among the sawdust and tinsel. And that ragbag, for me, has always been the traveller's real luggage, his map and compass, sustenance and ticket. In opening it, and rummaging about suitably, we may draw our real co-ordinates, plot where we are now and so travel on with more accuracy and assurance.

As for the old house on the hill, my foster father – thinking of Elizabeth Bowen's familial histories and novels and the absolute ruin of her great house in County Cork – has written: 'Every life that has been recorded acquires a short lease of immortality and a house that has been loved and written about, room by room, will survive its physical destruction.' So be it with this house: one way, or another, it will survive.